D0375079

WHAT WOULD BEYONCÉ DO?!

WHAT WOULD BEYONCÉ DO?!

LUISA OMIELAN

CENTURY

1 3 5 7 9 10 8 6 4 2

Century
20 Vauxhall Bridge Road
London SW1V 2SA

Century is part of the Penguin Random House group of companies whose addresses
can be found at global.penguinrandomhouse.com

Penguin
Random House
UK

First published by Century in 2016

www.randomhouse.co.uk

A CIP catalogue record for this book is available from the British Library

ISBN 9781780894454

Typeset in India by Thomson Digital Pvt Ltd, Noida, Delhi

Printed and bound in Great Britain by Clays Ltd, St Ives plc

Penguin Random House is committed to a sustainable future for our
business, our readers and our planet. This book is made from Forest
Stewardship Council®-certified paper.

'To thine ownself be true' – my man Shakespeare

Hello You. I wish you could see how powerful you truly are. Every breath, curve, bleed, laughter, tear. Every inch of your skinny, fat, saggy, toned river of skin. Every curve, breast, cunt is beautiful. *You* are beautiful. Nurture your kind, your gentle, your strong, your bossy. Embrace it; embrace every aspect of your female form, inside and out. When in doubt: Be Yoncé.

PS Don't worry, I only use the C-word once. PS It's actually not a bad word, it's not my fault someone made it derogatory, I think it's actually a very beautiful thing to have one. Mine is lovely. HELLO NEW FANS!!!!

PARTITION, PLEASE

Hi babe, my name's Luisa and I am 33 years old – well, I'll be 34 by the time you read this, maybe even 35, who knows when this book will get finished? I'm a comedian and I do live shows, that's what I'm good at. Some comedians are really good at writing jokes on Twitter, I am rubbish at it, but when it comes to writing live solo shows, mate, I'm your girl. Saying that, I am currently typing this on my way back from York, where I played to silence in front of 400 people, so I guess it really depends which day you catch me.

With stand-up, you start with five minutes of material and then work your way up, a 10-minute set, a 20-minute set, and then the big one is writing an hour. My debut hour was pretty epic; it's called 'What Would Beyoncé Do?!' Oh hello cheeky book title!

So how did this book start? Good question! (When will it be finished? Even better question!) So there I was, doing one of my many sell-out runs at London's Soho Theatre (I've had 7), and after my shows I like to stand by the exit and say bye to the audience and sell some badges. This woman called Francesca comes up to me and is like 'Hi, I work for Random House' and I'm like 'Ahh, that's really cool #neverheardofit. See you later. Bye!' That was the first step in the birth of this book.

At the time I was touring my WWBD show and was in the process of writing the follow-up show 'Am I Right Ladies?!' My brain was mashed; I had no time to take on any other projects. You see, my shows are all-consuming, I put everything I have into them. They are pretty much parties with jokes in, you should come. I love them, they are a hoot. Francesca came twice, and then again and then again. I was like, mate, you are making this awkward, please be cool. She said, please consider writing the book, Random House is a massive publisher and I would love to help you get this story out there. I laughed in her face and told her no, but I'm pretty sure I eased the rejection with a free badge.

Now when it comes to writing things down, I am rubbish (see Twitter and my Facebook page. What do you mean you haven't liked my Facebook page? How did you even hear about this book?). I get bored so easily and have the attention span of a flea. When I am not doing shows, I just wanna get lost in American TV. I'm really into *The Good Wife* at the moment and keep saying 'Objection overruled' in confusing circumstances, like in Starbucks: 'Would you like chocolate on top of your latte?' OBJECTION OVERRULED. PS Do not watch Season 5 unless you are ready to CRY.

I also love *House*, and every time I get sick I'm like, I swear this could be lupus, which is a ridiculous idea; it's never lupus. I even tweeted Hugh Laurie once saying 'Please can we have sex? Keep the limp and bring the stick.' But he never replied. He's probably still grieving over Wilson, Sorry, spoiler alert, I should have warned you.

I have just finished *Sons of Anarchy* – THERE'S A BLACKBIRD PERCHED OUTSIDE MY WINDOW *taps nose to all the *SOA* fans for the reference* (see what I mean about my attention span) – and I cannot cope. I keep calling everyone brother and saying 'Let's bring this to the table.' Mate, that final series was like Shakespeare, it's beautiful. Watching box sets is one of the many things I have been focusing on in an attempt to avoid writing this book. Here are some others.

1. Rewatching *Criminal Minds* . . . wheels up in 20. PLEASE CAN PENELOPE AND MORGAN KISS?
2. Painting the skirting boards at my mum's house.
3. Learning all the words to all the *Sons of Anarchy* albums.
4. Putting together a 90s playlist including 'MMMBop' and the NSYNC version of 'Everything I Own', and Usher's 'Separated' (I'm sorry we didn't make it).
5. Watching *Lemonade*. Yes queen. Beyoncé, you are a goddess. This wasn't a distraction, this was imperative to my personal growth.
6. Washing my make-up brushes. I even found a make-up brush cleaner on eBay, it's really cool, like a mat you wipe the brushes on. I digress . . .

What was my point again? Oh yes, I have a short attention span. So when it came to my first solo show, I basically wrote a show that would appeal to someone with a minimal attention span who's a sucker for pop culture references. Turns out there are loads of us out there! Hello ADHD! #notathing #totallyathing #whosaidthat

Fast forward to 2015, I am still very grounded and humble and still catch public transport. I was invited out to Australia and asked to perform for three minutes for Australian TV. I performed three minutes of pulling my pants down and telling a joke about the thigh gap. At the gig, no one really laughed and I was just a mental woman with a London accent and no trousers on. However the people of Facebook loved it, it got shared and shared and has since amassed over 35 million views. After all the years of work and the hours I'd put in trying to master comedy, it was pulling my trousers down that got the mass appeal. Dreams really can come true.

Once the clip went viral, I got really excited and thought, wicked, maybe finally I'll be able to earn some money and take the cling film off my windows because I can't afford the heating bills (double glazing on a budget). Maybe I can buy my own place, maybe this is it!

I called my agent Debi: surely this thigh-gap viral clip will help get me on telly now? *Live at the Apollo*? Jonathan Ross? *Loose Women*? Come on, body image is huge and the views of my jokes are going up by thousands every day.

'Sorry Luisa, the booker for Jonathan Ross needed to see you live but couldn't get a babysitter. And *Live at the Apollo* say you're not ready.'

'Not ready? What do you mean, not ready? I'm on millions of views from one joke; show me another unknown *Live at the Apollo* act that has had that.'

'Maybe it's because you say bitches a lot?'

Oh FFS.

By the way, if like me you hate these pre-story ambles – JUST START THE BOOK ALREADY – you can always skip this bit and then come back to it at the end, it will probably make more sense. But this prelude is imperative to the book, as I have a word-count deadline.

Anyway, back to the thigh gap. I was so happy it went viral, 35 million views and counting, and yet so disappointed that I wasn't getting more opportunities off the back of it, hello?! I should be famous by now. I have been training in performance my whole life, and doing comedy since the age of 19. Come on, I'm 33 now. I am tired of getting the bus.

Why is it taking so long? So I didn't fuck a footballer or go on *Big Brother* – OK, I auditioned but didn't get in, and I did once have sex with someone that played for Sunderland, but apart from that, I have gone the long route and you know, developed a skill.

So then my agent called me in for a meeting and what do you know, Miss Big Shot Random House was there and the pair of them accosted me. I wasn't ready, I was ill prepared, I don't know if I had even washed that day. Big Shot Random House was like, Luisa, hi, please write the book *What Would Beyoncé Do?!* Oh how I laughed in her face: listen honey, stop being so desperate, it's not going to happen, I am not a writer, hello? I am an artist, you need to see me live for the experience, you can't bottle me into pages . . . I clicked my fingers, flicked my hair and left.

The next day I was leaving for a gig in Singapore, and as I walked around the airport looking for something to read, I was like, man, there really should be a book called *What Would Beyoncé Do?!* Instead I picked up *How to Become Rich* and *Think Like a Billionaire* and went to pay for my new purchases. My card got declined. Motherfuckers. The irony that I should have bought these books sooner was not lost on me.

I called my agent. 'Fine, tell Big Shot Random House I will write her stupid book, but tell her it's because I think it's really important that I share my story and reach out to the people and not because my card got declined in an Asian Waterstones.'

THE END

#Jokes. That was the prelude.

LET'S START OVER

Here is the beginning. PS I am really sorry if you think this book is going to be all about Beyoncé. In this book, *I* am Beyoncé. In fact this book is my Adele *21*, bitches.

AND WE START.

So growing up I always thought I'd have the same lifestyle as Beyoncé, I thought I'd be really rich and famous, but God decided to give me a very different set of cards, ah she's hilarious. It's weird, because I've always had an affinity with Beyoncé, like in many ways me and her are really similar: we're both fabulous, both have booty and both our mums still make our clothes. In fact very often people get us confused; only the other day someone stopped me on the street and said:

'Have you had an accident or an injury at work lately?'

I was like 'I have hot sauce in my bag, swag.'

At 21, I graduated from uni with a first-class degree. Even though I didn't have an agent and was living in a run-down estate in Salford, I was adamant fame and fortune beckoned; just give it a year or so Luisa. I mean, look at Keira Knightley, she was like 19 and became huge. I mean, sure, I am a little older, but that's OK, you just wait, in a few years' time I am going to be massive. I genuinely thought that by 28 I would have it covered. Career, marriage, a house with two garages, babies. Tick, tick, tick. That was where my 21-year-old self saw me.

So when at the age of 27 I found myself moving back to my small home town of Farnborough and sleeping in my old room, even though my mum had turned it into an office (it was really fun sleeping on the photocopier every night), I wasn't where I'd thought I would be at this stage of my life. The photocopier did come in handy when I found myself making up waitressing experience on my CV trying to score a job in Costa with a first-class degree (who the fuck needs to write a CV for a coffee shop; what qualifications do I write down? I bet Beyoncé isn't in her local library typing 'warming milk' as one of her skill sets. It's just coffee, FFS, I prefer granules anyway. No, I didn't get the job).

This is how it started.

My brother (who is 26 and also lives at home, though he actually doesn't mind as his biggest ambition is to do handstand press-ups) blocked the toilet with a really big poo, you know, one of the massive long, thick ones, like if it was a penis, you would be well in, but it's not, it's a poo. He ran out of the house and my mum told me it was my job to clean the toilet. Me? Why is it my job? It's his shit!

'Yes Luisa, but he isn't here and you can't sit around doing nothing all day.'

'What? But that's not my fault. It's gross, can't you make him do it when he gets back?'

'No, he's too lazy, you know better; now clean the toilet!'

So I'm there with the toilet brush, desperately trying to make it go down the one-way system, but it's not moving and the water is spitting back in my face and a splash lands on my eyelid and I nearly vomit. It's not budging.

My mum comes in to check on me, like she wants to make sure I'm doing a thorough job. She's Polish, the stereotype is true, they do make the best cleaners. She actually teaches English as a foreign language, which is ironic really because she always gets her English wrong, but hey, don't hate the player, hate the game! My favourite English she ever got wrong was 'Luisa, I've noticed you have been going through lots of toilet roll recently. When you go, how many slices do you use?' Classic. Anyhow, she is the worst to clean for as her standards are unmatchable. So there I am, elbow deep in the toilet basin trying not to vom, and somehow I have managed to get rid of all the water but not the giant shit.

'Luisa, that's not going to work, you have to do it properly. Go to the garden and fetch a stick.'

'What! FML, I'm not getting a stick!'

'Listen, if you want to achieve anything in life, you have to work for it; whether it's a career and being famous, or unblocking the toilet, it's all the same, it's your attitude that counts. So do it properly, go fetch a stick.'

That's how, at the age of 27, I found myself walking around my back garden looking for a reasonable-size stick to break up my little brother's poo.

Luckily, just at that moment I got a text from my equally jobless best friend Zana. I have known Zana since I was 18. We met at a temp job and spent a summer in Zante together. She had just moved back home after a year's travelling hiatus. She'd been really hoping the experience would help her 'find herself'. All she found was how quickly nine months' worth of drinking fresh coconut water on a beach in Thailand can feel like a long-distant dream once you're looking for semi-skimmed in the local Co-op.

Zana saved me from my shit-stick search and suggested we meet up. So fast forward to 1 p.m. and we

4

are in our favourite bistro, Le Weatherspoon's, drinking Blue Lagoon out of the jug with a straw, swapping tales of Thailand and poo sticks. It did not take long to get reacquainted. We ordered another pitcher and laughed about the last time we were on this high street. It was four years ago; we were two stone lighter and filled with hope about getting out of this small town. Oh how convinced we were that our first-class degrees would be our ticket to a brighter future.

It was at this reminiscing moment that Zana said something that blew my mind; it was like I had my very own personal Jesus sat in front of me, like I was speaking to Gandhi himself as she uttered wisdom that changed the course of my life for ever:

'Do you remember when you had anal sex with that personal trainer on that bench over there?'

'It was an accident. I was very drunk, I'd had like three Smirnoff Ices!'

That wasn't the mind-blowing bit; I'm just trying to give you the context of the banality of the conversation so that when I tell you the mind-blowing bit it blows your mind too. She said – wait for it:

'Hey Luisa, you do know we are the same age as Beyoncé?'

'WHAT THE ACTUAL F?!'

'I bet Beyoncé never had accidental anal on Camberley High Street.'

'Of course she hasn't, when Beyoncé has anal, skittles pop out.'

'Ahhh queen!'

It was at that moment in my life that I made a promise for the future ahead. It's a two-part promise:

1. Never let a guy accidentally give you anal. I don't care how many Smirnoff Ices you've had; you either do it planned and prepared for or not at all.
2. If she couldn't sing and she couldn't dance but she found herself at 27 living at home and breaking up her little brother's poo with a stick, when life gave her lemons, WHAT WOULD BEYONCÉ DO?!

PS FYI, yes, now we know, she would write an album that becomes a cultural, ground-breaking phenomenon which is so close to what I did it's not even funny: babe, the whole 'When life gives her lemons, WWBD?!' is the first line in my solo show which I wrote a good FOUR YEARS before *Lemonade* even existed. I swear me and B are psychic twins.

2

ONCE I WAS 7 YEARS OLD (WELL, ABOUT 9)

Born in 1982, I was originally one of four children. I have three brothers, so I grew up with boys, all boys, and trust me when I say boys are dull. I was hilarious. I have only ever really known funny women; some funny men, but predominantly funny women. I used to watch anything with Whoopi Goldberg in it and Lord does that woman make me howl.

My parents got divorced when I was very young. In the week we lived with my mum in Farnborough and at weekends my brothers and I would go see my dad in Bristol. He lived on his own round the corner from my granny. She is also Polish and hardly spoke any English.

Polish was my first language, but I went to an English school. I felt really embarrassed to be one of the only foreign kids in the school (along with my bros), plus I had divorced parents. I didn't want another reason to stand out, so I learnt English and quickly disassociated from my Polish roots. At school at least.

My babcia (Polish for granny) would often look after us when we were in Bristol. She was beautiful and very Catholic, with a wicked sense of humour. We would have the *Carry On* films playing all day and she would howl. My brothers would always try and sneak 18-rated films on to the VHS; not the porno ones, just the ones with lots of blood and gore. My babcia didn't speak English but she cottoned on pretty quickly that the opening scenes of *Robocop* weren't suitable for four kids under 12. Instead, she put on *Sister Act* because she thought it was about church. That became my favourite film of all time. When Sister Mary Robert gets the high note in 'Hail Holy Queen', oh boy, what a pause and rewind moment; they nearly topped it with Ahmal's go at 'Oh Happy Day' in the school hall performance in *Sister Act 2* – those are two of my favourite scenes in movie history. 'Give it some of that deep shoulder, action!' Well, plus the 'scared of leaving this room and never feeling' in *Dirty Dancing* and 'Dad, dad, come on, you gotta get up' in *The Lion King*, but I digress.

I loved being with my granny at the weekends; sure, it was great to see my dad, but hello, the real hero was Babcia. She would stay over at my dad's house whenever we were in Bristol and I would share a bed with her. We would sleep back to back as it kept us both warm. Often before we fell asleep we would play mime games like charades. One of our favourite games became to recite scenes from films or TV we had watched that day. I would recite lines from *Sister Act* with act-outs, and she would really laugh; she loved it, and I loved how this made me feel. Selfish really, making other people laugh because it made me feel happy, but rather that than, I don't know, making them cry.

The next day after church her friends would come around and Babcia would get me in the living room and ask me to act out the film again. Her friends would smile politely with expressions that can best be described with acronyms like WTF?! But I didn't care, it was fun entertaining my grandma and that was what mattered.

At school, though, I was still the awkward Polish kid. I didn't feel like I fitted in, so I created my own world. I was quite happy entertaining myself. I had always wanted to perform, ever since I was really small. I was a shy kid, but I loved showing off when I was comfortable. I would put household objects on the couch and perform to them (milk bottles and a Hoover are surprisingly great laughers). As a child, it was simple: when I grow up, I am going to be a famous artist. As long as I am always comfortable and there is a Henry in the corner, that is what I am going to do.

Around this time, if people ever asked me what I wanted to be, I would always say an actress. My parents divorced when I was seven, and it was a turbulent, drawn-out process. I grew up in a house with a lot of arguments, tension and uncertainty, but I found that being funny could quickly eradicate and relieve the tension. I hated the transition of being playful and free with my grandma at the weekend and then feeling totally withdrawn and like the class weirdo at school.

My mum did the best she could with four small children and broken English; she went to classes in the evenings and eventually met my stepdad, Johnny. Johnny is a kind British man; he knew of my acting aspirations and decided to sign me up to dance classes, which he thought would help me bond with other girls in my school. I was nine years old with a crew cut; all the other girls were so pretty and pristine and I just rocked up with a frown on my face like someone had farted. I felt so awkward all the time, to be anywhere near British girls in leotards.

When I went to the classes, something weird would happen. I could follow the class, but as soon as the teacher stopped to turn around and watch us, I felt so self-conscious and wanted the floor to swallow me up. The fear was debilitating; I would freeze, every time. People would be dancing to the routine and it was like my limbs would go 'No' and I would just stand there and front it out. I learnt very quickly, when I was scared: don't show fear, just don't show anything. So I would stand there, hold a pose and not dance, fronting it out.

It was so weird. At home, at my granny's house, I could sing and show off for her friends and not care that they didn't like it. I felt good because she did. But here in Farnborough, I felt completely out of my depth.

Some weekends, when we weren't at my dad's, we would go and visit Johnny's sister; they lived in London and were pretty well off. Private-school-educated, million-pound house, well connected. Me and my brothers would rock up, have a delicious lunch and then as we would leave, Johnny's family would offer us hand-me-downs. Not in a bad way at all, they were lovely to us, but it was Johnny bringing his new partner and her four small children, and it just always felt weird. We were never really part of the family; as hard as they tried, I always felt like an outsider with my brothers.

One of these cousins was an actress. I was so excited to meet her and tell her that that was what I wanted to be too! She told me that to be famous and successful as an actress you had to go to drama school and it cost a lot of money and not everyone could get in. You could only do well if you had an agent, and it was hard to get an agent. She was speaking generally, and in hindsight I can see her own struggles with it. But at the time it just made me feel so embarrassed to admit that acting was what I wanted to do. And she was right: we had no money, there was no way I could afford to get into drama school, and there was no way my freeze dance moves would get me a scholarship.

However, there was a secondary school down my road that was a private school known for its drama department. When I left primary school, I was desperate to go; I'd heard that the school had links with people at the BBC, so if I could get in, I could end up on *EastEnders*. The only problem was the school cost £11,000 a year. You could do a test to try and get a scholarship, and I was desperate to sit the exam, but my mum wouldn't let me. She said it would be a very difficult test, and even if I got the scholarship, she wouldn't be able to afford all the uniform.

So instead I caught the bus every day and went to a comprehensive seven miles away in the next town.

I felt like an oddball at school, though I loved Fridays. Fridays the tuck shop was open and you could get a bag of penny sweets for 10p. My favourites were flying saucers. Sometimes if you were really lucky you could get a bag with *two* flying saucers. Flying saucers and pink lemonade, the Fridays of dreams. Apart from that, I wasn't a fan of the rest of the week; it was the weekends that shaped me.

My parents seemed to have the longest divorce, it went on for a few years and it made it very difficult for me to make sense of the world. It seemed to me that my dad had a lot of hate towards my mother and would call her all the names under the sun whenever he would mention her. We were all under 12 at the time.

He would come and pick us up on a Saturday morning, but he would never come to the house. He didn't want to see my mum and so wouldn't come to the door. It was before mobile phones, so he would arrange the week before to pick us up at the bottom of the road at midday. Me and my brothers would take it in turns to run down the street and wait for him. Sometimes he would be there at 12, other times at 3 p.m.; you never knew. When I saw his shiny Orion come round the corner, I would feel so excited and run towards the car.

Social workers were involved and there were lots of court dates and legal battles. It all left my mum pretty broken. My mum always felt he hadn't allowed or encouraged her independence, it was all about staying at home with the children, so she wasn't allowed to drive or to work. Friends were not allowed over and although we had a phone line, my mum wasn't allowed to use it. The first thing she did when she left was to have one installed. My father hated it.

I, on the other hand, was in love with him; he was my hero, I couldn't have adored him more. I found him really funny and loved being around him. Often when he picked us up I would sit in the front as I was the only girl and he would put on Cher tapes. I would sing my heart out and my dad would laugh and applaud. I loved making him happy. He would be like 'Luisa, do a show for us' and that meant I would sing and dance along in the car to whatever '80s power ballad he was playing. It would drive my brothers in the back of the car crazy but my father loved it.

He hated that my mum had met someone else so quickly and got pregnant with my awesome little sister. But Johnny saved my mum; she says that if she hadn't got away when she did, she wouldn't be here now. Johnny encouraged her to live independently, to have driving lessons, and he would buy us takeaway kebabs at weekends. I liked him.

My mum had Asia. And I was delighted, yay, a girl! My father was furious. He used it against my mum in the courts and then filed for custody of me and my brothers. We didn't know at the time that he had fathered two other children; they used to always be at his house whenever we stayed, but he denied they were his kids and just said he was babysitting.

We kinda got suspicious 19 years later when he had photographs of him attending their graduations, but hey, some babysitters are just really passionate about their work.

One of the memories that sticks out the most was when my dad asked me where I wanted to live. We were sat in the garden of my grandma's house, and he pulled me to one side, put his arm around me and asked me which of my parents I wanted to live with, him or Mum. I was so confused. I loved him, but I loved my mum more, and she had just had Asia and Asia was really fun, plus she let us have kebabs and my dad never let us order takeaway ever. I remember weighing up the pros and cons and literally because my mum was nicer to me and I preferred her cooking I said, 'Er probably best if I stay with Mum?'

My dad unwrapped his arm from around my shoulders and didn't speak to me for the rest of the weekend. On the car journey home there was no singing, and he didn't ask me to do a show. He just played really sad music, suggested I was no daughter of his and then refused to talk to me. I was heartbroken. Looking back now, I guess he was too. But I didn't know that at the time.

The courts decided it was best to split us down the middle, so my elder two brothers with my dad and me and my younger brother with my mum. The weekend before we split it was agreed we would have one last big Christmas together at my mum's house and then my dad would pick up the two boys and that would be the start of the custody.

We had just had the first half of the holidays at my father's and he was dropping us off for the final week at my mum's. Johnny walked past the car as we were saying goodbye. He interrupted, words were exchanged and they ended up getting into a fist fight. I managed to grab my little brother and ran up to the house to get my mum. She ran out but as she did my dad locked the older two boys in the car and drove off. It was Christmas Eve.

It was all pretty horrible. I will never forget the pain etched on my mother's face as she chased my father's car and ran after her sons as he drove off with them. I think my father hated it that his family was broken up and my mother hated it that her family was broken up and everyone seemed to be to blame but nobody could seem to fix it. I learnt not to trust my own instincts after that; I didn't know who was right or wrong, what to believe or how to make sense of anything. It made trusting reality very hard.

I guess comedy and performing to objects in the living room was my way of escaping the real world. I loved it, I loved anything that was showing off by myself. I used to sneakily watch *Band of Gold* when I was younger, a TV show about prostitutes, and I remember thinking the women were so glamorous; they had male attention and validation. I had no idea what they were doing, but would spend afternoons dressing up in my bedroom and rolling my skirt up with my hand on my hips. Lord, I was a paedophile's dream. I read somewhere how Dolly Parton said she once saw the town tramp and decided that she wanted to be just like her. I figured I was in good company.

My dad knew of my aspirations to work in acting and he would often say, 'Well, if you lived with me, I could have put you in a school where they have a great theatre, not like your mother who put you in a comprehensive.'

I would feel really anxious that I was missing out on something because I chose to stay with my mum. It wasn't my fault I liked kebabs so much. At weekends, when all four of us were together at my dad's, I would be in my element because I had my boys back. My brothers were happier at my father's; ever since Asia was born, Johnny had become really strict towards them. My mum said it was because he was jealous of the attention she showed them. I never understood that, how a grown-ass man could be jealous of a child, of a mother's love for her children. How fragile are these guys?

My dad didn't seem fragile; he was the opposite, he was so alpha, but he wasn't strict at all, apart from the ban on takeaways. He just left us to it really, which was cool as we could just hang out with my granny, and we loved spending time with her. It was one of the reasons the boys moved to my dad's, 'cos my gran was so amazing. But she died a year after they moved in and slowly things started unravelling.

Weekends at my father's involved babysitting his 'non-children', playing Sega and going to Tesco to buy big bags of Wotsits. But our favourite thing to do was to go to Makro; before my dad got custody, he would take us all and buy us loads of sweets. Makro with my father was one of my favourite childhood memories. Some kids love being taken to Alton Towers. Not for me mate, get me with my dad to a wholesalers and I will show you a happy face! I could get a massive box of my favourite flying saucers and they would last me for weeks.

My dad got really upset and angry after the custody though. I think he was hurt that me and my little brother were still living at my mum's. I remember one time in Makro I picked up a colouring book and went to put it in the trolley. He took it from me and put it back on the shelf and said, 'If you lived with me you could have that, but you decided to live with your mother so she can buy it for you.' And then put two colouring books for the boys in the trolley.

Leaving him and my brothers at weekends was hard. I would cry myself to sleep every Sunday. My mum loved us very much but she had Johnny now and a new baby, and I felt quite isolated. Johnny had bought the house next door and they'd knocked the walls through, so now instead of a semi, we lived in quite a big detached house with two sets of stairs, one to go up and one to go down, or vice versa.

I would come back from my dad's with my little brother and just run to my room, put on Cher music and wait to fall asleep. I would feel awful on Sunday nights, but knew that as soon as I was back in school, I would snap out of it and be a different person. Sure enough, on Monday I would wake up and not feel the urge to cry; I would be fine, a new and different Luisa, who functioned and went to school like a normal person until it was time to see my dad and brothers again. It was difficult having all these feelings of sadness but having none of the maturity to understand my surroundings or other people's pain.

At 15, I took GCSE drama classes. I loved getting up and improvising and imitating classmates. The room of people laughing gave me confidence. At 16, I went to college. I had to pick three subjects, but I only really wanted to do performing arts, so the other two were just filler. Psychology because I thought it would help me understand characters and emotions better, and French because ... I don't know why I chose French. I think I fancied the teacher.

In performing arts, we did a lot of drama, all that stand-in-the-middle-of-the-room-and-pretend-to-be-a-tree shit.

That wasn't what I wanted to do; I wanted to get up and move people, get people to emotionally react and engage. But for now, I guess, being a really good maple would have to do. I loved it when we could improvise, that was when I felt in my element. It was only ten minutes of any lesson but it was my favourite ten. Any time I could do funny, that made me feel good.

I signed up for a local amateur dramatics group outside of school. It was held every Tuesday in an old man's pub and consisted of three men in their sixties and two women in their forties putting on a production of *Peter Pan*. One of the older dudes wanted to play Peter. I thought with my crew cut I would be the obvious choice, but apparently this guy, the 60-year-old, really had never grown up! Oh how they laughed every time he said that. Every time.

They wouldn't even let me play Tinker Bell; instead I became part of the 'boat ensemble'. I tried to talk to my mum about it, but she was busy with the stress of being a mum, and she was grieving my brothers I guess. Even though she saw them once every two weeks, she never seemed happy and was always sad about it.

I talked to my dad about acting, but he said it was a stupid idea and it wasn't too late to study to become a lawyer. I had never expressed an interest in law, but for some reason he seemed to think I would excel at it. He reminded me again that if I lived with him I would get an excellent education like my brothers, but I'd chosen to live with my mother.

So I spoke to Johnny, who said I should be grateful, and that I was lucky to be in the *Peter Pan* production.

He tried to inspire me with 'I once saw a play where a woman had no lines but came on stage and moved a chair, and she stole the show!' but all I heard was 'I once went to see a really shit play.'

I hated seeing my mum sad all the time and I hated how conditional my father's love seemed to be. I didn't like life, and something inside me kept telling me that I was meant for more. That it shouldn't be like this. It can be so hard trying to figure out what you want to do in life, what your place is. But I always felt that I had to know happier times than I was having now. Here's the thing with me: in a weird way I feel like I have lived the life I want before. I used to cling on to that thought, that I knew there was better out there because I had experienced it in a past life. Despite all the crap, there is a part of me that knows I deserve and can have better. I might not know the name for it, I might not know how to get there, but what I did know was that whenever I got to play, be that improvising in front of my classmates or re-enacting *Sister Act* with my grandma, time stood still. I was present and I liked it. So I spent most of my teenage years and early twenties trying to find that feeling again.

I signed up to dance classes, but they didn't feel right as once again I would freeze like an awkward antelope. The am dram society was depressing. But put me in my drama class and the teacher was like 'Luisa, get up, start a scene' and that would feel just right. It wasn't learnt; it was something that I assumed I was and would be. I just loved the feeling of people watching, and showing off, but only ever in the safety of rehearsals, my grandma or the Hoover. Not really the basis for a successful career in cinema.

So I'm 18 and leaving college; time to audition for drama schools. I figured I would need a student loan anyway if I wanted to do further education so I may as well get the same loan for drama school. Besides, anyone who I spoke to said if you wanted to get anywhere in the acting world, you had to go to drama school.

I lined up a bunch of auditions – Mountview, RADA, Edinburgh Uni and Manchester. But on the day, cue dance class all over again. Something happened, the panic of feeling like I didn't belong. The people in the waiting room were all flexible-limbed and had great posture; the straighter they stood, the more I curved. I didn't have money or an eating disorder. I didn't have a posh accent and I didn't keep saying 'I just live for the art.' I was just a weird Polish kid who really wanted to be famous, because hello, in a past life I must have been?! This didn't go down well. I froze at every audition; even if I didn't freeze, I didn't read well. I didn't get in to any of them.

Hurt, lost and confused, I called my father and he said he wasn't surprised and suggested again that I try and do law. I nodded and said I'd look into it and went elsewhere for help. Help came in the form of a little module I saw when scouring university prospectuses. The module was called 'Stand-Up Comedy'. These words shone out on the page as if they were highlighted. I looked at the school. Hello land of dreams, Salford University, a BA Hons in Performing Arts. Yes, I am Destiny's Child.

I rocked up at Salford for the audition. The uni was rough as fuck, paint peeling off the walls; the skies were grey, terraced houses and council flats lining the streets and the air full of northern grit. For a girl from a small town in the south where the sun shone every day and people waved to you, this was a shock. It was not the glamorous drama-school lifestyle I had dreamed about, but in a way it was better. It had stand-up as a module. It wasn't going to be until year three, but nothing else felt as good as the idea of doing this course. As I walked around the council-estate campus, I asked the universe for a sign. I found myself on a street called Strawberry Road, and as I love strawberries, I thought, that will do.

My audition was with a guy called Mark Bishop, smoker, pot face, middle-aged, gross, receding hair. Who for some reason I found sexually irresistible. I warmed to him instantly, I don't know why, but I remember liking being in the room as long as he was in it. Later down the line he gave me a lift home once and reverse-parked with one hand. I nearly came all over the seat. Jesus, I have daddy issues.

Mark made me do a Shakespeare monologue, so I did the same one that didn't get me in to Mountview, RADA, Manchester or Edinburgh. You would think I'd have learnt to perhaps try and change my technique, but I thought, fuck it, it's Salford, what are they gonna do? Say no? They can't – the gods have spoken, Strawberry Road was my in! I read through it once, standing in front of him. He then suggested I read it again, and for some reason I chose to lie on the floor.

In hindsight he must have done something to my hormones as subconsciously my womb spoke to me, saying, 'Brace yourself; you should lie down for this one as you need to get pregnant.' So I did, I lay down and looked up at him as I quoted it. It was sexually charged, poorly recited Shakespeare, and as I was coming to the end of the monologue I got up, stroked his face and held his gaze. I was a really horny 18-year-old.

I got an unconditional offer from Salford about a week later. Fast forward to results time, I got 2 Bs and a C. I called Salford to secure my place, the phone rang twice and I panicked and hung up. What the fuck was I going to do at Salford? It was so rough and why do I have to be poor, I don't want to be poor. Sure I do love strawberries and that lecturer stirred weird feelings in my vagina, but that's hardly the basis for a life-changing decision. Also, is it worth going somewhere for three years just for one stand-up module?

I mean, come on, I should be able to go to a good drama school, I am meant to be a famous actress. Like hello, what would Beyoncé do? She wouldn't be going to some shit-hole. I am meant to be in movies already, not Salford. I am not going to some rough institute even if it does do comedy. I'm Beyoncé. I am meant to be Yoncé. Why does this not feel Yoncé? Salford is not Yoncé!

I called up Salford and rejected their offer. My mum said I should do a TESOL certificate, teaching English as a foreign language. Well that sounds much more Queen B. So I went through clearing and found the solid career choice subject of 'Communications'; they were offering a

TESOL cert as part of the course, so even if I didn't like the course I could travel and teach English. Even though I never liked the idea of travelling and I could not care less about teaching English, I called Salford and said sorry, my bad, I am securing a better future for myself: I am going to Lincoln to get a degree in communications. That'll show 'em.

My first day at Lincoln and the halls were rough as fuck. I opened my bedroom door and I cried. It was gross. There was a dirty dark grey carpet, a stained single mattress next to a massive window. A plastic chair with Tipp-Ex stains, and a broken wardrobe. There was a sink in the room with a cracked mirror, and as I opened the desk drawer, the desk came apart and rat poison fell on to the floor. My mother's cleanliness had turned me into a snob. I didn't want to be at Lincoln. What the fuck am I doing here? I should be at Salford. Oh FFS.

My mum, stepdad and little sister left me at uni, and rather than feeling excited, ambitious and ready for all the casual sex that was promised in freshers' week, I felt lost, isolated and shat myself. As I went back into the dorm from the car park I met a girl called Pas. I looked at her and said 'Ahh, you're pretty' and that was the basis of the lifelong friendship that followed.

A month in and going to classes on linguistics, which I really had no passion or attention for, I kept thinking about performance and how I wished I was acting, or getting up in a room with an audience and making people laugh. I went to look for Pas in the dorm and passed this pink fairy-lit room with the Destiny's Child *Survivor* album playing, I went in and looked around. I liked it. In popped this woman with a slicked-back ponytail and the most amazing drawn-on eyebrows I had ever seen. This was Delia's room.

Delia and Pas were the reason I went to Lincoln, to pick up those two bitches. We have been best friends ever since. At the time, I was so upset and angry with myself that I couldn't get into drama school, that I didn't have money, that I was living in a shit-hole. But in hindsight, everything happened for a reason: meeting Pas and Delia, that's why I went to Lincoln.

Despite meeting the two girls and my discovery of pear hooch and the '80s classics that they played in nightclubs (mind blown), I couldn't stay. Two months into the course I rang Mark Bishop at Salford and confessed I had made a terrible mistake and would like to come back the following year. He said he remembered me and would welcome me in September. I quit Lincoln. See, remember I told you I was bad at trusting my own decisions? Case in point.

So after those long Lincoln months, and 19 years young, I moved back into my mum's house, called the whole thing a gap year and decided to look for a job. I got one, selling massage machines in department stores. Little thing you should know about me: I'm a hustler. I've always been really good at winging life and winging jobs; when I was 16 I was on £6.80 an hour when most of my friends were on £4. Speculate to accumulate was my motto, even though it had nothing to do with me earning £6.80 an hour. I just remember hearing it once and then using the expression for everything.

My massage job meant standing in a garden centre or department store and convincing old people to sit down and have a free massage. I then had to encourage them to part with £289 worth of machinery which for today only was £200. For every machine I sold, I would get £80.

Technically to get a healthy day rate of £80, I only needed to sell one a day. You would think this simple maths would bring out my inner Wolf of Wall Street and drive me to try and sell four or five in one day. But I am lazy, and this only confirmed my laziness; to be honest, I just looked forward to the lunch breaks. I agree with the notion that you should always hire lazy people to complete a difficult task, as they will find the easiest and quickest solution.

I would be massaging customers in the aisle of a Debenhams or a Daniel's and they would ask me what I really wanted to do (I don't know what it was about my aura that gave them the impression I wasn't satisfied in a career selling massage machines). I would tell them I wanted to be an actress and they would laugh and say they would look out for me on TV. I liked them saying that. I like it when people say good luck and wish you the best. I felt like their good wishes and intentions were putting messages out to the universe. That all these would collect and I would be an actress.

If only I could find a way in. The arts seemed like a club to me. It's not always very nice. I have never liked people telling me that I am from a certain class, or opportunities are out of reach for me because I don't have money. That suggests that my dreams and aspirations are out of my hands. I always found these people stupid, like what are you talking about? Of course I am going to achieve everything I want and live the lifestyle that I want. But that lifestyle seemed to be behind the doors of this club. And the gatekeepers to the club were the drama schools, a system put in place to keep people like me out. Why? I couldn't understand: how could they not see that I belonged?

But at the same time, when it came to the crunch, I couldn't deliver; the fear I had in those dance classes years ago carried on to acting. I would get nervous, and although I could do well in rehearsals, it would get to stage time and I would be so aware that everyone was looking at me and I would freeze. Leaving Lincoln and having a year to work myself up for Salford just made me more anxious. And when I was anxious I was funny and then I would relax again.

That was comedy. In my auditions with drama schools, even though I didn't get in, I could get a laugh – not enough of one to warrant a scholarship, but enough of one for me to feel acknowledged. Addressing the wooden performance, commenting on how awkward and awful it was, the relief of pressure would exhale through laugh. And that moment, that moment I really loved.

Laughter was my form of mindfulness.

3

WORKING 9 TO 5 (P.M. TO A.M.)

So my massage job didn't work out. As much as I was happy with my sell-one-machine-a-day intention, my boss was not in the business of hiring someone with such a low sense of ambition. I got fired, became depressed and was sharing a room with my little sister. Which I actually enjoyed; she was ten and fun. I would get upset over some guy who hadn't texted me and ask her for her advice, and she would reply, 'I don't know, I'm ten.' She's a legend.

I started temping in a call centre for about a month or so (that's where I met Zana) before my mum signed me up to a three-week intensive TESOL course. My mum offered to pay for the course on the condition I would help her teach at home. My mum was running a home-stay business. So we would have people from all over the world stay at our house and she would teach them English in the morning then go show them the sights.

I qualified and despite my mum's appeals decided to fuck off to Greece. Absolutely nothing to do with teaching English and everything to do with fear of missing out. You see, at the grand old age of 19, when everyone had done their group holidays to Ibiza in matching T-shirts three years beforehand, I'd never been there, done that or got the T-shirt.

I didn't ever really have a group of girlfriends. I was always the odd one out at school and I kinda felt like I was flying solo a lot. My mum would give me a haircut like my three brothers had, so while the rest of the girls would come into school with their hair in a French plait, I would be rocking the latest in the bowl-around-the-head cut.

Think Beatles in the '60s, but before they were cool, i.e. never. Saayyyyy whhhaaattt! (hello I love Cher?!) But my mum wouldn't let me dress up in a black see-through lace bodysuit to straddle a cannon, so Beatles-inspired it was.

It's amazing how much of a beacon for sex appeal a bowl haircut can be, so much so that when we used to play kiss chase in the playground, I would walk really slowly and they never managed to catch me. I can remember clearly Valentine's Day, aged about eight, and Daniel Woolmer brought in Valentine's cards. I was so excited as he gave them out. I was the only girl who didn't get one. Daniel Woolmer turned out to be gay. I couldn't get a Valentine's card from a gay guy; maybe giving it to me would have been too obvious and outed him. Still, at the age of eight, I was like whatever and just did a headstand in the corner of the room.

So when it came to my holiday, I did what I have always done and thought, if I can't go with a group of girlfriends that I don't have, I will go by myself. I booked a flight and a two-week holiday to Zante. What was the worst thing that could happen? Apart from getting mugged, attacked, cut open and left for dead on a beach, or worse, getting lonely?

On the day of my flight, my stepdad Johnny dropped me off at the airport. I gave him a cuddle and said bye, then I started crying as I didn't know why I was going and I hated change. Why do I always make stupid choices? I don't need to go abroad by myself just to experience life. He said, Luisa, I have never known you to do things by halves or not land on your feet. If you hate it, you stay for a two-week holiday and then catch your flight home.

As it happened, I loved it and stayed out for the season. My first day, I walked past this shop offering cruises around the island, with this tall, skinny gay guy handing out flyers, calling, 'Cruise around the island.' I had just landed and had no tan, and no make-up on because I wanted to get a tan. (PS Who are these bitches that go to the beach full face?! PPS I love tanning, tanning is my jam; besides, cellulite has never looked sexier than when it's orange, am I right ladies?!) So there I was looking rubbish and he had no time for me. Conversation went as follows:

Me: Hi sorry my name's er Luisa and I just got here, you can probably tell from my pasty skin, haha, er sorry I haven't got any make-up on and so look awful but I er sorry just wanted to sorry get a job, haha, sorry . . . (My assertive skills were on fleek.)

Daniel: Right . . .

Me: And er well you just look British, sorry well I mean you stand out 'cos er sorry you are, you know, well burnt like a lobster and sorry I thought maybe you could give me some pointers? (Again nailing it.)

Daniel: Riiight, listen, just go into bars, make an effort with your appearance and ask for a job. You can get one like that.

Me: Oh, OK, sure, yeah, I do scrub up well, anyway sorry for er my face, er thanks OK er bye.

And I strutted off like the strong, independent woman I am.

That day I spent hours on the beach, caught a bit of colour and then decided to get dressed up to the nines. Armed with a cute butt and a winning smile, I was gonna try and get anything: a job, a boyfriend, a dream.

On my way out, I bumped into the shallow gay guy. He was like 'God damn, hi babe! You look amazing!'

'I know, right,' and we became the best of friends for a season.

There is something really honest about shallow people, you can kinda tell straight away where you stand, and for a woman by herself in the middle of Zante, having a gay best friend who told me when I looked awful was better than having no friends at all. Dan and I started hanging out every day, always hustling for a way to make money. He would flyer for cruises, and I picked up a job pretty quickly in a bar called Ghetto Club. It had an outside seating area, a square bar and a dance floor under a roof, TV showing football on every wall, neon pink lights, a smoke machine and the loudest Destiny's Child remix playing from the speakers. It was perfect. This was fate, I was home.

I was the only woman they hired, and I worked alongside five gorgeous local guys. They took me under their wing and I felt in my element; it was like being a little sister again, but a fancied one. I know, right, dreams really can come true. These guys found me attractive, I had a tan, I looked mixed race and beautiful and my body was slamming. I started having the time of my life.

My job was to be a hostess and greet people, get them to come into the club; I would go round with a tray and offer them free shots. I loved the attention of getting groups of men into the bar, but it was always more friendly than sexual. I feel very comfortable around groups of men. Growing up with brothers, I like having guys as friends; they make me feel safe and like I am at home.

It was an easy enough job: give out shots, clear glasses, serve drinks, dance a bit, €15 a night, cash in hand, done. I'd work until about 2 a.m., then meet up with Dan, go dancing for a couple of hours and then head to the burger café for breakfast/dinner before going back to my apartment to sleep. The next day I'd wake up at noon, get my bikini on, go down to the beach, practise sunbathing half-naked, getting paranoid and covering my boobs with my hands every time someone walked past, then head on back to the apartment. And then do it all again.

Dan and I would talk about how we were going to be rich and famous. But for now we needed a game plan, a business idea, something that could help us make fast cash here on this beautiful island. Speculate to accumulate, remember? Loads of other people were doing it, why couldn't we? We just had to be creative, think outside the box, get edgy, get current. The locals were walking around flogging tours, ice cream, shots and sunglasses; there must be something we could sell. Everything is for sale in Greece. (INSERT GREAT POLITICAL JOKE ABOUT 2015. Oops, how did we miss this before it went to print? Shame. Would have been a great joke, I'm sure. Lols.)

One afternoon, tired of being broke, I was lying flat on my back in the street while Daniel sang his 'cruise around the island' jingle. He decided to step over me, which I found hilarious, so I lifted my feet in the air and touched my toes with my hands and said if he wanted to step over me again, he needed to 'open my bridge'. I don't know what I was doing, but he got it. He would walk towards me, I would open up like a bridge and he would step over me. This quickly escalated into 'Step over lady 50 euro, step over lady for euro.' It was without doubt one of the funniest things I have ever done. I think we made 10 cents once, that was a great day. Admittedly you probably had to be there. But if you ever see me lying on the street, just whisper 'Step over lady 50 euro', and like magic, a bridge of legs will appear and the pathway to your enlightening future will be lying right in front of you.

A mini parable entitled 'The Night I Stole'

So we were feeling particularly poor one day, more so than usual. 'Step over lady' wasn't taking off and my €15 a night was quickly absorbed by apple sours and 5 a.m. burgers. The lack of funds was getting frustrating and must have been playing on my mind. One particular shift at Ghetto Club, I welcomed in a group of lads and got them all inside with the offer of a free shot. As they took their seats, I went and grabbed their watered-down peach schnapps and brought them over. One of the guys turned around and gave me a couple of euros for the drink, but instead of saying 'No, it's free' and returning his cash, I sneakily hid it inside my miniskirt pocket, ignoring my pang of guilt As I turned around, though, I saw my manager staring at me. He had seen the whole exchange.

Oh shit. I felt so guilty but also kinda relieved that he had seen me, as my Catholic upbringing kicked in. Maybe I was hoping for absolution. He gestured with one hand, like a Mafia don, and called me over. He told me how disappointed he was, as we got on well, but I'd stolen from him and was no longer trustworthy. I tried to explain that it wasn't stealing, I just saw the donation as a tip, and anyway it was only two euros! He said that wasn't the point, it was still technically stealing and he didn't want thieves on his property. He told me to get my stuff and leave.

I felt awful because I *am* trustworthy, and I loved this job. I was gutted. As I started to leave, one of the bar guys shouted 'Luisa, table four' and put two cocktails on the tray. I didn't know how to say 'Sorry, I have just been fired' so I collected the tray and took it over to table four.

As I put the drinks down, they said 'Oh, can we order two more please', and I still didn't know how to say 'Er sorry I have just been fired' so I went back to the bar and ordered two more cocktails, all the time unable to look up as all I could feel was my manager's eyes burning holes into me. Then a group of lads outside the bar were deliberating whether or not to come in, and I couldn't just stand there and say 'Sorry, I've just been fired' so I said all I could say in that situation, no not step over lady 50 euro but, 'Hey guys, you wanna come in and get a free shot, lots of sexy ladies indoors?'

Essentially I just kept working; I ended up staying the whole shift. At the end of the night, my manager put €13 in my hands and told me he would see me tomorrow.

He never mentioned it again and I continued to work at Ghetto Club for the rest of the season. Without stealing.

So what have we learnt from this parable?

1. Beyoncé would never steal two euros.
2. Beyoncé doesn't have to.
3. If she did and got fired for it, I think she would do what I did and just keep working.

4.

NASTY PUT SOME CLOTHES ON

After I'd been in Greece a few weeks, my friend Zana came to stay. You remember her from chapter 1 – she is one of the funniest people I have ever known, and the only person I knew in Farnborough who understood my Beyoncé struggle. Everyone I went to school with seemed so settled and happy with their cool jobs living in the big local city of Southampton, getting on the property ladder, having boyfriends, and being maid of honour at each other's weddings. Whereas me and Zana just wanted to be really fucking rich and famous.

Zana decided to come out and join me in Zante. ZANA IN ZANTE!!!! And LUSIA ALSO IN ZANTE we would sing. We promised ourselves that we would have the summer of dreams, suck a lot of dick, drink, dance, be really hot and hair-flick out of every bar we walked into. Even though by this point I had only ever sucked one dick and I didn't even know how to do that. I remember reading somewhere you should do it like you're eating an ice cream, but the problem is I bite ice cream, so I guess my analogy would be eat it like it's crispy aromatic duck, i.e. devour it slowly and don't let anyone interrupt you whilst doing so.

But don't forget at this point at age 19 I hadn't been introduced to the art form that is crispy aromatic duck and so was still sucking dick like biting ice cream.

So Zana got a job in a bar down the road from me and became part of mine and Dan's gang, though she refused to play 'Step over lady 50 euro'. I know, what a killjoy. Killjoy Zana as she became known.

One afternoon, myself, Dan and Killjoy Zana were out trying to pick up boys. Now ladies, this is a tip I will pass on to you if you're looking for the best place to meet men in the middle of the afternoon. Er, in the summer of the World Cup, my friends, rock up to a bar with all the hope, body and dreams of a 19-year-old wearing nothing but a bikini and a feigned interest in football. Bam, you're welcome.

Our lack of funds had made us very resourceful and we'd become friends with some bar workers on the strip. They would serve us cheap drinks at their place, and we would return the favour at ours. So there we are, the three of us sharing a cosmo out of a pint glass, when we spot these two guys walking into the bar eating sausage rolls, though who eats sausage rolls in Zante, I don't know.

The boys started chatting to us and buying us drinks; we kept pretending to offer to pay but they were having none of it. Thank God they didn't call our bluff. Roll on a few hours, Zana and the white guy, Mike, are getting on like a house on fire, which is great, but I was sat with Egor. And he is still eating a sausage roll. Egor was this beefcake of a man with tattooed arms, grey string vest, fat sunglasses and a big head. He was ugly, but you would notice him because of his body alone, built like a brick shithouse. He was confident in a way that only ugly men can be when they know they've got something to offer that is not overtly visual. He had that 'I've got a big dick' aura.

So Mike and Zana are flirting and Zana turns to me and is like, I really fancy this guy Mike, and I'm like, well good for you Zana but I don't fancy Egor. Zana is like, don't be so frigid Luisa, come on we are 19 and in Greece, I'm not asking you to marry the guy, just be normal, stop spoiling your own holiday and step up.

It's now 4 p.m. and me and Zana are slowly getting pretty drunk. I say slowly; it hits me really fast and hard, but she is hard-core and gives me water every other drink to keep up. Both of us have a three-hour shift at seven. We rock up at work steaming, the boys follow, we give them lots of free shots and all keep drinking. We dance badly, laugh loudly, and then they invite us back to their hotel. On the way they stop at the shop, and ask if we want anything. We're brass broke, so we ask for washing-up liquid, toilet roll, shower gel and some sun screen. It's not quite the packet of gum they were thinking, but we get some of that too.

At their hotel, shopping bags in hand, Zana and Mike start getting it on. Meanwhile Egor is talking to me about puff pastry and I'm really not into the conversation. I have been drunk since four and kinda just want to sleep, but Zana, who has consumed four times as much alcohol as I have, says that we have to keep partying and that it's my first holiday and I should relax my crack. Also she whispers to me that she has always wanted to have sex in a swimming pool, so she goes outside and leaves me alone with Egor.

I wanted to leave but she is very clear that I am 19 and in Zante and this is supposed to be the time of my life. I go to the balcony overlooking the pool, just to make sure Zana doesn't drown or anything. I can see them fucking in the pool, Mike's weeny white body causing ripples in the water. Egor sees this as an opportunity to take his pants off and start walking around the hotel room butt naked. I'm disgusted and think 'How dare you?' but at the same time, oh my God, look at the size of his penis. Admittedly I had only ever seen like two, apart from my brothers', but that was as a child in the bath, and this looked very different.

I didn't fancy him at all, but something about the heat and his penis size and the fear that I was in Zante and should be living it up and having fun meant that I fucked him. I fucked Egor. And I can say hand on heart it was some of the best sex of my life. Because I didn't fancy him, I had no emotional tie to him (if anything I found him repulsive; he had pastry down his chin FFS); it was just the gratuitous act of sex for sex's sake. Animalistic almost. I saw his hard dick and I wanted to sit on it.

I loved it, it was so liberating to have sex and not second-guess his emotions or feel like I was being judged. It was sex how I wanted it. I had never experienced it like that before, and because I had no feeling for him, I didn't care, I was brutally honest. He was on top of me pounding away and I was like 'Oh you disgust me Egor, you can't even fuck me properly, call yourself a man, this is boring.'

He would reply, 'Sorry Luisa, I'm trying my best.'

'Well try harder.'

'Yes, oh my God, you are amazing.'

'What am I?'

'Amazing.'

'Amazing and what, Egor?'

'Amazing and beautiful, Luisa.'

'Damn right, you are shit and I hate you.'

And here is when I learnt a very valuable lesson about the male ego. You criticise a woman when she's having sex with you, she will probably start crying and you won't hear from her again. You criticise a man when he is having sex with you, the fucker works harder.

5

UPGRADE YOURSELF

I love sucking dick; teabagging is one of my favourite pastimes! Love playing the D, too much d fun. Yay to the D time, what time is it? Oh it's D time! The aubergine is my favourite emoji.

Here is a narrative that I am so bored of, women getting slut-shamed. I like sucking dick, dudes love getting their dick sucked; why am I called a whore? A while back there was a story in the national press about a young woman who went on holiday to Magaluf and sucked off more than 20 men on a nightclub floor. She was annihilated in the press and on social media, people calling her a slag, a slut, a whore. I found the whole story really uncomfortable; it was like a modern-day witch hunt.

It should never have made the national press; they vilified her, named and shamed her and posted her picture for everyone to judge. Not once were any of the men whose dicks she sucked held accountable or pictured, and there were more than 20 of them, you would have thought they could find a picture somewhere. Not once was the venue manager or the proprietor of the bar held accountable for not looking after people on their premises; these are the men that encouraged the behaviour, offering alcohol as a prize, these venue owners were profiting, cashing in on the publicity at the girl's expense.

Now I am not saying the girl was blameless. But she was 19 and an idiot, and who hasn't done messed-up shit when they were young and on holiday? I know I have. OK, admittedly I didn't suck off 20 dudes in a nightclub to win a free holiday – I was too busy playing step over lady with my BFF – but I have done other embarrassing things.

What I'm trying to say is that I hate how women are subjected to and vilified at the expense of their sexual attitudes, desires and behaviour. This was a vulnerable 19-year-old. I hated that this was front-page news, that it was all over social media. A lot of my guy friends were sharing the story on Facebook, and they were posting it with updates like 'Check out this dirty slag,' 'Check out this dirty whore.' And I'm thinking, this is so repressive, because I can't imagine one of these dudes being put in the same situation and having the decency and self-respect to go 'Excuse me, excuse me, let me be the first to put my dick away, here, have some flowers.'

So why is it that men are so quick to call women slags, sluts and whores? If you want your woman to be good at sucking dick, well that takes practice. And it's not just men, it's women, we call each other these names. It's exhausting and damaging.

A woman can be sexual if it's for the pleasure of a man, be that in porn or in advertising, but the second it's natural – e.g. breastfeeding in public – it's inappropriate. Or worse, the second a woman's sexuality is for her own pleasure and satisfaction, she is vilified. Why? What is the world so scared of?

I appreciate we need a way to understand our world, and so I think it's just a case of upgrading the terminology. In the same way you don't call a nightclub toilet cleaner that any more, you call them like a hygiene attendant or a sanitation consultant, I suggest we do the same with slags, sluts and whores; let's upgrade the terminology.

'Hi, this is Mary, she is a pleasure angel.'

'Hi, this is Suzi and she is a climax fairy.'

And by all means you can still keep it real.

'This is my friend Katerina. Katerina had sex with my ex-boyfriend a week after we broke up and she is a spunk bucket, a cock guzzler, an anal-gaping princess.'

6

YES!

So Zante is over, I have since enrolled at Salford, two years speed by and it gets to the year I have been waiting for. It's September 2005, I am 22 years old, a size 10, and it's day one of stand-up comedy class. I have spent the previous two years in classical acting training and women in media studies, as well as masturbating furiously over Mark Bishop, who I still found sexually irresistible and could do absolutely nothing about it.

On my first day of uni, the first person I spoke to was Zoe. Zoe became my best friend. I saw her waiting in the corridor and thought 'Ahh, she's pretty' again, a brilliant basis for a lifelong friendship. Zoe was from Stretford, Mancunian born and bred. Her dad is Pakistani and her mum is white from London. Zoe is fucking beautiful. She introduced me to Luzia, who was from Angola and the funniest, most beautiful person I had ever met. Luzia would call me her little African queen and I would call her my Polish princess. Zoe was our Pakistani prince. These two women became my royal family for the next three years.

So it's day one of stand-up class. Zoe is in the class with me; Luzia was too chicken to sign up and was having too much fun dating a Lebanese guy who worked in the local salsa club. There are ten of us in the class, two men and eight women; my lecturer keeps saying how refreshing this is. I don't understand, as to me those stats are obvious. The lecturer (not the sexy one – sorry Lloyd) tells everyone to go outside, you have ten minutes to think of your first stand-up routine, I want you to think of a funny story or a joke, and then I want you to come back into class and perform it for everyone like it's your first gig.

All the girls ran to the loo and were trying to think of what to talk about whilst the hand-dryer was going off. We all went back into class. The boys were more nervous than the girls, one of the lads, Larry, said he spewed in the toilet a little bit. I was nervous but also excited; it was something I had wanted to do for years. It was really important to me that I get this right. I didn't know what I wanted to say, or how I wanted to say it, but for that moment I wasn't worried about anything other than the sheer panic and excitement of getting up in front of people and performing.

I got up and told a story, a simple story, an obvious story; it was a sex story about me wanking. My punchline was 'Oooh, Mark Bishop!' Aka I told my class a 'joke' about me wanking over my lecturer (the sexy one). It got lots of big laughs, and the joy was contagious. Apart from Lloyd, who I think was a bit jealous that no one wanked over him (sorry Lloyd ... though I'm sure Zoe said she did once).

I sat down and Zoe turned to me and said, 'You are a natural, it's like you have been doing it your entire life.' It felt so right and so good and so on point to hear. After all the auditions and failed dance classes, the awkward am dram meetings, the massage machines and the vodka shots in Greece, finally here I am. Here in this classroom, a room with no windows, a broken television in the corner, a room in the middle of Salford, with paint stripping off the walls, I felt like I had finally showcased my voice, that out of my whole life, this one day meant something. It was one of those moments where you feel like, yes, finally I'm alive. This is living. Today I matter, I am making a contribution and I can see a glimpse of what a good, real life should feel like.

7

I WAS HERE

I genuinely believe that if you have a vocation or a calling or a dream, something that keeps you up at night, something that leaves you restless for daydreaming about it, something that the universe and life keeps drawing you back to – whether it be performing and you find yourself walking past a sign for drama classes; or maybe it's painting and drawing and you realise that out of your group of friends, it's you they always ask to do their hair and make-up or customise their old dresser; or maybe it's working on bikes and feeling passionate about riders or languages and you study abroad and always feel an affinity with foreigners – whatever it is, you will do it in your spare time, where you are not getting paid, you will do it when you are broke, you will do it when you are sick, you will do it when you are tired. Maybe it's cooking, maybe it's design, maybe it's medicine. Maybe it's motherhood or fatherhood (yes, I am aware there is no spare time in parenthood). But that thing that you do, that you keep coming back to, that you are naturally good at, that thing, whatever it is, is part of your being. It's part of your core genetic make-up, it is what makes you the beautiful unique individual that you are. It is your gift to the world.

It's when you don't listen to the voice within that is desperate to follow your calling that you will damage your heart. Your soul becomes depressed, bored, disheartened and lethargic, you question who you are on a daily basis, why you are here; you feel easily exhausted in the grind of life. You wonder what the point of life is and your happiness is limited to fleeting moments of freedom that only come when you momentarily forget the reality you have become accustomed to. Reality that you are just part of the machine, working in a job that you don't care for, earning money just to pay the bills and keep a roof over your head; you are literally waiting to meet someone, procreate and die.

It is harder to endure this reality than to listen to your vocation. It takes more effort to kill your soul in a long, slow daily process, gently chipping away at the fabric of what makes you beautiful. People think that following your dreams is hard; I think it's the opposite. Not following them is harder. Because it is only when you allow yourself to do the thing that makes your heart sing that life falls into place. No matter how many people have told you it's not for you, or you won't make a career out of it, or that you are not good enough, your inner voice has to be louder, stronger and more consistent than all the doubters. Because the second you live your authentic life the way you are meant to, the second you allow yourself to follow a suppressed vocation, something magical happens. It stops the feeling of time. It is no longer living to die, but dying to live. This is who I am. This is where I am meant to be. It makes every moment of crap worthwhile, because here, in this very moment, you allow your soul to sing.

And here in this shitty room in the middle of Salford, where there are no windows and the paint is stripping off the wall, I felt more alive than I had done in years; my soul was singing her little heart out.

The feeling lasts for approximately the rest of the day until I wake up in my student dorm and have to get to voice classes with Dane. Fuck the voice classes with Dane; I was already looking forward to my next stand-up lesson. 1.30 every Thursday became my new favourite time.

The fact that I fell in love with my stand-up class was good, as I didn't have much luck anywhere else. I was in love with a married man called Marley. I didn't know to begin with that he was married, though it should have been obvious when he would never answer his phone between the hours of 6 p.m. and 8 a.m. I met him in a bar, he played for a local football team and everyone around us was staring at him. I thought it was adorable and said, 'Aww, this is what it will be like when I'm famous.' He laughed and clapped at everything I said, I loved getting his attention.

After a few weeks of what most people would call a couple of dates and a few exchanged text messages, and what I preferred to think of as a whirlwind romance, someone dropped the bombshell that he had a wife and children.

The next day I kept getting text messages from him, which I ignored. And I could see myself looking at the situation and thinking: I have two options. I can just carry on ignoring him and move on. Or I can answer his messages, continue a dialogue.

To this day I wish I'd carried on ignoring him, but I didn't, and I spent the next year choosing to be heart-broken over a man who would call me once or twice a week and have sex with me twice a year.

It was self-destructive, but it was easier to be in love with Marley; on some level it was a pain I felt I deserved. I had only learnt negative things about love from my father: that women can be disrespected, and that I was not worth fighting for or having in someone's life. That was damaging, and my relationships with others reflected it.

One day Marley showed up at my student halls with a football shirt with *Lulu* on the back. It was his nickname for me. I was over the moon and really felt a T-shirt with my name on it was a sincere sign of a married father's affection for me.

Turns out Marley had girls up and down the country; it was actually him that told me about them. One time on the phone, when I was complaining about why he acted so weird with me, he said, 'Why can't you be more like Lulu?'

'Eh? Lulu? I *am* Lulu!'

'No, the other one.'

There was another Lulu; I was technically Lulu number 2. I cried for months. It was OK for him to cheat on his wife with me, but not for him to cheat on me. I think of that shirt now, and how worthless it is. It means nothing; the fabric offends me.

Be it a shirt, or a pair of shoes, or a car, or a ring, or a house, nothing bought is ever as valuable as self-love. Someone can buy you all the gifts in the world, but if it is at the expense of your own self-esteem, you are indebted to that item. You are worth more than a T-shirt; you are worth more than a house. Please know that value.

But at the time, I was young and I thought this active purchase proved Marley's love for me. I was heartbroken when I found out. And felt like an idiot. I remember being sat outside the Arndale in Manchester, it was 10 p.m. at night and I was eating a kebab, chips and cheese on a bench. I gave my older brother Adam a call and was crying down the phone to him. He gave me this nugget: 'Aww don't cry Luisssaaaa. Listen, some people might say there's plenty more fish in the sea, but I think for this occasion there's plenty more footballers in the league.'

I digress.

I completed the stand-up module; part of the exam was to do a live show in front of a real live audience. No longer just playing to your classmates, but in a proper comedy club, on a proper stage in front of a paying audience.

The university hooked up with the Jongleurs comedy club and our showcase was booked for Jongleurs Manchester. It was a sold-out event and there were about

250 people watching. My lecturer said I was one of the strongest and so wanted me to go up first.

I did well for a first time – I didn't kill it like I had done in class every week, but I did well. Then Zoe went up and opened the second half, and she annihilated it, like the audience went absolutely crazy for her. And despite feeling really pleased for my mate who moments before was being sick in the toilet from nerves, at the same time I felt a pang of jealousy that I couldn't rouse that reaction.

Afterwards at the bar, a friend of ours, a guy we both kinda liked flirting with, came up to Zoe whilst I was stood next to her. It was a really noisy bar and he whispered loudly to Zoe, 'Oh my gosh, you were the best one on tonight Zoe, by far.' My heart sank. I was crap, I had been good all year and here I was stood next to my best friend and I was crap. This is how I measure myself. I don't think it's a need to be the best; I think it was because I didn't do as well as I knew I could do. Why is it every time I try to get up and perform, I fuck it up by not being as good as when I practise? In real life I can do it effortlessly and have the confidence to deliver, and yet the second there is the pressure of a real audience, I don't do as well, or because I didn't get the reaction a friend got, I feel like I have somehow failed.

After that I played a few open mic nights, but I had lost my confidence a bit and they weren't as good, and someone posted a blog about it online and called it a 'smutty set by Luisa Omielan'. I hated it, I hated myself, and I felt mortified that I'd put myself on stage just to be ridiculed. It was hurtful and I was embarrassed for myself; this wasn't how comedy was meant to make me feel.

But despite not nailing it outside of the classroom, I graduated with a first-class degree and was selected for a final-year industry showcase, where 20 students were chosen to perform to maybe 100 or so agents and industry professionals.

I loved the rehearsals and felt confident about how it would all go; I'd found this brilliant monologue of an emotional woman that I thought I could do justice to. It came to the showcase and I did all right, but by no means did I wow the crowd. I came outside afterwards for the drinks reception and wasn't approached by anyone. I went up to an agent and asked what he thought of my performance, and he said, 'Yeah, sorry love, I've already got brown hair, brown eyes.' I remember thinking, not mine you haven't.

Despite that, my lecturer Mark, the one that I loved and was amazing to me, brought me into his office and showed me my grades. I'd got a straight first, top scores across the board, one of the highest overall grades in ten years at the university. I was delighted. I ran out and called my mum. She was over the moon for me. And then I called my father. I wanted him to know that I'd done all right, that I wasn't a failure. My older brothers had graduated a few years before with a 2:2 and a third, and they had since cut contact my father. He hadn't spoken to them in three years. He said he was waiting for them to see sense.

When I told him about my first, he said 'That's nice' and then stupidly I said, 'I know, but remember how you said I wouldn't do very well and that if I lived with you I would do better? Well the boys got a 2.2 and a third, and look, my lecturer said I got the highest first in ten years!'

He replied, 'Yes Luisa, but they did BScs and you did a BA, don't think I don't know the difference.'

I hate how the arts are dismissed, how there is a snobbery about those subjects. It's a gift to be an artist, it is as important as any science. You can't discover or learn without art; it is too intrinsic, too insular, too feminine. Art is creation. And it's fucking hard.

Anyway, graduating with my first and not getting an agent or the Hollywood blockbuster movie offer that I had hoped for, it didn't make sense to stay in Manchester. Sure I could work as a bar girl and dance on tables, or sell perfume in Debenhams. But if I was going to do that and be depressed, I may as well do it in the comfort of my mum's house. So I moved back down south.

Back in Farnborough, when people asked what I wanted to do next, I didn't have the balls to say 'comedian' so I would just mutter something about acting and seeing what happened. I didn't want to do a temp job; a local recruitment company was advertising a graduate scheme in London. I thought, well at least I could lead the fun City lifestyle, and, you know, meet boys and go out for drinks. Whatever. The schemes were so down with the kids they held auditions as opposed to interviews, and you could earn up to £18k in your first year. So I applied to all of them.

One particular interview/audition was with a very kind old man. It was a graduate scheme with a start-up tech company of some sort, and my job would be in computers or hard drives or something. We had a big long chat and he asked me about all my skills; we seemed to get on really well. He said, 'Luisa, you are doing a great interview and I think I would happily hire you, but I get the feeling you don't really want the job.' I didn't want him to get in touch with the agency and blame them for wasting his time, so I said 'No I do, I really do' and then found my face winking for me. He half laughed and wished me well.

The recruitment company said it was all about transferable skills, and that my training would make me a great candidate to be a recruitment consultant: it was people-focused, with good earnings and an easily established clear career path. But I didn't want to sell things; my gap year of massage machines had put me off for life, and the thought of working in recruitment made me want to dig my own eyes out with a spoon. But I did like the idea of having money, so, dead inside, I applied.

I went through the interview process and got quite far by displaying my enthusiasm for recruitment and targets. What do you know, I am a good actress. I got to the third round of interviews and was selected to be seen by a senior recruiter in a central London corporate office. Having had what I thought was a successful half-hour talking to a lady in a suit, she then asked her male colleague to step in.

He was a proper Del Boy in an Armani suit, think fast, talk fast, Essex accent, brown shoes, and coke at the weekend kind of guy. He must be the company's best-kept secret, I thought. There was a chair opposite me behind the desk, but instead he chose to sit on the table in front of me.

'So, says here you got a first in acting?'

'Yes.'

'Well if you are an actress, why are you here?'

'Because it didn't work.'

'And what, you just gave up?'

'Er no, it's just really difficult and unrealistic to get in to.' I was quoting the rhetoric of aunts and uncles everywhere.

'So you don't want to do it now?'

'Er no.' My heart winced. 'I really want to work in recruitment.'

'Interesting. If you came to me and said I'm 40 and it hasn't worked, I would believe you, but if you can't even be bothered to work and fight for your own dreams, what makes you think I want you working and fighting for my company?'

Sometimes, when someone says something really truthful, it can be embarrassing and annoying. Especially when it comes from a suited-up 20-year-old who's earned more money in the last three days than you have all year. But at the same time, it can feel like a relief. The game was up, and although I had no face left to save in this situation, it felt good. I hated him because he'd showed me up, but I loved him because he was right. He should be a recruitment consultant, he was absolutely excellent at it. I should not.

So I quit all the graduate training programmes and parked the dream of working in London. My mate Alison from college had set up her own recruitment firm and she could help me out with temping. It was enough for now. I got three jobs a day, spending my mornings as a postwoman, my afternoons in the stock cupboard of Wilkinsons and my evenings working in a bar.

It was at this time that I started thinking about going to America. I did some investigations and rang this school called the Comedy Institute, where they teach a masters in comedy, sketch, joke writing, improv, stand-up, the works. Just reading about it made my heart sing. I enquired about coming out for a year and getting a visa, and they said, 'Hey you should totally speak to a really good friend of ours, I believe he's in London at the moment, a German guy called Klaus Hans, oh you'll love him! Want us to pass on your email?'

And here, my friends, is the first plot point in my story.

8.

DADDY . . . ISSUES

Klaus was a comedy promoter from Germany who had spent a year in the States doing the course at the Comedy Institute before deciding to set up his own touring company. He booked shows in Berlin, Gdansk, Helsinki, Romania, Singapore, you name it; he was a good guy to know.

He met me in a coffee shop above a bookstore. I don't know why, but I had goose bumps around him. We had a coffee and I bought him a slice of rocky road and we chatted for hours about comedy. Now I wouldn't necessarily associate German with being the sexiest accent in the world (sorry Germany), but for some reason, whenever Klaus opened his mouth, something about his harsh, gravelly tones had me. He literally had me at *guten Tag*.

Klaus said I didn't need to go to America to do a course; in fact I could do a comedy course right here in

London. He said London has one of the best stand-up
comedy scenes in the world and if I did a class here, it
wouldn't necessarily be to learn more about stand-up, as
I had already done that at uni. He said the only way to
truly learn stand-up is by doing it, but that a class would
help me find my feet, it would give me the confidence I
needed to start in London, and I could meet a network
of people on the London circuit. There was a man called
Logan Murray who taught an excellent stand-up course.
Klaus gave me Murray's number and I signed up. He then
handed me a copy of *Time Out* and circled all the gigs
that I could call and try five minutes at. We talked about
everything, I told him all about Salford, he told me all
about the US. We spoke about our hopes and dreams,
about failure. He told me what it was like trying to sell a
show and having acts on that people wanted to see as
well as taking risks on acts audiences had never heard of.
I talked about being crap and judged, and how it kept me
feeling trapped and prevented me from trying.

He said, 'Darling Luisa, maybe it is not fear of failure that
you have, perhaps it is more to do with fear of success.'

Sometimes believing for a lifetime that you can achieve
something becomes a daunting prospect when you actually try and execute it and it's not happening. I didn't
get an agent, I didn't get signed, I wasn't funny on stage,
but put me in a room where I can just play and I am at
my happiest; surely that's got to be a sign of something.
So I took Klaus's advice and looked for a room where I
could just play, free from judgement and just play. So
I signed up to the stand-up course. It cost £495, a month's

postwoman wages, but like I have always said, you got to speculate to accumulate.

I stayed in touch with Klaus when he travelled back to Germany; he would call me, I found him so easy to talk to and he was so passionate about me starting my comedy journey in London. Before I knew it, we would be Skyping for hours. But it's safe to say that on that first day, the first day I met him over a rocky road that I went home and said, 'Mum, I've met the most amazing guy, I think I may have found the one.' And for me, he remained the one for the next four years.

THE ONE

Listen, haters gonna hate, when you have found the one, embrace it. I think it's really unfair when people say 'He's not the one for you.'

How dare you?! How do you know he is not the one for me? 'Because if he was the one, then he would like you back.' Er hello, what planet do you live on? This is hugely inflammatory and not only inaccurate but incredibly offensive. 'How do you know I am not the one for him?'

'Well because he says you are not the one for him.'

'Yes but just because he says I'm not the one, doesn't mean I am actually not the one. He doesn't know what's good for him, he doesn't know I am the one yet but I am still the one. I have to show him. Look, it's like when your kids don't want to eat broccoli, they don't know it's good for them, so you have to chop it up into tiny pieces and hide it in their favourite crisps.'

'This sounds very rapey.'

'It's not rapey, it's broccoli.'

'So you are equating yourself to broccoli?'

'Yes, actually, I am his broccoli, he might not know it yet but I am good for him and he will want to eat me eventually.'

"How do you know you are good for him?

'Because I'm the one for him . . . jeez, keep up.'

'So you are going to just waste your time until he realises you are the one for him? Don't you think he would know it already if you are?'

'It's not a waste of time! And obviously it would be helpful if he caught up to my oneness sooner, some men get it straight away and others are slow, so I have to play the long game, the broccoli game, oooooo, open wide, here comes the aeroplane, aka, Skype him and talk for hours, play it totally breezy, take at least an hour to reply to his messages, look gorgeous every time I see him, then on a subconscious level, he begins to realise how good I am and slowly but surely falls truly, madly, deeply in love with me. Mate, I'm broccoli.'

This charming German man with his weird accent and odd taste in shoes had come along and just like that unclipped my wings and said go. I felt like I was a knotted water hose and someone had just released me and the water was free to flow. It's a shit metaphor I know, but I was in love and he's German, and they love engineering, so it will have to do.

In August, Klaus was back from Germany and producing some shows for the Edinburgh Festival. He was helping a few acts put on their solo shows and suggested I come up and see how it all worked. I was pretty sure this was German for 'I love you, Luisa, come and work with me.'

The festival takes place during the month of August and the whole city turns into a great big party performance space. You cannot walk down the street without being flyered for a show, theatre, comedy, dance, the lot. Every bus and taxi has performers' faces slapped all over them, and if you want to get anywhere in the city centre you have to allow yourself an extra ten minutes as you will be stuck in crowds walking at a snail's pace.

Klaus helped me find somewhere to stay for the month and offered me a job flyering for one of his acts. He was so impressive; here he was, a German, not in his own country, looking after five acts at the Edinburgh Fringe Festival. None of them were big names but they were all doing solo shows and Klaus was running things! His assistant Gert was really sweet and lovely to me. She had just started dating a Danish comedian and was totally besotted with her.

Klaus would run from show to show, making sure the rooms were set up properly and the acts were happy. He would meet me at 5 p.m. every day to hand me some flyers, then I would go out on the street and give out leaflets and say things like, 'Fantastic comedy show, 8.45 tonight at the Three Sisters pub.' OK, so flyering for Klaus wasn't exactly what I had in mind as my course for true love, but it was a good start. I don't think Klaus ever noticed how much effort I made to look good for flyering, I think he thought the tutu was to attract attention; actually it was to subliminally show him what I would look like in a wedding dress.

Five p.m. became my favourite time of day. I was working for the man I was totally in love with, he was my boss, I was his worker, oh role-play undertones drove me mad. I thought, well if I can impress him with my leafleting technique and get him audiences every night, he will be like, wow, now that is a woman I want by my side to help me build my comedy empire. I must marry Luisa. That's how I thought it would pan out, but I'm not very good at this whole predicting life thing.

The Edinburgh Festival runs for about three and a half weeks and most performers do the whole run with one day off in the middle. It's frowned upon to take more days off as industry can come and see you at any time and that's the big point of the festival. People perform in Edinburgh so TV, film, casting people, agents and promoters can come and scout for talent. It can set you up for the rest of the year. Some acts even get a run at the Soho Theatre, which is the most prestigious place for Edinburgh acts to play in central London.

A massive part of the festival, which every comic I met talked about, is the comedy awards. Awards are given out every year for best newcomer act and best show. You only qualify as a newcomer if you are performing your first solo hour. The pressure to be nominated for the awards has become so huge that it has started a trend of 'trying out' your first solo show during the festival at 45 minutes so that you can come back the following year with a full 50–55-minute bullet-proof show and still qualify as a newcomer. I always thought this was a wimpish way out as it was pandering to and playing to the industry and not for you own artistic development. Klaus had several acts just doing 45. I wanted him to have more confidence than that, but it didn't lessen my love for him. As far as I could see from my first year, Edinburgh was all about getting an agent and TV people to come and put you on telly.

Now there are two ways of doing Edinburgh. One is by having a big agent already and they put the money up to hire you a room for the month. They pay for all your posters, a PR and flyers; they then spend the evenings networking to get industry people to come and see your show. You are placed in one of the major festival venues, where tickets start from £12. All you have to worry about is performing; your agent takes care of everything else. You just need to get good reviews and make sure you're nominated for the awards so your career for the rest of the year stays on track. No pressure.

The cost of this privilege was around £12k for the month back then. Edinburgh is extortionate. Acts are indebted to their agents and/or their venues and spend the rest of the following years paying back the money by doing 20-minute spots for £80 here and there up and down the country. That is the system.

Now to get an acting agent, you go to drama school and get picked up. In the comedy world you just need to be good at showcases. Enter new-act competitions, win then, get some buzz around you as the next big thing and sign to one of the major agencies. Once you have an agent, they're the ones who will promote you, otherwise the doors to the comedy world are closed. It is my belief that it generates an elitist system that leaves out a huge number of people who are good but who may have not been discovered because of lack of opportunity and financial circumstances.

And that is where the 'other' way of doing Edinburgh comes in. No agent, no promoter, just an act who is willing to put on their show for free. It's called the Free Festival Fringe. There are some politics around calling it the free fringe or the free festival, so to save you from being bored by the details, let's call it the Laughing Horse fringe or 'free shows'.

Essentially Alex, who runs the Laughing Horse, controls several venues in Edinburgh: pubs, restaurants, bars, cafés with a function room, or, in recent years, shoe cupboards. These rooms come equipped with sound and lights but no technical staff and no door staff and no front-of-house staff. You, as an individual, can rent a room from Alex for £50. You also need to pay a £500 registration fee in order to be part of the Edinburgh Fringe Festival and be in the main festival brochure, but apart from that your costs are what you make them. If you need someone to do sound and lights for you, i.e. be your 'tech', you can hire someone. If you cannot afford to, you do it yourself. You are responsible for the design and printing costs of your posters and flyers. You put them up yourself, you go out flyering your own show, you set up your own room, you do your own tech and at the end of the show you hold a bucket at the door and ask audiences to leave a tip. After an hour's work, you can leave with anything from £3.10 (tough crowd) to £200.10 (great crowd), you never know!

Something about the Laughing Horse fringe immediately resonated with me; I felt much more affiliated with it than I did with seeing people in the big rooms. Watching Klaus fill his comics' free rooms to the rafters with audiences, I felt so excited to be watching him work. Klaus offered to come and watch me do a five-minute set before one of his shows; I took the gig. I was super nervous and panicking that he was watching and just did really gregarious material about sex but with none of the swagger to pull it off so I just looked like a screeching child.

Some Stand-Up Terminology
Died/Bombed: Means no one laughed, it was embarrassing for everyone involved and why would you even think that someone as worthless as yourself deserves a platform to have a voice? Stop trying to be funny, everyone hates you.

Smashed/Killed/Annihilated: Means everyone laughed, the audience loved you, you are the funniest bitch they have ever seen, everyone in the room wanted to be near you, and you are a gift to mankind and a goddess at life.

On this particular occasion, the only occasion, that Klaus decided to watch me, I died on my arse. He watched a bit of it but then left. That's how bad I was, he didn't even want to watch my whole set at his own gig.

Now here's a thing, I don't mind dying on stage. In fact I kinda love it; there is a freedom in dying on stage which I only discovered once I started doing more and more comedy.

In the early days of me doing stand-up it was all about not dying, just please don't die, please don't be awful. But once you die, once, twice, a hundred times, the fear is no longer about dying, so you kinda have to learn to enjoy the deaths as much as you can. Deaths can actually be quite invigorating; it becomes a 'status-off' between you and the audience. You are literally in the lion's den, one woman vs a hundred booing, jeering people. It's actually kinda fun. No heartier laugh or tighter bond can be made from comedians than by hearing their worst death stories.

However, here in this moment, being in love with Klaus and telling him about all my aspirations to be a really successful comedian and him seeing me for the first time just die on my arse. This was horrible, I was so embarrassed. I don't think he actually cared, comics don't tend to because we all die at some point, but I was too new to the game to realise this.

Besides, Klaus was always way more focused on what he was doing. Something about that felt like home to me. He was an authoritative figure who could make me feel good and then just ignore me; #hellodaddyissues. It just made Klaus more attractive and confirmed my belief that it was true love; as far as I had been conditioned, being ignored and having to work to earn someone's affection was what true love was all about. This was catnip.

So Edinburgh, I did the flyering job and started hanging out with a few other open-mic'ers. I was getting paid £6 an hour. I met another flyerer who worked for one of the big venues. She had access to the stockroom where they kept the flyers for all the shows. In there she found some Smirnoff vodka vouchers offering a free shot with every flyer. She stole about 200 and we split them. Oh yes, my friends, the days of feeling guilty for stealing two euros were long gone; I was on to the big money now, 100 free vodka shot vouchers. Speculate to accumulate, bitches, even in crime.

That night I got really drunk and was high on life from not spending a penny (figuratively; literally I was weeing constantly. I don't know which is literal and which is figurative in this sense, I must remember to ask my editor. Oh man, another thing I missed for the print!). I got talking to some guy, and it being Edinburgh and a festival filled with show-offs, we decided to swap clothes. In my drunken state I thought this was hilarious. (Someone in Edinburgh actually still has my favourite black-and-white dress.) Then I took the guy home.

When I woke up the next morning, my one-nighter had gone, my favourite black and white dress wasn't there and his clothes had left too. Why would he take my dress as well as his own clothes? Weirdo. Then I noticed that I only had about five vouchers left.

Confused, I rang my friend.

'Mate, how much did we drink last night?'

'Loads mate, at least five each.'

'What? So why do I only have five vouchers left . . . Oh fuck.'

I had been robbed by my one-night stand. I found him two days later, with the flyers my mate had stolen, buying rounds for everyone, dickhead. So you see, karma is real!

I told Klaus about my one-night stand hoping he would be jealous, but nothing. If anything, he looked disgusted. All right Germany, I said, I have seen your porn and I thought you would be more open-minded. Yes Luisa, but in Germany we do not sleep with people who steal from us. We are not British hahahaha.

Oh SMH (by the way, some people think this means 'shake my head', but I'm going to use it as 'shave my head' as that's more fun. Guys, it's my book).

One of Klaus's acts was a guy called Patrice. Patrice was a 40-something skinny man with the biggest heart of gold. It took about ten minutes to see that he was as playful and ridiculous as I was. He was so impressed with my flyering skills, he offered me the chance to come and work for him.

What my job boiled down to was to be his hype man. I would meet Patrice at lunchtime and do a couple of hours of flyering, but actually my job was to keep him motivated. Now please let it be known that Patrice is completely capable of motivating himself; he is the most selfless man I have come across. What actually happened is that he gave me the job in order to keep *me* motivated, but did so with the ruse that I was there for him. He could see my unrequited obsession with Klaus and wanted me to have my own thing. So my job description was to flyer, prepare the room, clear away old glasses, lay the chairs out and let the audience in so he could get in the zone for performing. Then stand by the door and not let anyone else in so he wouldn't be interrupted.

The reality went more like this. I would rock up, usually hung-over and either elated or tear-stained depending on the drunken escapades of the night before, dance with Patrice in the rain (welcome to Edinburgh summers) then get him to flyer his own show whilst I slept off my hangover and broken heart at the back of the room.

The room was small, approx. capacity 50, and when Patrice only had five people in there I felt really guilty because I had done my job badly; I hated not doing well for Patrice. And yet every show, no matter how many people were in, or how much money he made in donations, Patrice would take out £6 for himself for lunch and give the rest to me. I'd make anything from £6 to £37 an hour. Every time, without fail. Patrice was an angel.

It was coming towards the end of the festival and I felt like here was my last chance. If I was in love with Klaus and if it was ever going to work, I needed to share my devotion with him. Klaus had met some woman from Manchester and was dating her; he introduced me and couldn't understand why I was snappy and annoyed with him. Eurgh, his girlfriends were so annoying. They were really plain Jane and had no personality; they would just look at him like he was the best thing since sliced bread.

MEN: HOW TO TELL WHEN YOUR GIRL FRIEND FANCIES YOU

1. She is with you all the time.
2. She happens to look amazing every time you see her.
3. She offers to work, translate, study, cook for you.
4. She laughs at all your jokes.
5. She disappears to the toilet for ten minutes after you tell her you went on a date.

It got to 5 p.m. and I met Klaus in our usual meeting place. I was sarky and he told me to snap out of it. I said, 'Look, I love you, I have been in love with you since I met you.' He said, 'Ahh, that's nice, but also not true. Anyhow, you know I like Woman from Manchester.'

I ran off crying and went looking for Patrice. Patrice had become my unlikely best friend superhero. He was like a big brother who looked out for me. He said not to worry and it's good to be honest, just go back and flyer tomorrow and you'll be fine.

I rocked up the next day and my German amour/ employer was handing flyers to another girl.

'Er, what are you doing?'

'I need a flyerer Luisa, and she is good.'

'But *I* am your flyerer!'

'Yes but I didn't think you would come back so I replaced you.'

Fired by my one true love. I spent the rest of Edinburgh in tears and being absolutely useless for Patrice. He still paid me though. The legend.

Despite all the drama, the next time I saw Klaus I did some damage limitation and explained that it was the festival and obviously I was just tired and emotional and that I wasn't *actually* in love with him and obviously we were 'just friends'. He seemed to swallow it and we continued to be just that, friends.

The festival finished and I went back to living back at my mum's and temping as a postwoman. I loved being a postwoman; it's so nice to get up that early and greet people with their mail. Plus, hello, I was a really glamorous postwoman. It was getting difficult with gigging in the evenings though, so eventually Alison got me a 9-to-5 job with an IT firm, where they paid me £10 an hour and I just had to log complaints about poor internet service. I would answer and pretend to know what an IP address was and then just pass the complaints on. The job was really fun because the team I worked with were awesome, plus every Friday the company paid for Domino's. I don't even like pizza, but I quickly liked Domino's. Companies, if you went to motivate your unqualified staff to care, give them free pizza Fridays.

It didn't matter that I was rubbish at the job; it paid for my travel to gigs. Several nights a week I would take the hour train to London and back to do a five-minute set. Sundays were my favourite, the Exhibit bar in Balham run by an old man called PJ. PJ is a character, who would fill you with confidence by saying, 'Next up we have someone who is shit – oi Luisa, it's you, take your bangles off, they're too distracting. Sorry ladies and gentlemen, sometimes she gets it but most of the time she is shit, so good luck Luisa, get up now and do twenty!' And I would run up on stage, heart pumping, all wide eyes and excited with sore wrists from where I ripped my bracelets off. PJ was really good to me, he would throw me in the deep end and I would scrabble trying to fill twenty minutes to a room of 12 or 100 depending on the Sunday. I loved every second of it, it would take me three hours to get there and back because of the Sunday train service, but I didn't care, it was worth it and I did it religiously for years.

I would Skype Klaus and tell him all about it and he would be genuinely delighted that I was out and about doing stand-up. I felt the happiest I had been in ages.

My stepdad was proud of me for working and gigging in the evening and he helped me buy a car. I saw this gorgeous MGF convertible for sale in an Asda car park for £3k. Wow, I thought. Only £3k for a convertible. I started doing some research and found one for £2k. Johnny looked at it with me, and made sure it was safe; it was Tahiti blue with cream leather seats, gorgeous!

I had savings of £1k and Johnny paid the rest and my insurance. He wanted to motivate me, and thought maybe the car would help me with my travelling. Him and my mum were breaking up at the time. I think they had been unhappy for years but stayed together for Asia's benefit. To be honest, I don't think my mum ever recovered after my dad got custody of the boys, but she loved Johnny and he had helped her so much, they just weren't good together, they were mating each other miserable.

It was a stressful time, and my mum had no financial security of her own. Her side of the house was in a mortgage with my dad's name which he transferred into a trust fund. As far as I understood, my father had never taken his name off it, and when they broke up, he took out a second mortgage on the house and used the money to set himself up in Bristol. So the 20 years she had been paying off the mortgage, she was paying off my father's debt. Now, with the prospect of breaking up with Johnny, what would happen to the house, the children, where would we live? Johnny is kind though, he moved out and let my mum and my little brother and Asia live in the house for as long as she needed.

I never want to be in that position, I want everything in my own name, so no one can ever hold any contract over my head and use it against me. I never want to pay off someone else's debt. I like having my own money and my own things, I don't like loans and I don't like credit cards, have never had one. Obviously I love an overdraft, but that's different. When I buy a home, it will be in my name, married or not, I will make sure I am secure.

As I got older, I stopped speaking to my dad. He would never call me either. I used to make the effort to call him regularly, I didn't mind. Before mobile phones, he didn't want to call the house phone in case my mum answered, but ever since mobile phones, well, I'm not sure what his reasons are.

My dad would always say he loves us very much. Whenever we see him, I can see he cares and that he wants a relationship when I am stood right in front of him. But after a while, I got so tired of what felt like chasing him, and when I would look at the situation objectively, there was no valid reason for him to not stay in touch. So I stopped running after him. If I don't call, I just don't hear from him. I have learnt to be OK with that now.

But coming to that conclusion took a lot of learning. After the whole falling in love with Klaus thing, I was annoyed at myself for chasing someone unavailable again. I wanted to get to the root and try and fix it, so I called my father.

A therapist said that if your father is unavailable, you are attracted to men who are also unavailable, because that's what you think love is. Well I didn't want love like that, not any more. I wanted to fix my future and not be destined to be the child of divorced parents who never had success in love.

So I decided to go and visit him. It was time I cleared the ghosts with him. I was engaging in shit relationships and surely he was partly responsible for that. I was bored of having 'daddy issues' and I would keep telling myself that everything that had happened happened years ago so it was time to move on. However as much as I repeated this rhetoric, it didn't affect my actions, as my daily behaviour was a reflection of those past hurts. Maybe if I could get some clarity I could get some control.

I went to visit him for the day. He was back on speaking terms with my brothers, and they were gonna meet me at his house. I had spent so long planning what I was going to say when I saw him. I wanted to sit him down and have a good, healthy, calm conversation about all the ways I felt let down and tell him that I would like to start a relationship with him.

I pulled up in my sexy new car. I had the roof down, hoping to impress him, hoping he would see that even though I wasn't a lawyer, I was doing all right. He came out to meet me and the first thing he asked was about my car and how could I afford it. I mumbled something guiltily about Johnny helping me out, and my dad made a snide remark. I quickly sniped back, 'Well at least he's been there. So he paid for a car, good, I needed a car. You've got four kids and I've never seen you so much as pay child support for one of them.'

And that was the beginning of the end. The 'good, healthy, calm' intention went out the window and I started crying. I couldn't stop; we weren't even through the front door and I was shouting at him, asking him why he was never there, why he never called, why he didn't seem to care or love us.

He just looked at me stone-faced. I could see him taking all of me in. I was the spitting image of my mum when she was in her twenties. As he stood in his doorway, in a low and quiet and very calm tone he said, 'You are nothing more than a common harlot wailing in the street. You look and sound like a prostitute, so much like your mother, how very proud I am of you. Stop yourself before someone tries to pick you up.'

I was distraught.

My brother pulled up and saw me in tears. He grabbed me and gave me a cuddle and told my dad to fuck off. Half an hour later, we were all sat in the living room and the gloves were off. I looked around and he had pictures of his other children, pictures of him being at key events in their lives, birthdays, sports days, graduations, not even key events, some pictures were just of days, regular, normal days. So he was capable of being there for his other kids, just not me and my brothers. I don't get it, why them and not us?

My dad said he was ashamed and it wasn't too late for me to go and study law. I told him I didn't want to do law; I wanted to be a comedian. He laughed and made some quip about being the fool whilst the kings laughed. I used to always switch off when he spoke in riddles; to this day I am really good at zoning out. It must have been a self-preservation feature, as I knew that if I processed it it would probably hurt. But in that moment as my dad was going on about what a dumb bitch I must be to 'be a laughing stock' all I could do was zone out, and as I did I visualised myself so clearly on stage.

I was stood in a bright spotlight in a beautiful old theatre, with gold lint all around the edges of the audience's red velvet seats, the room was packed and people were just clapping and cheering and laughing and they were doing it all for me, with me. I held on to that image, I took a snapshot of it in my head like a photograph and used it to protect myself from the negativity. I didn't want to absorb any of it, it just looked like I wasn't listening. I was, just to myself.

I left soon after that and drove my little car home. I didn't have the roof down on the way back, I felt embarrassed, I didn't want anyone to see me. I drove back to Farnborough and ran straight into the arms of my mother. I cried for hours and told her everything; she laid me on her lap and stroked my hair, saying 'My darling, you are very capable of anything you set your mind to, you will achieve everything you have ever dreamed of' and she held me until I slept.

9

I'M NOT A GIRL . . .
NOT YET A WOMAN

I felt driven and encouraged by my mother's support. I was going to be the one to give us both a better life. My first year of comedy quickly passed and I was itching to get back to Edinburgh. I learnt so much from being in touch with Klaus and Patrice. How much you have to fight to get what you want and never let a rainy day stop you. I started going to Edinburgh every year. How could you not want to go? It was the only time of the year when I could get up on a stage and perform every day and no one could tell me otherwise. If I was shit, I owned it and I learnt from it. If I was great, it fuelled me to keep going. Edinburgh became the place where I could follow my dreams; the rest of the year didn't really matter.

For my second Edinburgh, I went with another comic and we did 25 minutes each. It was a massive deal for both of us: how was I ever going to handle being funny on stage every day for 25 whole minutes?

But something about doing the free show and having control over it meant that I stepped up. I loved every detail: organising the photo shoot for the posters, putting the posters up, flyering for my own audiences. Every aspect I adored but most of all I loved performing my set, whatever it would be. We would often get a crowd of around 20 people and I could just stand up and talk to them. I learnt so much in my first year. It didn't matter if you were shit, you had to go straight back up and do it again. Also it didn't matter if you killed it; you could get straight back up and die the next day. All that mattered was that I was doing it.

I invited every newspaper and agent and PR I could think of, but no one came. That was OK, but to be honest, I wasn't ready to be showcased, I needed time to cook. I still need time to cook. I just relished the freedom of finally doing what I loved.

I spent the next three years temping from my mum's house, regularly in touch with Klaus, and playing the Edinburgh Fringe Festival. I got involved in a children's play where I was a tree. An improvisation show for kids, an improvisation show for adults. One year I did four shows a day and learnt so much. It killed me, but I loved it. Every year I would continue to be in touch with Klaus. It was so nice to see him regularly at the festival. I could hang out with him every day, as outside of Edinburgh he would either be back in Germany or touring with his artists. He had a different girlfriend this time around but she was pretty much a carbon copy of all the others. I affectionately called them 'Paint Dries', because they were about as interesting.

By 2011 I was gigging regularly, about four or five nights a week. Now most people in comedy are the kindest, loveliest, salt-of-the-earth people. But every now and then it can feel a little bit intimidating. I remember one time these open mic'ers asked me to go for a drink after a show. Open mic'ers are comics that are still new and on the unpaid circuit. The two males started waxing lyrical about joke construction and 'what you need to be a great comedian'. They then started congratulating themselves on their knowledge of American comedians, dissecting and analysing famous people's jokes and explaining to me why it was funny.

I just sat there trying to keep my Smirnoff Ice straw out of my eye. Then one of them turned to me and asked me who I liked. I said I love Whoopi Goldberg. They laughed and one of them said, 'You're not a comedian, Luisa.'

'What? Where has that come from?'

'You can't call what you do comedy.'

'Oh. I like it.'

'Haha yeah, you clearly don't know comedy. You are awful, you need proper jokes, you just screech on stage. Listen, send me your stuff and I can write some punchlines in for you, because you don't know what you are doing.'

Both of them laughed and I went home and cried my eyes out. I was too embarrassed to mention it to other comics in case they thought the same. I called Klaus. He said, 'Luisa, no comedian worth their salt would ever say anything like that to you or anybody, fuck them, they are not comics, trust me when I say comedians on the circuit do not behave like that.'

It made me fall in love with Klaus a little bit more, to see he was supportive. As for those two guys, I haven't heard of them being on the circuit since.

Comedians are pretty special people, there is a beautiful solidarity amongst comics, it's an isolating job, being alone on stage, so it's nice that off stage most comics are absolutely lovely. One of the loveliest is Rachel Anderson. Rachel has the voice and face of an angel and would do killer jokes and amazingly funny songs, my favourite being 'Shit on my Tits and Feel no Shame'. It is genius.

In stand-up, when deciding a line-up and running order, you always open with a strong act. In the middle, when the audience has settled in and warmed up a little, you have a newer act; the middle spot is often a really nice one as the audience are more receptive. Then you close the gate with a headliner, someone who's on at the end because they are difficult to follow.

In February Rachel asked me if I wanted to do a show with her at Edinburgh, sharing an hour together. I had already booked myself in to do a *Whose Line Is It Anyway?*-style improvisation show, and the timing of Rachel's slot meant that if I was to do a show with her, I would have to go on after her as I wouldn't make it across from my venue in time to open. The decision to say yes took for ever. I felt so honoured, because Rachel was amazing, she was one of the best, I would learn so much from doing a show with her, but at the same time, the thought of following her scared the shit out of me. I hated the idea of turning down something performance-wise because I was scared, and the whole point of this festival was to challenge yourself, so I accepted. I am so glad I did, as Rachel became one of my closest friends and is one of the sweetest, kindest, most beautiful women I know.

So it's August 2011, myself and Rachel were booked into my favourite Laughing Horse venue, the Meadow Bar. Zac, the chef there, would make my usual meal: a veggie burger with a fried egg instead of salsa, and cheesy wedges instead of chips. Clare and Michael from down-stairs would just ring the kitchen and tell him that Luisa was in, and my burger would come down the hatch. I felt at home here with these guys.

Rachel's sister mocked up a poster using Photoshop and some old Facebook photos, we got them printed up and we were in! We would both do the improv show half a mile down the road, then Rachel would leave before the last improv game and run across the bridge for our two-hander, which we called 'All Over Your Face'. She would set the room up as the previous show was exiting, clear the glasses, rearrange the chairs, open the windows for some air, stick some music on the iPad and start letting the second audience in. Meanwhile I would finish off the improv show and arrive just in time to welcome Rachel on stage.

Like I mentioned before, when you do paid shows, the venue has staff who do all this for you: the sound equipment is tested, there is a technician throughout the show, the room is cleaned and set up, there is someone taking tickets at the door. In free shows, you are the venue staff, the ticketing staff, the cleaner, the musician, the sound tech, the bouncer, and the performer. And I loved it. I loved doing things for myself. I loved the pressure and stress of setting up your own room, I loved running from one venue to the next. I loved all of it.

Now with free shows, you have no idea how many people are going to turn up. My improv show was attracting anything from zero to 50 people. With our two-hander, I always arrived late, so missed out on seeing the queue outside the door. You can tell a lot about how a show is gonna go by the length of the queue. Also, you can get a feel for the energy of the audience before they've even entered the room.

My show with Rachel was a lot of fun. Rachel is one of the most talented comedians I know. The prospect of playing with her, let alone following her, was daunting. As soon as we had done a few shows together, though, I started to relax. It became a joy to follow Rachel because she got the audience so hyped. I would often arrive dishevelled, soaking wet from rain or sweat, and would introduce her with a straightforward 'Ladies and gentlemen, please welcome to the stage . . .' One of my favourite memories from the run was Rachel's face at one of the introductions. It was the last Tuesday of an exhausting festival run, I was really late, the room was full and I was flustered as I ran on stage. I wanted to say 'Ladies and gentlemen, please welcome one of my favourite comedians' but my brain panicked. Instead of 'favourite', I started to say 'female', and I didn't want to say 'female comedian' because she is a comedian, 'female' is annoying unless I say 'male comedian', so instead my mouth quickly changed 'female' to 'finest', and then I was spewing words before my brain knew what I was saying and I came out with: 'Please welcome to the stage one of the femaaaa . . . ffeee . . . finest comedians of our generation, Rachel Anderson!'

Rachel's face was a picture, I found it hilarious. To me she absolutely is one of the finest comedians of our generation. But she is also incredibly humble and would never allow herself to be referred to as such. There we were, in a sweaty room above a pub, where our stage was opposite the toilets and we got interrupted by the hand dryer every ten minutes, here in this magical room, and the audience could see, for free, one of the finest comedians of our generation. If that's not an incentive to visit the festival, I don't know what is.

So what did Edinburgh teach me this time? I learnt that I loved improvising and interacting with the audience, I was beginning to get comfortable calling myself a comedian, a new one yes, but a comedian as opposed to someone just doing comedy. The question now was how to make this feeling last for the rest of the year.

Speaking of Rachel, I helped her get married. I wrote her dating profile for her on MySingleFriend.com. How it works is you write your friend's profile and they write yours.

Here is the profile I wrote for Rachel. It has been proven to work, so feel free to copy and paste:

> Rachel is sexually aggressive and seldom washes. By all means try and be the man to tame her, but do so at your own peril, she is not a woman to listen.

Rachel then wrote a witty reply, something along the lines of 'Haha, thank you Luisa for that lovely introduction.' She got several dates and a boyfriend who then became her fiancé and is now her beloved husband.

For my profile Rachel wrote – and I would advise you not to copy and paste this, as it never worked; in fact it's safe to say that Rachel sabotaged me, I want to say it's payback for 'finest comedian of our generation' but she will deny it:

> Luisa is a wolf who at midnight turns into a hairy beast.

I responded with what I thought was hilarious witty banter: 'Owwwwwwwwwww' (as in a wolf crying).

Nothing, I got nothing, not even a smiley winky face. Moral of the tale, Rachel is a rubbish friend. She will say I didn't get any responses because I didn't write a normal reply, but I think we both know who is lying.

Anyway, back to the chat. So I finished Edinburgh and was back in Farnborough. Throughout the year there are industry showcases and new-act competitions, remember I told you about them? It's where young comics (young to the game, age is but a number) compete with lots of other comedians with a three- or five-minute routine; eventually you might get into the final, and that's where industry and agents will see you and show interest.

I entered the Laughing Horse new act of the year competition. As always, I was so nervous and just shrieked like an idiot, classic Luisa, I wasn't funny at all, which is annoying because I swear it takes extra effort to not be funny. For some reason whenever there is a competition or people are judging my performance, I turn back into that kid who fronts it out at dance class. *Holds the mic and thinks, no, why don't you make me laugh for a change before stamping off*

In hindsight I don't know why I bother with competitions; it should be more about showcases. You can't have the best act; you can have best-received person of the night, but comedy is so subjective, and when you start working in clubs, it's not a competition, more a group effort to make an excellent night out. So I don't know why competitions are necessary (FYI, if I was good at competitions, this line would be changed to 'Comedy competitions are imperative to seek out the best person who is the best at comedy and they deserve everything in life.'). Like it's comical how badly I can fuck up and not be funny when there is a need to prove something or there is pressure. The more natural and unstressed I am the better I am at being funny.

This love affair with comedy – am I good, am I awful? – is probably one of the reasons it is so addictive. Though most art funds and schools and colleges don't agree, stand-up comedy is an art form, and one of the most intelligent, delicate, perfectly balanced, beautiful, human art forms anyone could ever hope to try and master. It is the most honest art form, because it's immediate. Failing is absolutely a part of it, and there is failure at every level.

Now I don't really do puns or wordplay, I tell stories. For a while I was nailing the whole neurotic woman scene, but then it annoyed me, because when it didn't go well I just looked like some person coming off the street having a meltdown. That's the worst bit, when you die on stage and you are embarrassed for yourself. There is no one there to scoop you off the stage, so you have to pep-talk your embarrassing self and be like 'Come on Luisa, put your pants back on and let's get out of here,' it's so humiliating.

Performing stand-up on the open mic circuit and at festivals gave me confidence and opened me up to a whole new network of people on the London comedy scene. Eventually Klaus encouraged me to take the plunge and move to the big city.

A friend I had met on the comedy circuit had a place in West Hampstead. The room was only £80 a week, which in West Hampstead is stupidly cheap! Thanks to Klaus, I took the leap of faith and moved in. I got a temp job working for the Rugby Football Union in the IT department where I could not have been more useless, but they were paying me £15 an hour so who is the real loser?

Klaus had just finished with his Swedish girlfriend and was having a dinner in town to celebrate his birthday. I was so pleased he had finished with her. It was my first week living in London and his parents had come over from Germany. He invited me to come and join them. I figured if this wasn't a sign that the clogs were finally turning (nose tap, clogs, nose tap, German, nose tap, clogs aren't actually German, nose tap, oops), I didn't know what was. Hello? Parent meeting. Mate, it's love.

It took me about three days to get ready. I picked the perfect outfit, nice black dress, fitted but below the knee, had that 'hi, I would make a really good daughter-in-law' look for the parents, but also a 'wow, I want to have sex with you' feel for Klaus. I picked out a present; it was a plastic microphone he could use to sing in the shower. I knew he was anal about microphones as he always made his acts buy a really good one. Plus he hated that in London he didn't have a bath, only a shower. I thought this would be the perfect combination of hilarious yet stupid, playful enough to show I hadn't spent that much money, but also thoughtful enough to show that I cared.

I arrived at the restaurant and to my surprise there were already four people sat there: Klaus, his mum, his dad and Paint Dry *sound the trumpets*. He brought the

Swedish girlfriend, the Swedish-oh-I'm-sorry-I-thought-you-were-no-longer-going-to-be-a-problem-ex-girlfriend.

'Hey, great to see you!'

She gave me the look of 'Bitch I know why you are wearing that dress' and I gave her one of 'Don't know what you are talking about, Paint Dry, I'm just a really good friend!' I squeezed Klaus, trying to look extra pally, that's me, friendly old Luisa! sat down smiling a lot more than I should at his bewildered parents. I knew they thought I was mental when they said, 'You don't act very British.'

I laughed it off heartily as a compliment, trying to hold myself together without feeling like a complete moron for arriving dressed to the nines for a dinner with Klaus, his parents and his not-so-ex-girlfriend. If I didn't smile heartily, I would cry and I was not about to lose this one. No siree, not today. Today I smile politely and will nail this horrendously awkward dinner.

I got through the meal without being sick and went home and cried for approximately three hours. The next day Klaus called. I ignored him. He called again a few times over the next three weeks. It took everything I had not to pick up. I changed his name on my phone to 'Do Not Answer', but that didn't really motivate me as I often do things I am told not to do, so instead I changed it to 'The Gym'.

It got to Christmas and I got a text message on Christmas Day but I didn't know what to say. I didn't want to reply, but I didn't want to not reply, so I went with the classic *Thanks x*. That was my attempt at saying 'I'm not ignoring you because I am not immature but also my one kiss should tell you that I am totally ignoring you, but actually I don't care any more.'

I hated not talking to Klaus. I really missed him. But I liked him too much and he had a girlfriend, or at least he didn't have one but he still invited her to dinner with his parents (who does that?). I felt bad, as I loved him and wanted to be a good friend, but at the same time, being a friend meant hiding how much I liked him and it was exhausting.

Roll on the new year and I am feeling a little bit less heartbroken over Klaus. I am living in West Hampstead and starting to gig more regularly. Then I got hit with really bad flu, and I had been in bed for about a week when the universe decided to test me and I got a call from 'The Gym'.

I was ill and feeling super sorry for myself; it was only because I was weak that I answered. His first words were 'Thank you for answering me, my darling beautiful friend, how are you? I have missed you, and before you speak, I know you are upset with me, but I do adore you so I just wanted to call to see how you were. We don't have to talk, I just want to say hello.'

Now I had mentally prepared myself for this conversation and had planned many a time in my head what I would say in this situation if Klaus was to ever to call me. My articulate and prepared response was to be 'Hey there, you! Old buddy, old pal! I'm great! Been so busy, in fact I better run as I have a really important gig tonight, yeah it's 7 minutes in an old man's pub in Finsbury Park but if it goes well he will give me ten minutes so I really can't stop and chat, after all success won't wait for everybody! Haha! OK! Speak to you soon. Bye!!'

That was my plan. What I did not intend for was the following. Don't judge me, I had been in bed for a week, in London with no mumma to comfort me, I hadn't washed in two days and was ODing on Night Nurse and Lemsip.

'Hi, thank you *starts crying*, I just, I'm fine, I just *crying gets louder*, I just really miss you and you invited me to meet your parents and I thought that meant *crying uncontrollably*, it's just I've been sick and no one is here, flatmate's away, completely on my own *starts snotting down phone* and I could be dead and no one would care *erratic now* and I was thinking I could die right now and no one would even find me, and even if people knew I was dying, and I had like a run-up, I still would be lonely and then I thought, well I would be OK with feeling like that If I knew you were around, because *hardcore can't breathe crying* even if I had cancer and lost all my hair and my sight I would be OK as long as you are next to me and I could hear your voice.' *Wails off inaudibly.*

Yes, ladies and gentlemen, that was my killer line. Shakespeare's sonnets eat your heart out. To the man of my dreams, a promoter from Germany, my great love letter was 'If I had cancer and lost all my hair and my sight I would be OK as long as you are next to me and I could hear your voice.'

Now you wouldn't necessarily think German dudes are the most emotionally on-it people, but actually Klaus was pretty brilliant. 'Luisa, you are cold and lonely and wet' – I mean I was, but that's because his accent killed me, though he meant as in sweating, I know, I understand him, it's one of the reasons we should be together – he continued, 'Have some rest, don't worry, we are good, I do love you, you are my friend, shall I come over and see you, would that be OK?'

It's amazing how quickly you can snap out of flu when you need to. Roll on two days and there was a knock at my front door. I'd decided to wash, do my hair, do natural-looking make-up, which took me an hour. I got my nails shellacked the day before, wore skinny black jeans and a vest with no bra on. Had the window open to air the sickness and keep my nipples hard. I'd scrubbed the flat the night before but took out a mop to look like he had caught me in the middle of it.

Klaus ended up spending the whole day and the night.

10.

CRAZY IN LOVE

We dated for about five months and I could not have been happier. I called my brother to tell him about Klaus and me finally getting it on. He said, 'Well done Luisa, just goes to show, if you wear a man down long enough, eventually he will just give in.'

I spent my nights following Klaus around comedy clubs and forgetting all my own gigs and my days daydreaming about seeing him again. We went all around London and up on the Millenium Wheel, it was so romantic. Well actually it was quite long and boring. But it didn't matter – I was with Klaus!

I loved his voice, I loved his smell, I loved him calling me baby. He developed a nickname for me, 'Badger'. I loved being his badger. I was a badger, I was as happy as a badger in badger land. I loved sucking his dick and being held by him. I loved how when we walked down the street he held my hand and our feet walked to the same step. I loved how our fingers interlinked easily. I loved how in sync we were. But with every moment of loving it, there was a small part of me that felt constantly on edge. Like maybe, on some level, I wasn't good enough to be his girlfriend, like at any moment this magic and love that I was feeling was going to be stripped away from me. Self-fulfilling prophecy knocking.

I lost my job with the Rugby Football Union (they cottoned on to my uselessness, you can only play the 'just turn it off and back on again' card for so long) and had to move out of my friend's place. It was at this moment that another comedian told me about this wonderful government scheme called 'Housing Benefit'. Basically if you go to the job centre and say you can't get a job but are looking, then the government will pay your rent for you. Why had I not heard of this wonderful initiative before?! So I skipped along to the job centre and sure enough, for a 27-year-old single person, they would cover up to £250 a week rent.

Now Noddy here, rather than finding somewhere I could afford once I got a job, went 'Wahoo! £250 a week!' And found a one-bed flat in West Hampstead. Johnny helped me with the deposit and I tied myself into a six-month contract. Now the only way I was going to be able to afford this new love nest was by either working every hour God sends and not make the rent or not work at all, keep signing on and have a nice flat to live in.

I chose the latter. Probably the most soul-destroying, negligent thing I could have done. My plan was to use this as an opportunity and really concentrate on comedy and go to the gym every day. But my plan was ambitious and flawed. Instead, with too much time on my hands and no sense of routine, I just allowed myself to get completely besotted with Klaus. My whole world became about him: seeing him, cooking for him, sexing him. I loved him; I had never felt more love.

He was earning more and more money and working with bigger comedians. I felt like an idiot because I wasn't good enough to work with someone of his status yet. I didn't mind too much though, as I felt I could make myself more invaluable as his support.

I would try and kiss him in public, which he didn't like. At comedy gigs he didn't want me to kiss him as it's important to be professional at work events, but I really wanted to show off in front of all my friends that I was dating him. I used to get really frustrated. I remember one time a girl was eyeing him up. Unaware that we were dating, she whispered, 'Klaus is looking sexy.' I said, 'Well of course he knows how to work it, he's gay!' 'IS he?! Oh man, all the good ones are!'

A bit tipsy and feeling smug I walked past Klaus as he was chatting to another promoter and whispered, 'Don't worry darling, no one will know we are dating, I just told Claire you are gay.'

I thought he would find it funny, but he quickly ended his conversation with the promoter and told me we were leaving. We had a massive fight. He hated that I would publicly mock him like that and I hated that he didn't want to kiss me in public. I felt like he was ashamed of me because I wasn't big enough in comedy and because I couldn't get an agent. In hindsight, these were all my insecurities for putting someone on a pedestal. Of course, from where I placed him, the only way he could see me was by looking down.

I had two months left of my lease in London and was looking forward to working without the constraints of signing on because of my stupid rent deal. Klaus had just moved into a new place in London and I came to help settle him in. I went round and cooked him dinner. He did some spreadsheets of tour budgets and I just watched him. He had been a bit quiet and distant, so instead of leaving him to it and giving him space, I deliberately missed the last tube home and stayed with him, all night. He complained that he was too busy to even unpack in his new place and was sorry he couldn't give me more attention but he had to get work done. I didn't mind, I just sat and watched him work. Like a weirdo.

The following morning he left early for Germany. I stayed and unpacked all his belongings and rearranged his room, set it up how he liked it.

When he got back on the Monday he called and said, 'Oh my gosh, Luisa, thank you! I love you, that is so thoughtful of you, Badger! Can we meet tonight? I want to talk'.

I had found this T-shirt with a picture of a badger on it from New Look and wore it because I thought it would be cute. I meet him at Piccadilly Circus, he takes my hand and we go and sit on a fountain. Word to the wise, never trust a meeting with a lover at a fountain, you only get your hopes up. Boys can be so dumb.

Hey guys, here are my handy hints for places not to dump someone.

1. On a fountain
2. At a wedding
3. On/near/before their birthday
4. At a funeral
5. On the day of their big promotion
6. On a fucking fountain

He said he was sorry, but he just wasn't ready for a relationship and he couldn't give me all the things he felt I needed. I was upset but surprisingly I felt OK. I gave him a peck and left. You know sometimes when something bad happens and you feel sad but at the same time you are like 'I am surprisingly OK about this, that's weird.' *cue snowstorm that will hit you when you least expect it*. I had one of those moments.

I threw myself into gigging. I decided to enter a funny women competition and do my best to step up. The owner, Lynne Parker, called me and said, 'Luisa, I would love to put you through to the semi-finals, but looking like you do, you shouldn't be talking about what you talk about, it's not nice for young women to be so crass. Why don't you send me your material and I will edit it for you and consider putting you through.' I found myself saying thank you on the phone and feeling absolutely crushed. I never sent my material and she never put me through. Why do people keep wanting to change my voice?

I entered another competition and, for once, I got through to the final. The next day a review came out in *Chortle*, the online comedy bible; the head guy Steve Bennett said I would amount to 'being the novelty nutter baffling the *Britain's Got Talent* judges'. Scathing. I knew Klaus would read it; he loved and respected Steve.

And so here I am, dumped, in a flat I can't afford, getting nowhere in comedy and my ex-boyfriend will see a review of how shit I am. I bet he is relieved he dumped me. I left my flat to go pick up some boxes to pack and bumped into a comedian called Juice. Juice was an open-mic'er and a bit of an idiot. He once tricked Sky TV into doing an interview with him by telling them he was in a bank when it got robbed. He was nowhere near. He's either an idiot or a genius, seldom in between. His dad owns a chain of kebab shops in south London, so he sees himself as having working-class roots even though he lives with his mum in a three-storey house in central London.

Juice called to me on the street and I told him about my review; he said, 'Bennett is an idiot, fuck him, keep going, you are brilliant, don't worry.' I could have kissed him. I moved back home to my mum's that afternoon.

Back in Farnborough, I wept in my pants for a week, then got a job at the local radio station in Guildford, Eagle Radio. I figured at least it related to the performing arts. I enrolled to be part of the promotions team and then got promoted to receptionist. I would see all the celebrities coming in for interviews and it was so much fun. I would always feel like I was one of them, even though technically I was making the tea, but that's cool, I'll do that even when I am famous.

The station took part in a nationwide scheme where ten employees would be picked as interns and be taught about all aspects of the medium. My station nominated me and I got into the programme called 'Route into Radio'. Three months hard-core training with the best people in the business. I went to stations around the country and learnt about every aspect of the artform.

Klaus and I were no longer together but he started calling me again. He said he was proud of what I was doing; he was also impressed as he was interested in radio advertising and how it worked for small businesses. So I would use my training days with the radio sales team as an excuse to ring him up and spout statistics at him: 'Did you know radio advertising is 50 per cent more effective for small businesses than TV adverts alone? PS I love you.'

I liked working again; I liked having my own money and not feeling guilty about signing on. It wasn't the most glamorous job and I wanted to be behind the mic as opposed to on reception, but I was much happier here than I had been in years. At least I wasn't lying to myself with undergraduate recruitment programmes. Even if I couldn't be an artist, at least I could immerse myself in that world. Plus all the team were super supportive and proud of my aspirations to be a comedian. The office would always ask how my gigs in 'the big London' went. It was long getting home late after gigs and being in for 8 a.m. to answer the phones but I loved it. I was making friends in the office and picking up pals on the circuit.

I met a girl called Katerina Vrana who was Greek but has the best British accent, and Suzi Ruffell who was from Portsmouth, They quickly became my comedy besties.

At one of my gigs Doc Brown, another comedian, saw me and he said he wanted to recommend me to an events company who were looking for a host. They were offering £80 a night and were looking for someone flexible who could step in at the last minute. I called them up, they were in a panic. Meet Musical Bingo. It's pretty much regular bingo but ten times more fun and with music instead of numbers. They had a game format that involved a host presenter, a DJ and music. They had a corporate gig the following night for the BBC in Brighton and their host had done a runner.

Jonny, the man who'd created the format of the show, was gutted. He didn't want to pull out, as it had taken him ages to get in with the BBC. They had everything for the event apart from a host; they even had a script and Jonny asked if I could learn it in time, he was aware he was throwing me in at the deep end. I said fuck the script, let's have fun with it. It was hard as the crowd were all strait-laced business types who liked the game but weren't so into the drinking aspect. But Jonny was pleased enough and so in 2011 I became the face of Musical Bingo.

It was a rough time for Jonny as the previous host had gone off with a similar format and started running nights.

I never understand people like that, who take someone else's idea and sell it as their own. But we quickly made Musical Bingo our own and turned it into one of the best nights out in the capital.

Jonny ran events every month, with a residency at Concrete in Shoreditch. A hundred and fifty drunk Londoners would come in and want to have a party. My job was basically to manage that party. For a small-town girl from Farnborough this was intimidating as fuck, but also fucking awesome. We would play music, give out fun naff prizes, like a slow cooker or novelty glasses, and people would just get absolutely shit-faced. What amazed me was how pumped up and excited people would feel about getting shitty novelty glasses. Grown adults would lose their tiny little minds over a song and be so excited to win a box of After Eights.

I started having real fun developing the show; we threw away the script and I just did my own thing. I would have Jonny there, and Abel and Olly DJ'ing – those boys became like my Musical Bingo London family. We would have so much fun doing the nights. The events just got bigger and bigger. As I became more confident, I started throwing in rap battles and dance-offs and competitions for prizes. The audiences loved it. I even picked up some jokes from it.

For example, one of the questions to win a grand prize was 'Cows have different accents depending on where they are from ... true or false?' It's actually true, so in my sets I started doing cow impressions: cows with a British accent, Scottish accent, Australian accent, etc. It's really funny but you have to be there.

The Musical Bingo business grew and Jonny booted more and more shows and brought in more hosts. I loved being part of this team. I was doing it whilst still heartbroken over Klaus and wished he could see me rock a room; maybe then he would see that I was good enough to be with. It gave me so much confidence to perform in front of a large group, improvising and bantering with the audience. Here I am in a room full of drunk people and I can get them to go crazy over novelty glasses; surely there has to be a way I can get people to go as crazy over my jokes.

It's strange, isn't it, I can be the biggest office clown and make people around me howl, say the right thing at a funeral, a wedding, a bingo gig and people will laugh and be putty in my hands. But getting up on stage at a comedy club and trying to be funny is a different ball game. How do I merge the two? How do I make one transfer into the other? At comedy clubs audiences don't give you their love or laughter so freely, it's not enough to offer After Eights, you have to prove yourself. But in bingo they go bat-shit from the off.

That's what got me thinking. How can I make my stand-up gigs like a party? How can I get people pumped?

11

MIDNIGHT TRAIN TO CHICAGO

Klaus and I had finished months ago but we were still talking regularly and so that made me feel not too hurt about it but instead just more of a constant dull ache. We kinda went back to being friends again and just sleeping together holding each other, I mean literally just sleeping together; he wouldn't let me have sex with him as he said it would confuse things. I was confused anyway.

After months of being in this weird limbo of hanging out but not having sex but then having sex but not being together, he finally put a full stop to it in July. It was now officially officially over. All my friends were tired of me talking about my breakup; they'd seen it coming for a long time, they knew it had been over for ages, whereas I was always hopeful. In my head, the harder I have to work for something, the more real it is, so I believed that all the effort I made and the hurt I felt was validation that it was true love. We had gone from being best mates to lovers to weird best mates again, and it was a complete head fuck.

I couldn't stop crying. My mates were tired of hearing about him, they thought we had split up months ago and I didn't tell them that I had been seeing him again and staying with him in London after Musical Bingo or gigs instead of catching the last train home. I didn't tell my friends because I didn't want to hear it, I didn't want them to tell me off and talk sense into me. My mum couldn't understand why I was so upset over him. She thought it was over a long time ago and as I had stayed friends with him, I was happy enough. But now my safety blanket had been cut off and I hated it. I missed him hugely, he was my best friend and everywhere I looked just reminded me of him.

I remember being at Piccadilly Circus, and thinking, oh this is where he dumped me the first time. I cried remembering how sad I was when he dumped me the first time. I was melancholic over all the reasons that clearly showed why we couldn't be together. I would see couples in Five Guys and just be sad because Klaus loved Five Guys. One time, when we were together, I took a bus and walked what felt like a mile to his house to deliver his favourite Five Guys. It was cold by the time I got there but I figured he would appreciate the sentiment, but he wasn't in and so I just left it on the doorstep like a weirdo and ran off.

Or there was the time we tried to be all sexy and he poured champagne down my vagina but it started to burn and sting and I had to hot-skip to the bath and sit in it for ten minutes until my vagina calmed down. Or the time we had an argument at Leicester Square tube station because he didn't like me singing Celine Dion at him in front of people (I know right, WHAT IS WRONG WITH HIM??? Maybe 'cos it was Celine . . . If it had been Cher maybe he'd be less embarrassed), or the time at Finsbury Park tube station when I was embarrassed that he was singing Frank Sinatra at me in front of people (oh how the tables had turned. I wouldn't have gone as red if he had sung Celine). Everything reminded me of him. Oh what fond memories. And here they are, all around London.

And now I had nothing to take the edge off, no meeting up, no phone calls, no Skype. He stopped calling me completely and he didn't reply to my messages. I was broken. I could handle being split up as long as I still got to speak to him every day, but this, this was rubbish.

So I thought, what would Beyoncé do in this situation? And I did it; I decided to leave the country.

Chicago has famous improvisation schools – Second City, IO, ComedySportz Theatre – and it's where all the comedy greats go. Tina Fey, Amy Poehler, Mike Myers, John Candy, you name it; they've all been through improv school.

All my comedy heroes are American. In the UK, people never really got me when I said I wanted to be massive in comedy like Whoopi G, my idol. They didn't seem to get how much of a reality that dream is for me. So I figured I am living at my mum's and heartbroken; if now's not the time to fight for a big ridiculous dream, when is? I couldn't make it into the finals of competitions or get an agent, and the only review of me online said I should be a runner-up on a talent show. When you're at the bottom, fuck it, you may as well shoot high.

So I thought, I know what I'll do, I'll move to Chicago and do comedy classes, and whilst developing my skillset, what a beautiful side effect that Klaus will be jealous and impressed. Because he's a German fighting for an international career and here I am being, you know, international. People were like 'Wow Luisa, you are so ambitious and determined to drive your own career.' Little did they know it was just because I couldn't handle walking through Finsbury Park tube station and remembering cold Five Guys. Break up, leave the country. Genius plan.

I signed up at Second City, IO and ComedySportz Theatre. Chicago cost me £4k. You gotta speculate to accumulate. I figured I had nothing to lose. I'd sold my MGF for £500, got £1k deposit back from my London flat and saved some money from the bingo and the radio work. Plus I had a £2k overdraft, so I figured I would use half of that and just live off the rest for three months.

I went on Craigslist. Everybody warned me about Craigslist and how serial killers post on there and I would end up dead. This was really comforting for a white girl from Farnborough. I found a young mum who had a spare room; I told her my plan of coming out to study at Second City and gig. I explained I would be getting home late at night after gigging and she assured me that would be OK. I called her several times and even Skyped her. Her kid went to a local school, I googled it, it seemed legit enough, so I sent her my deposit. She was really cool and even picked me up from the airport when I arrived.

My classes were as follows:

Second City (grandad of improv school!):
- Improv for Actors: using improv to develop naturalistic scenes
- Comedy Writing: sketch writing
- Clown and Physical Comedy: learning about elements of clowning to provide the funny!

ComedySportz Theatre (*Whose Line Is It Anyway?*):
- Musical Improv: improvising songs and musicals of different genres including hip-hopera, er hello?!!!
- ComedySportz Games: short form improv games with a competitive element

IO:
- Talk Show Portfolio: writing course, one-liners based on topical news
- Cook County Social Club: improv course using traditional and experimental techniques designed to challenge!

At these schools, the terms last eight weeks, so I could just come in for the term and stay out my visa and then come home again, and that's exactly what I did. I flew out by myself, signed up for the courses and went to meet my new landlady.

When she said I had my own room, what she meant was that in her bedroom there were some steps up to a mezzanine floor where there was a bed, so if I looked over the edge of my bed I could see her there sleeping. My first thought was, how am I going to masturbate when she can clearly look up and see me? (DRAW DIAGRAM – OF BEDS, NOT ME MASTURBATING.)

I stayed there for about a week before finding a room at a businessman's place. His best mate was a comic and that was how I heard about it. My new landlord had a gorgeous two-bed en suite round the corner from the IO. He worked away Sunday to Friday and so essentially I had my own place for the rest of my stay. My comedy angels were looking out for me!

When I started going to classes, people thought it was kinda strange that I'd just come out there by myself. True comics (I think they are true because they get it) thought I was a legend and really liked my spirit of pursuing comedy. I could tell quite quickly who I wanted to become friends with. It felt really nice to start creating my own world without Klaus in it. Here I was being successful in my own little way and I wasn't beholden to anyone else.

You see, back home I had made everything about Klaus, our relationship, his career, how well he was doing, I got consumed by it all. I remember one morning coming out of his flat and he had a car picking him up to take him to an interview for Radio 1. They were super impressed that this German promoter was managing all these British acts and flying them back and forth. I was so happy for him; I waved him off in his fancy car whilst I walked to the bus stop. I wanted him to do well, though I also was like 'Wow, I can't wait until one day I get a car sent for me.' But I was happy for him that he was doing well. A small part of me was embarrassed that I wasn't successful, so it was easier just to big him up and make him feel good.

I think avoidance was a key part of it. Avoiding my own life, my own aspirations. It was easier to think what could I do to impress Klaus: what shall I cook for him, what shall I wear for him? I so quickly became one of those women I mocked and swore I would never be. I just wanted to make my world him. Totally unhealthy.

Or maybe not that unhealthy, if it was reciprocated. But it wasn't. I guess that was the problem. I think it is difficult when two egos get together. I would watch him as his acts got standing ovations and I could see the pride in his eyes, but the more I saw him succeed the more embarrassed I would be at the thought of him watching me perform in a room of 12 people. I used to think, wow, he is so special, what is he doing with me?

I wasn't independent or fierce, or running things. But I always believed I was the right woman for him because no one could love him more. And that was true in a sense; no one would love themselves less in order to love him more.

That wasn't Klaus's fault, it was mine, hindsight is a beautiful thing, but at the time, I still wasn't prepared for the snowstorm that was about to hit.

Klaus had found some Chicago contacts and emailed them across even though we weren't talking. In fact, he kept emailing me. Why it is guys have this radar? Almost the second you are feeling good and happier without them, they sense it and have to get in contact with you just to fuck it all up again for you.

I ignored him, I ignored his emails and called my friends. They were delighted; the conversations went like this . . .

'OK, so you need to go to Chicago, which is AMAZING, and totally not talk to him, it will drive him wild! He will go crazy and miss you and realise what a mistake he has made.'

'Yeah, totally, if you ignore him, he will be gutted and in your head you can be like, it's OK, I will talk to him when I'm back at Christmas, but don't let him know that, let him suffer.'

'Oh my gosh, if you ignore him for three months, he will hate it, nothing a man hates more than being ignored.'

'Oh my God Luisa, you are totally gonna fall in love with an American who will think you are adorable and Klaus will be soooo jealous!'

'Stay strong Luisa, you can do it! You can do it for all of us!!'

So I ignored most of his emails, especially his last one – *I'm so proud of you* – and got on with my plans.

My first night in Chicago I rocked up at this open mic night, maybe 12 people sat on sofas and chairs watching the acts perform, and the MC, a guy called Brian, who was lovely but way geekier in real life than his hot profile picture suggested, was beaming to see me, he was lovely and so welcoming. I met another comic called Atta, who was a huge *Doctor Who* fan, was a virgin and wore corduroy trousers. These two were not quite the American romance fairy tale that I had in mind, but they were gorgeous human beings who took excellent care of me.

As I watched from the back, the act on stage got out his toothbrush and started brushing his teeth. I howled, this was weird and awful, and very American. It was not the American dream as I knew it, if anything, watching this man brush his teeth on stage was the opposite of my vision of the American Dream whilst simultaneously being very American: nut bags, just complete nut bags.

And as I sat in this room of 12 people with the geekiest male comedians who kept saying 'all right guvnor' and asking me *Doctor Who* questions, I thought about leaving Klaus behind. I didn't need him any more. Here I was watching an old man brush his teeth on stage. I felt excited, I felt happy and excited, that I was somewhere, that I had come on my own and I was part of a comedy scene, in its perfectly backward form.

I did the gig, 15 minutes, and I smashed it, they loved me and I had a ball. I felt like I had made the right choice. I walked back to sleep in my new American mum's weird bed, got honked at for looking at the wrong side of the street when crossing, and I felt good, scared, petrified and good. Klaus texted me to ask me how I was. I was strong, I didn't reply.

I started the classes and I loved it! I met a woman called Susan Messing who is a comedy genius and improviser legend; she totally took me under her wing. I was totally in awe of Susan, she is inspiring to watch and just so ridiculously talented. The classes were brilliant, I was so happy. For the first time in about three years I was feeling excited because I was doing something for myself. I was in improvisation classes and I was dying on my ass. Every time I would nail something, I would fuck up again, and I loved it. I loved feeling like Play-Doh, like I was getting mashed and beaten and moulded into something beautiful only to be mashed up again. I loved every second. It was watering my soul.

I started growing in confidence. At the time, I had really long hair, I had hair down to my waist, and on a whim I went to the hairdresser's and thought, I know what will show 'em! I will cut it all off! So I had it hacked into a bob. I felt like Samson. I cried for days, it was my biggest regret. Someone posted a picture online and Klaus emailed saying, oh my God, you look beautiful. I cried harder and sobbed into the mirror, imagining shouting at him: 'Look what you made me do!'

The worst part about cutting long hair off is when you wash it for the first time and you are like whhaaaat, I don't need so much shampoo any more?!! And then you cry again. I mean, I know in the grand scheme of things it's not that significant, but for a first-world problem it's pretty traumatic. I forced myself to leave the house and make the most of my time.

I was about six weeks in now and was starting to tire of the loneliness. Just having no one else to go 'Isn't this soo weird' with. Little things, like when I ordered lemonade at the bar and they gave me this weird lemon drink, aka real lemonade as opposed to Sprite. And then I would say, 'Oh no, that's not what I wanted, I wanted *lemonade* lemonade, like, you know, Sprite.' And they would be like 'Oh well then in that case you should have said Sprite.' Or when I tried to buy a ticket for the train but didn't have cash and so asked one of the station staff if I could pay by card.

'Waaaa??'

'Can I pay by card for a ticket?'

'Noooo.'

'Oh OK, where can I get cash from?'

'Da bank.'

Helpful, really helpful. (God bless London TFL staff. They are the best and underrated and so fucking educated on everything around their station, you don't appreciate them until you try and buy a train ticket in America.)

I was fine when I was in my Chicago classes but the novelty of being on my own so often was starting to wear off. I enjoyed the gigs and people were lovely to me but I hadn't made any long-term friends yet. I was desperate to speak to Klaus. He emailed me a few times and I tried to ignore him and focus on my adventure, but at the same time, why would I want to ignore the very person I was missing and pining over? Talking to him made me feel better, even though he still didn't want to date me.

I would go to the cinema by myself and imagine he was with me. I went to see that film *127 Hours* and the whole time thought Klaus was like my arm that I needed to cut off in order to survive. (Oh hello spoiler alert!)

I caved in and called him. We were both delighted to speak to each other and talked for hours, romanticising our pain with stupid movie analogies. How could it not work when we were both hurting by not being in each other's lives? My friends were right: going away did seem to change things. We didn't talk about all the reasons he could never date me, we just talked about what we had been up to; how I was loving Chicago, how proud he was of me for gigging out there, how he was opening a comedy club in Berlin. And then we talked about me coming home.

'You know when you come back, it's going to be Gert's wedding.' Gert was his assistant, who I'd first met in Edinburgh. I got on super well with her; she knew about my undying love for Klaus and was always hopeful we would get together.

'I know! I can't wait.'

'I could meet you at the airport, take you home.'

'Ahh, that would be lovely, I'd like that.'

'Yeah, it would be nice, we can go to the wedding together. You never know, maybe afterwards, how do you know I'm not gonna propose to you?!'

My heart skipped a beat. This is it, it's happening, Chicago worked, the universe loves me, this is it. And I was on cloud nine for the entire day, I could not stop smiling, he'd said 'HOW DO YOU KNOW I'M NOT GONNA PROPOSE TO YOU?!' Those actual words.

I mean it was kinda in jest but also, you wouldn't even joke about something like that unless there was a hint of truth. Oh my God, this is it. Do I want to marry him? Don't worry about that, he wants to marry me, potentially. NO, he was joking, wasn't he? I don't know, who cares, he said it! Yay! I am in love again, scrap that, not again, it never left, I just suppressed it until I got depressed and now I can let my love run free again, yay love!!!

After that initial break in the no-contact rule, we would start calling each other regularly. Just shoot the breeze about his day and my day. I would finish my Second City class and run outside on the street to get reception and make the call. I could only grab him at certain times before he would get busy with his day. Me and Klaus were back on and I could not have been happier.

There was maybe a week of bliss, and then we got so comfortable talking again, we had the following conversation. It's a Tuesday, 9 p.m. I have just come out of my clowning class where the exercise was to make a rose out of tissue and go and give it as a gift to someone on the street without telling the person or asking permission. It was awesome. I was buzzing after the class and was stood outside Walmart talking to Klaus.

'God it's soo good to talk to you. I just don't know Luisa, I don't know what I want. I wish I was in love, I want to be in love, like really in love.'

Oh. Hang on, say what? That's different. Here I am stood outside a Walmart in the freezing cold, they don't call it the windy city for nothing, and here he is rabbiting away as if I am just some old platonic friend and he drops that little bombshell. 'I wish I was in love.' I mean, I know English isn't his first language; he must have got it wrong. Maybe he meant like he wishes I was there and we were going on dates like a loved-up couple? No. Maybe he meant like he was in love with me but it's not easy. No. Maybe he didn't think and of course he loves me, he tells me all the time he does. No. That doesn't sit right either.

I asked him to clarify, you know, give him a chance to correct his English, but no, he did it again in that clumsy way of his: 'I just wish I was in love, you know?!' Bam. You can take the man out of Germany . . .

Part of me felt sick and resentful and was desperate to get this man out of my life. But the other part of me was so desperate to talk to him. Which one would be the lesser evil? Talk to him? Don't talk to him? Listen to what he is saying, Luisa! I couldn't get over that line. As much as I tried and tried, I couldn't twist 'I wish I was in love' into 'I love you, Luisa'.

My brief comfort from hearing his voice quickly turned into cold isolation. In that moment I felt lonelier listening to his familiar voice on the phone, than I had done the whole time living by myself in a foreign country.

12

LIKE A VIRGIN (SORT OF)

I feel very happy at the back of a comedy club, listening to the audience as I wait to go on. Doesn't matter where I am, that feeling of being huddled in the back of a dark room on a comedy night is very familiar, and it's universal, pretty much with every comedy room in any bar in the world. Being there at the back of the room is very comforting.

I tried to convince myself to make the effort and have sex with someone else. Ideally fall in love with them, that would get me away from Klaus. I would go to a couple of bars and just sit there and wait for Prince Charming to come and chat me up, it would make such a great story of how we met for the grandkids. But it never happened. I never did get the fairy tale, even the *Pretty Woman* one where I'm a prostitute and a client falls in love with me. From day one I have only really gone after men who weren't right for me.

I was 19 when I lost my virginity. I always wanted to do it to 'Time of My Life' from *Dirty Dancing*. I love music; songs are my emotional soundtrack and diary. I always remember a feeling from a song. It's my favourite thing to do sometimes, just listen to old playlists and remember like a diary extract the feelings from my life.

When I was younger and used to love Cher, I would always listen out for her songs as a sign. I would listen to 'Save Up All Your Tears' and would think of her telling me not to cry. As I got older, my Cher sign song was 'Believe'; whenever a relationship was definitely over, that song would come on. That's how I knew it was definitely, definitely over, because 'Believe' would come on.

Anyhow, when it came to my virginity song, I played my favourite game: predict your future with song shuffle (you'll notice I play this game a lot!). On this particular occasion I said, 'Next song that comes on the radio is the song I am going to lose my virginity to' and lo and behold, 'Time of My Life' came on.

I put on the CD when I had sex for the first time. I hated every second of it. The sex, not the song (at least I had experienced that before). It was awful and he treated me like shit. It was a man called Dave, drug addict, rough childhood, mentally unstable Dave. The first man to pay me attention, and I was so willing to love, I jumped on him. He was the kinda man who on New Year's Eve, when I was working, went up to my best friend and said, 'Tell Luisa I am going home with someone else tonight.'

I was a virgin at the time; nine months later I slept with him. I can call him mental, but you attract people for a reason. If I'd had a healthier opinion of myself, of love and relationships, I would have bounced. But for some reason I decided he was the one I would have sex with.

So I did, on his grandma's living room floor. I put the *Dirty Dancing* soundtrack in the CD player and the final song came on; afterwards he said 'I can't deal with this Luisa' and went to sleep in his grandma's room. Didn't see him again after that.

I don't know why I was in such a hurry to lose it, other than the fact that I didn't want to be 19 and the only virgin at university.

Maybe if socially we were encouraged to enjoy a healthy sexual appetite and relationships, virginity wouldn't be such a huge ordeal and there wouldn't be the pressure associated with it. Having sex should be normal, it should be educative and awakening, it should be healing and desirable and fun. It's something you gain, you gain insight. Not lose innocence. I can suck a dick a day and still have innocence. How about we stop making women feel GUILTY for taking part in what's natural? Such bollocks.

Sex is absolutely precious, and the person you share your body with, that is your choice, your life. It is sensual and powerful and a vital part of life to experience. I loved having sex in a relationship; I can see why people miss it so much. It's way better than doing it on your own all the time.

Eight weeks into Chicago and my plan to just meet someone else and fall in love wasn't happening. However I did fall head over heels in friendship with a gorgeous woman called Kalinda. I was sat at the bar, she was with a friend and we just hit it off and got on so well. She became my Chicago bestie. She lived and breathed kindness. At Thanksgiving she invited me to her family home five hours' drive away, where I was welcomed, fed a feast, went on a zip line and shot a gun. I shat myself and swore never to hold one again. They made me shoot at some wood, like they do it for fun. In America, it's their thing. Guns = Fun. ☺ 🔫 Irony is not lost.

We went to the local church, which was the most expensive church I have ever seen. Not in a laced-with-gold kinda way, no, it was way more subtle that that. It was enormous, bigger than a football stadium, and had some of the most advanced technology I had ever seen in a church. A massive stage, huge speakers, big white screen, iPads as you came in. It was like a concert stadium but a church. The pastor was preaching and I was amazed. This guy was like a headliner at a comedy club; he had the audience in the psalm of his hand. Get it, psalm? Oh never mind.

He was talking about virginity and how precious it is and how women should never give it away. Hold up? I was with you until that bit. Then in plain English (American) he went on: 'In my past devil life I slept with dirty women, evil women, where the Lord was testing me and I failed, I failed the Lord. I was with prostitutes and I regret the pain I caused the Lord. But then the Lord forgave me, forgave me and blessed me with a new life. A good blessed life. Being married, making love to my wife is like making love for the first time, every time. I speak to you young women of the audience. Give your husband God's great gift, let him love you for the first time.'

I felt sick. This was disgusting. I looked around hoping to see eyes of disdain, but all I saw was awe. Surely this dude shouldn't be allowed a microphone, let alone an audience of 1,000 people. Wow, welcome to America.

I watched Kalinda as she was looking on, not in shock, but in agreement, she was smiling in agreement. I felt like I was in 'The Emperor's New Clothes' and I'm going 'Am I the only one who can see this guy is naked?!!' Kalinda was just beaming at this preacher, her mother and father standing next to her proudly. They didn't intervene, they didn't hold her ears, they didn't say to her 'Sweet child, no'; they beamed. And Kalinda could sense that I was staring at her like I was watching a cow give birth. Kalinda, who I loved and adored, with a heart of gold, turned to me and whispered, 'Luisa I am still a virgin' and smiled. I wanted to cry for her.

I didn't like this church at all. A preacher who himself had enjoyed multiple partners was telling women to save themselves. I wanted to shoot him, but then I remembered I am not American, plus God wouldn't like that.

Jesus seemed like a cool guy, not an anally retentive misogynist. Why are men given this platform to spew such damaging venom? How is this legal? Worst of all, how is it mainstream? A man preaching to a woman on how she should use her sexuality. That is, a man controlling a woman's sexual behaviour. If a man has control of a woman's sexual behaviour, she is not independent and she is not then allowed to learn and take responsibility for herself. This is rape culture, where a woman's sexuality and worth are controlled by a man. Control is power. Rape is power.

I was brought up Catholic. The books at school were pretty standard: share, be nice, be kind, God loves you. But as I have got older, I have moved further and further away from the Church. It just seems very man-made and man-run. I don't feel it embraces all the facets and delicacy and beautiful infrastructure that is human nature and womanhood.

It's not been an overnight process, but as I have got older, I have started to question things I always took as standard. Art, for example.

Historic artwork in public galleries is all by men. Always dudes, guys, boys, men. Seldom is artwork by women depicted in the history floors. When I was younger I was like, wow, women must be really bad at painting, writing, designing things. A woman creates art and maybe if she is lucky, one woman in every generation will have it displayed. Whereas a man creates art, it is celebrated for generations. Throughout history how many female artists are there that are undiscovered, why hasn't their work been published? Why is a man's art more revered than a woman's? A woman wasn't even allowed to create art. Didn't have access to supplies or teaching and if they did and they developed, that would often be seen as something they do in the home, to pass their time. Sketching and knitting.

Why? The whole point of art is creation, and women deliver the ultimate act of creation I guess: pro-creation. Is that what it is? Womb envy on some level. We can create life, and that in itself is so powerful and perhaps threatening to the limitations of the male anatomy. What better way to regain control and ego than by undermining and controlling a woman's ability to create life. Shame her vagina. Judge bitches on sex. Are dudes ultimately scared of the vagina? I don't know. The guys I meet aren't, they quite happily bury their heads in one, but then why through history, and especially in religion, are women judged in this way?

This notion of virginity is just another means of control. A woman's virginity is precious and should be saved for a man to enjoy, whereas men are encouraged to lose theirs as quickly as possible.

I always got the maths confused on this one. How come boys can have loads of partners but a girl can only do it that one time with someone special? Surely that can only be achieved if there is like a five-to-one female to male ratio. Also the language, 'losing your virginity'. You don't lose something. Your virginity is for you to have sex, it doesn't mean you've lost anything.

There is no in-between, how could there be? A woman must not lose her virginity until she is married, and if she does have sex before then, she is a scandalous whore. I don't understand why the public perception of women's sexuality has been so controlled, perpetuated and narrated by men. Why? What are they so scared of?

I would like to think I am my own woman and can fuck who I like, but you are not going to make me feel shame for my body and how I use it. Like shaming women for breastfeeding in public. Why is my form up for public scrutiny, and not just my form, but my natural design as a woman? Why are you scrutinising my nature? Women around the world have their sexual organs used against them daily.

The sexualisation of women is a constant source of debate. Women's magazines, porn, breastfeeding in public. Our bodies are covered in shame. Who set up and started the rhetoric? My cunt is amazing; every woman I know in my life is amazing and strong and powerful. We are capable of giving birth. We are also capable of great pleasure. We are goddesses, and I say that with no uncertainty. You are a goddess.

I mean we all start as a girl in the womb. You would think as the bearers of life women would run things. It's the most powerful aspect of our being, the ability to procreate. But men have taken this function, the body form of breasts and a vagina, and instead of worshipping it they use it to control us. I wonder if that's one of the main reasons why women have been deliberately subverted rather than celebrated as equals: fear. And here, in the middle of America, is this man standing on a stage who has used and abused that pleasure and privilege and is now calling out for young girls to protect themselves and not become 'whores'.

A lot of men are oblivious to their own privilege. There is an arrogance in many of the men I meet, be it talking over women in meetings, dismissing their ideas, catcalling, feeling owed on nights out for sexual favours because they paid. Even on a basic level, having conversations with dudes who have no social skills or ability to read a situation, but just see their own reality. I have always thought women are so emotionally intelligent and evolved. We have had to work harder emotionally and are streets ahead, and yet show patience and love to the male form.

Women are seen as secondary. One in four women in the UK will experience sexual assault. One in four. That statistic is terrifying.

I love men, I respect men, I am not anti-men, but why am I being taught that my value, opinion and body are worth less than those of a man? Can I breastfeed in public? I don't know, it's up to the guys, they make the laws. I believe a lot of men struggle with the current notion of masculinity. I see emotionally weak men all the time. The men I have met who call women desperate are the same ones who are never out of a relationship for longer than a few weeks. They have all the bravado of being a player and yet have a poor girl at home waiting for them. Men who are married for 25 years become widowed and are in a new relationship a week later.

A woman's whole journey in this life is about self-improvement, whether that be physical, emotional or spiritual. Where is society's call for male self-improvement? For a man to stand on his own two feet and know himself, really know himself. His feelings, his fears, his sexual beliefs. His values, his worth, his truth.

The religious men who scorn scantily clad women are some of the weakest members of society. Learn about your own sexual repression and educate yourself to not touch what is not yours. Do not teach women shame, teach men control. I believe some men have got lazy. Some are just so emotionally lazy because women, mothers, have made excuses for their crap behaviour. Men have been praised and celebrated throughout history; we have museums filled with their creations. And now the current man, who is creating nothing, has an ego so fragile all he can do is, I don't know, become a comedy critic.

Obviously I couldn't discuss this with Kalinda, a virgin herself but I wanted to hear her opinions; after all, some of my sexual experiences weren't great, so if her way saved her from pain, go for it. She just wanted to fall in love, get married and then have sex. The pressure of that though: what if the sex is awful? Could you imagine, your wedding night and you get down to business and are completely incompatible. I have knobbed guys where the conversation is on point and sparks were flying but then you try and fuck and it's such an anticlimax. I didn't want to upset Kalinda so I respected her church and her feelings, but that's not what I want for my child.

Overall though it was a wonderful Thanksgiving, as sad as I was about not being with Klaus. Even after 'I wish I was in love'-gate I continued to talk to him, even though it often left me feeling drained and frustrated because I knew he didn't really want to be with me. Who was I to give Kalinda advice on sex and virginity if the relationship I was in was leaving me feeling empty and used? But old habits die hard, plus it would be nice to see him when he picked me up from the airport.

Career-wise, though, I ended up having the time of my life in Chicago. I grew so much and gained so much confidence in my comic abilities. I had learnt about Americans and their self-belief, and I loved that. I had always felt in the UK that when I said I aspired to be a comedy performer, I would get shot down. Whereas in the States, the attitude was 'Why of course you can, and you will.' I loved that.

I had learnt to embrace my natural inner clown, how to use all of my being on stage and not just my voice. I learnt rules in comedy that were definitive in my growth as a comedian. I learnt to commit, if you are going to do something on stage commit to it. If it feels awkward, make it even more awkward until it is so awkward that you start revelling in how awkward it is.

I started using this improv training in my stand-up, committing more to my voice and my ideas. I also found it incredible as it helped me whenever I was doing badly on stage. If an audience hated me and I was dying on stage, say it had gone past the moment of rescue and I had tried and failed to salvage it. Then I could use these techniques. You see, I am not at the level where I have been going long enough to have a repertoire of jokes that I could pull out. You will see it with comics who have been going for twenty years, they can come out, read a room and go 'Bam, this is the stuff you'll like.' I've not got that. There is no point in me changing halfway through my set. 'Oh, you don't like relationship jokes? OK, here are my quips on office life.' So instead I started using my improv skills.

For example, if you are dying on stage, and the audience hate you, don't get embarrassed and pray for the ground to swallow you up, instead die harder, keep doing what you are doing that makes them hate you. That's all you can control. I know this isn't the best advice for everyone, but it works for me.

Because there is truth in dying on stage, and the best funny always comes from truth. Now I still very much have just horrible ground-swallowing experiences, but when I can, if I can, when I am dying on stage I like to try and own it. I sign off by saying my name really slowly and then spelling it out: 'Thanks for watching guys, my name is Luisa Omielan. That's L.U.I.S.A. O.M.I.E.L.A.N. Please come and give me your feedback on Twitter, that's @Luisaomielan. I really look forward to hearing from you. No please, don't clap, why make it any less awkward now? We may as well continue as we started! I think I would prefer it if I just slowly left the stage to no applause, it's the least I deserve,' and then I will mock high-five them and slowly and purposefully awkwardly leave the stage. There is comfort in doing it like that; people hate it, but fuck 'em. Chicago taught me that.

I had completed all the training and it got to my last week. I knew I was going to miss Chicago. I felt I had changed and grown as a person out there. I'd gained confidence in my talents and was clearer about vocalising my dream to work in comedy.

Then three days before I was due to fly home, I got an email from Klaus: *I'm really sorry Luisa, I can't do this, I'm sorry.*

Motherfucker. The week I am flying home, the wimp bails. No meeting me at the airport, no kissing me and swinging me round at arrivals. It felt like another punch in the gut. Why had I not trusted my instincts on this one? Why had I let him back into my life?

I flew back to the UK and my mum met me at the airport instead. And we had our *Love Actually* moment, and she was really pleased to see me, and I her, and even though part of me kept thinking it should have been Klaus meeting me, I was so happy and relieved it was my mother, because she came with the best form of love. Pure and unconditional.

13

RUN THE WORLD

After having my mind blown in Chicago and wanting to embark on a career in comedy more furiously than ever, the last thing I wanted to do was to go back to temping. My radio job had taught me so much but I needed to be more focused and vocal with what I wanted. I had seen what I was capable of and now wanted to make it my lifestyle, full-time.

So I came up with a game plan. I decided to stay living at my mum's for now and commute to London. It would only take an hour on the train, not that long really. I could go back to working as a receptionist if I wanted, I was lucky as my mum wouldn't charge me rent. Some people called it spoilt, I called it loved actually. I mean sure, I am 27, trying to avoid a temp job. I am the same age as Beyoncé. Look where Beyoncé is, she is selling out arenas and I've got a teaching qualification and several books of notes from

Chicago. What would Beyoncé do in this situation? So I thought what if I utilised the two. I could run a workshop and show people some of the exercises I learnt. I am by no means an expert and wouldn't advertise myself as one, just as a facilitator.

I didn't know if anyone would want to learn from me, but I'm good at giving presentations and making things fun, I knew I could create a safe environment for people to practice and play.

I have always been a hustler, I always think there is money to be made, I want to create wealth. There is a big pile of money out there; it's just about finding a way to access some of that for yourself. However, this drive for a better life, for having nice things and good quality is always met with self-doubt. I think this is quite a British thing, to compare ourselves to people who have less. 'Look, there are people starving in Africa.' Be grateful, yes I am, but there are also people taking a year holiday in Cannes.

I am not saying I shouldn't be grateful, but why am I always taught to look down and never to reach up? There is a good life out there with my name on it. I don't want to be part of the machine and live to work. I want to have money in my bank, I want to look after my mum and my family, I want to make something of myself. But this is always juxtaposed with self-doubt and the 'but how?!"

I wish women felt more confident in their abilities. I have seen my mum make £100 last a month with four small children, I have seen her paint her own ceilings, build her own shed, cook, clean, work, repeat, all whilst having a migraine. And yet every day I come across women trapped in the system of nine to five hating their lives. I wish we had more confidence in our abilities.

Is it any wonder we don't have the confidence in it, when we don't even have confidence in our own skin? Why would we have confidence in our careers?

We fall short on our sex lives, our thigh gaps, our careers and our appearances. I will see a friend and compliment her on her dress, I say, 'Hey babe, that's a nice dress!' Do you know what her response is to 'That's a nice dress'?

'What? Oh this? Yeah, it's cheap, really cheap, I got it in the sale actually a few years ago, colour doesn't really suit me, you would look amazing in it, I mean it looks frumpy on me because when I bought it I was really skinny and I've put on a lot of weight and I didn't think I would see anyone today when I left the house and here you are looking at me and oh my God, please avert your eyes, I look like a monster!'

Subtext: 'I hate myself, I hate myself, I hate myself.'

After a compliment?!! That's the wrong answer, bitches; do you hear Beyoncé putting herself down like that? Hello, no. What would Beyoncé do?! Upgrade herself, that's what. If someone comes up to you and says 'That's a nice dress', your response should be 'Damn right it's a nice dress, and I'll tell you something else for nothing, it looked shit on the hanger.'

Why have we learnt to self-deprecate everything – our body image, ambition, goals and dreams? I see lots of my friends struggle with confidence in their careers. I don't see it with dudes. For example my friend Delia – you remember Delia, my Destiny's Child-loving friend with amazing eyebrows? She is one of the most talented artists I know, can draw anything, she's so talented. She does nail art and can paint Snoop Dogg on one nail and it's epic.

She works as a teacher, a great, wonderful profession, but any other waking moment she gets she is drawing or creating or painting. So I'm like 'Delia, quit teaching and run your own business, do nail art, you just need to start as a one-man band, build a social media following, go for it, you are too good to not do it, you'll end up selling your stuff to Topshop and be a millionaire in like five years' time.'

Delia's response is 'Don't be silly, I'm not going to set up my own business, no one is going to want to buy from me, plus I wouldn't know the first thing about the financing side of it. No, it's fine, I like teaching, besides, I'm in my thirties, I live in a shared house, I work to get paid to pay my bills, I am this close to moving back to my mum's house and on Saturday I failed my driving test for like the eighth time.

'I can't be fannying around trying to start again, plus I'm gonna be 33 in a couple of years, I should be thinking about having babies soon because apparently if I don't it's going to be very difficult, and have you been on Tinder lately?!! It's really fucking hard. Besides, I love teaching, I love my kids, it's fine.'

And I'm like, what?! But Delia you are so good, the world needs to see your gift, yes you are an amazing teacher and kids need that, but your vocation is art, Delia. I want people to know how amazing you are, like this is your unique talent, no one else can do this like you can; I want people to know you exist!

Delia is like 'It's fine, I'll retire when I'm 75 or 90, whatever they make the retirement age by that time and then I will just work in a sandwich shop.'

Then I will see a guy friend with a fraction of the talent Delia has and suggest 'Mate, you are good at that, you should think about setting up a business one day.'

Do you know what his response is, 99 per cent of the time? 'I watched *The Apprentice*, how hard can it be?!' No qualms, no questions, no doubts. Confidence in his ability.

And it's irrelevant if the dude pursues his goal or not, it's the immediate attitude of 'Yes, I can do that.' I love that confidence, I love my men feeling that sure of themselves, I love my men feeling that capable, I don't want to see men be brought down, I want to see women step up and match that self-assurance.

My childhood may have taught me to doubt my instincts when it comes to life decisions, but it made me stronger when it came to trusting my instinct in my work. Plus Chicago had changed my game. It encouraged me to believe in myself and believe in my comedy. I felt stronger than ever.

I didn't care that I was nearly 28 and moving back home, I didn't want to work for someone else, so I put an advert on Facebook and offered a six-week improv course, three hours a week, for £100 and waited to see who responded.

I had ten names. I had a course. People wanted to learn with me. I was delighted and petrified. I found a room above a pub I got for free and every Sunday I would travel to London and run the workshop. It became successful and I taught for the rest of the year whilst gigging in the evenings.

I'd been home for about six weeks when Klaus got in touch and wanted to meet up. He had been in Germany since I came home and had just moved to a new place in London. I wasn't going to see him but then I remembered I had no willpower, and we met. We met on Valentine's Day, and again maybe once every few weeks. I found myself getting caught up again. I was getting bored of it now. We would discuss all the reasons he loved me but couldn't date me because he was just not ready for this kind of relationship. He called it an 'impasse'. We would have a break, cut each other off and then a few weeks later meet up. It was on and off, on and off and it was exhausting.

Gert's wedding came around, which was in Germany, and Klaus and I were invited. We weren't together and this was going to be so awkward. I arrived in Berlin but got held up because of the weather. There were no buses or trains leaving the city and I didn't have the cash for a taxi to the hotel. I called Klaus and he sent his dad to come get me. His parents called me Smiley. I didn't have the heart to explain to them that last time we met I hadn't been expecting to see Paint Dry and that was why I'd had to fake it and smile, since then I was fucking their son on and off, so instead I just had to keep smiling more than usual so they just thought I was normal.

Klaus arrived the next morning. We went to the wedding, we slept in the same bed but he wouldn't have sex with me as he didn't want to lead me on. The next day as we were wandering around the streets of Berlin, we walked past a jewellery shop. I saw a pretty little silver ring; Klaus went in and bought it for me. He came out and said, 'Luisa, I got this for you as a symbol of our friendship.'

☺🔫

After the wedding, we came back to London and he invited me and my mum out for dinner. At the last minute he couldn't make it but he told me to cover the bill and he would pay for it. We spoke that night on the phone about our infamous impasse and how he was just not ready and then he just went quiet for about a month and a half (not on the phone; he said goodbye first. I mean in real life. Just slowly nothing). I was sad, but I was OK. I would tell myself he would call me by the weekend, but he never did. Not a day went by that I didn't think of him, but I figured this was his way of having distance. I would have preferred to have this in Chicago but never mind.

Instead I focused on my gigs and my classes. I wanted to expand the classes, so I thought about teaching comedy for kids. I called up my old primary school and asked if I could come in and do a free comedy workshop after school. I already had my CRB check from my teaching qualification; the school was lovely and invited me in. Before I knew it, I was running improv classes in three different schools. I called it Comedy Club for Kids. Very imaginative.

Improvisation is brilliant for children. Scrap that: children are brilliant for improvisation. They are naturals at it. As we have got older we have learnt behaviours to fit in and in doing so dulled our senses. Improvisation allows you to be free. It's especially good for kids who don't feel like they fit in or struggle to concentrate in class, or whose English is a second language. I loved getting letters from mums telling me how their eight-year-old never got out of bed for school, but on Tuesday mornings he jumped out because he knew he'd got a comedy class to come to. I loved it. I wanted to help these kids, the more oddball the better. I loved them. I didn't want the cool kids, I wanted the outlaws, the nerds, the non-English-speaking, the geeks. And I got them and they excelled. Running my own little company and making money gave me such a sense of confidence.

I was enjoying working in schools and it gave me freedom to still travel to London and gig. Gert booked me in for one of her London nights. I had a feeling Klaus would be there, as he always used to go and scout for new talent, so I took the gig. I was nervous about performing, especially if he was gonna be there but at the same time excited as it was an excuse to see him. It had been over a month since we last spoke.

I got dolled up, a nice skirt and boots, did my make-up and hair and got to the gig early. Margaret Cho was on. She's a famous American comedian and amazing. As we were chatting on the stairs, Klaus walked around the corner. He seemed nervous and embarrassed; I thought it was because Margaret Cho was talking to me. He introduced himself to Margaret and gave her his card. I told her he was a great promoter from Germany and then went to go find him to say hello to him properly.

The gig was about to start and I saw him leaning at the back of the room. As I started walking towards him, he turned his body away from me. I thought he was just anxious so I waved and smiled as if to say 'Hi, can we be friends?' but he didn't look up. So I just turned and faced the stage, knowing that Klaus was behind me and could see me clearly in his eyeline. I remember watching the gig and putting my hands on my hips and wondering if he was looking at my silhouette, as he always liked my phat ass. I laughed at a comedian on stage and turned to look at Klaus. This is ridiculous, I thought. I'm just gonna go up to him. As I started walking towards him, a young woman ran up behind him, wrapped her arms around his neck and gave him a massive snog. Oh, what's that? Is that snow? I thought I had escaped unharmed, whoops! Apparently not. Here it is – may as well welcome it with open arms. Hello snowstorm, I was wondering when you'd finally hit.

I slowly felt the wind being kicked out of me; you know the kind of pain you get when you don't notice it and you just function. And you're so aware that right now in this moment you *have* to function. Because if you don't, you will collapse. I felt sick, humiliated and embarrassed. I felt like a fucking idiot: everybody in the room was laughing at me. Like the universe was mocking me to my face. I was surprised that I wasn't wailing or crying. I just smiled and went on autopilot. As if nothing had happened. In hindsight, I don't know why I was surprised. Just because I was in heartache didn't mean he had to be.

I functioned. I turned back around and acted like nothing was wrong. My name was called up on stage. I got up and was a quivering wreck. I tried my best to do my jokes but I couldn't get the words out. I was just silent and still. I stood there for a moment in the spotlight and felt so isolated. I could see Klaus at the back of the room with his new girlfriend and I wanted to cry right then and there. I wanted to tell the audience that I had just seen the man I had lost my mind over, that I'd lost Chicago over, that I'd lost my self-respect over, in the arms of somebody else, but that wasn't funny. Well not yet it wasn't. It actually went on to be hilarious but you know the classic equation, Comedy = Tragedy + Time.

Instead I just stood there, delivered the material like a robot and took the hit of dying on stage. I made an excuse and left. I felt so stupid being dressed up nicely, trying to look good for him and just looking like an idiot. I felt angry and hurt and ashamed, and I knew that he could see that. I wanted him to see the mess he had made and feel guilty and ashamed and say sorry, say something.

I didn't let anyone else see that I was hurting, I remained still and calm. Margaret and some of the comics left and I left with them. Klaus stayed at the venue. As we all walked through Primrose Hill to get to the tube, the guys were talking and I was making all the right noises to show I was listening, but my mind was miles away, I was desperate to cry and scream. It was an autumn evening and there were leaves on the floor. I slipped and went flying, both feet in the air, and landed smack on my arse. Put my palms down to catch myself and instead not only whacked my hands but fell right on my coccyx. Yay. Now my physical and emotional states were in alignment, slumped on the floor in the cold, with my hands bleeding and feeling utterly humiliated and embarrassed to be me.

I was embarrassed to trip up in front of Margaret, I was embarrassed I'd caught Klaus with his girlfriend, I was embarrassed that I'd thought he still cared and there was going to be a reconciliation, I was embarrassed I'd got dressed up, I was embarrassed that I'd just died in front of an audience, I was embarrassed I'd had the wind knocked out of me and fallen smack on my arse in every way possible.

My eyes welled up from the pain of landing on my butt and this gave me the excuse I needed to cry. It couldn't be a long one though, I was not with people I could talk to about it. I quickly laughed it off and headed towards the tube, got the Northern Line down to Waterloo and caught the train home.

I was fine; all I could think was, well he's an idiot, a selfish idiot. OK so I went to Chicago to get away from him, OK so he called me the whole time I was out there. OK so he met me when I came back and we hung out a lot, OK so he bought me a ring: it meant nothing, he always said that I wasn't his girlfriend. He did always say I wasn't his girlfriend. OK so he would still hold my hand when we walked down the street, but he did always say there was no chance of being his girlfriend. OK so I would show up at his house and he would tell me off for coming over when I should know it wasn't a good idea and then he would still make me a cup of tea and hold me all night long. OK so he told me all the time how he wasn't ready for a relationship, he wasn't ready for a girlfriend and he couldn't give me what I needed. OK so he's met some girl, she probably doesn't mean anything. It's probably just sex, you know what guys are like, they need sex. And OK this was all me, I chased him and he knew it, and it's fine because I am the idiot who let all this happen, he didn't do any-thing, he hasn't actually done anything wrong, he's not cheated on you, he always said it didn't work out and this is all good. He's free to do what he wants. I am fine with it.

I went to sleep with my bruised palms and tried not to think about it.

I woke up the next morning and momentarily felt light. For about two seconds I was OK until my body felt really heavy and my chest felt really tired and weighted and then I just started to feel really sad.

I heard music coming from downstairs: 'I can feel something inside me say I really don't think you're strong enough.' It was blaring from the living room – it was *X Factor* and one of the contestants was singing 'Believe' by Cher. Here it was, my sign, it never failed me. The song was playing, it was over. I ran downstairs and cried my eyes out. I cried and I cried and I cried until I couldn't breathe, and then I cried again. I didn't stop crying for months.

My mum came in to ask me why I'd been crying. I told her about Klaus, and she said that he was an idiot and that deep down I knew it was over anyway. I did, but it still hurt. Ah yes, the past can hurt, but the way I see it, you can either run from it or learn from it. OK, too soon for a *Lion King* reference.

In fact knowing it was over didn't make any difference to me. I couldn't understand why he couldn't date me. He'd said he wasn't ready for a girlfriend but now he seemed to have a new girlfriend. I don't know why he didn't like me coming to work functions with him, yet here he was letting another woman kiss him in a comedy club. I just don't understand, why her, not me? That was the start of it. My depression had been building for months, if not years, but it was in that moment that it finally began to unravel.

14

PRAY YOU CATCH ME

Twitter filled me in. She was a singer from Switzerland called Anna, she was quite well known. It seems they met on one of her tour dates and now she was staying in England and delighted to be recording an album in London. Her tweets were all about her new comedy boyfriend who was showing her around London. She tweeted about comedy club gigs and how happy she was to be there with the hashtag #Proud.

What? Proud?? She's not allowed to be proud, she hardly knows him. I'm the one that's been there for him, I flyered for him for fuck's sake, I went to Chicago and he called me every day for fuck's sake, he bought me a ring for fuck's sake. I cleaned and sorted his bedroom for fuck's sake, I put up with all his shit, I'm the one who helped him. Who the fuck are you, a stranger! You can't be proud.

I cried, I tried to distract myself, watch a film, listen to music, but all I could do was cry. I couldn't even wank. I'd just imagine them having sex, start crying again, I couldn't touch myself after that.

A lot of my friends didn't understand, as they'd seen it coming. But I never saw it coming. I think it's one of those things – you have to experience it to get it. I rang Katerina. She was so patient and would listen to me go on and on for hours about the girlfriend's Twitter feed. She just let me talk and listened.

Social media is the worst when you have broken up with someone. I wish there was an app that could ban you from looking at all your ex's online presence for at least six months. Little note for my old self – just unfriend them, just do it. It's really not necessary to hurt yourself. If you are going to be friends again, you can be, but give it time, you don't need to see his life without you in your news feed.

I found I could rely on friends I never knew I had. Sajeela, a brilliant comedian who ran a comedy club and was like Mamma Showbiz, took me under her wing. I would ring her late at night and she would just listen as I talked for hours. I couldn't get it out of my head.

Sajeela and Katerina were incredible and never judged me. I don't think anyone knows me better than Katerina, I could tell her every sick, hurtful thought. Like how when I was making a cup of tea and watching the kettle boil, I wanted to pour boiling hot water in my face. I felt like I deserved it. I felt like I was unworthy. Lying in bed, I would imagine what it would be like if I jumped in front of a train. I couldn't hang myself and

I didn't know how to do the car in the garage thing. But I could probably jump in front of a train. It wouldn't really hurt for that long and at least I wouldn't feel this shit about myself any more. I didn't want to die because I didn't want to live; I just wanted to do something drastic to get some peace from feeling like this. I felt so bad. I would walk down the street and see people who were happy, and think, that must be how he looks now, happy.

I'd sold myself short in Chicago. I'd cut my hair off because of him, I'd let him back in my life when Chicago was meant to be mine. It was meant to be about me. I was meant to cut him off, and I didn't, and here he is. He's cut me.

This feeling went on for weeks. I hated getting out of bed; it was easier to go back to sleep than it was to face the day. Sometimes I would wake up and for a few moments I would feel all right, and then I would remember every-thing and I would feel shit again. And if I didn't feel bad enough that day, I would go on Twitter and see what they were up to. And then I would feel bad enough again.

I did't even want to go on stage, all my Chicago pas-sion went out the window.

It got to Christmas, which is quite a depressing time anyway because it's cold and windy and whenever the family get together all we do is talk about past issues and my father. I guess me and my brothers kinda miss him, but personally I have found it easier to just not have him in my life any more. Instead I just moved my wound.

This rejection by Klaus was my Achilles heel. It felt so familiar, this notion of being replaced. I felt like that 12-years-old kid again. I felt disturbed and to be honest if it wasn't for Katerina and my mum, I don't think I would have survived. I would put on a pretence on stage and with people who didn't know how real my pain was; they would just laugh and respond, 'Oh you're so crazy!' They had no idea that as soon as I left and got on the train home, my eyes would well up and I would feel so heavy and tired and think that if I killed myself then maybe they would understand how all-consuming my feelings were.

Something about Christmas is so hard if you are feeling sad or vulnerable. This particular Christmas was no different. In Poland we celebrate Christmas Eve more than Christmas Day, and so my mum spends the whole day preparing food and then when the first star comes out she lays the table and we sit down and eat a Polish feast.

It's a Polish tradition to keep a chair spare, just in case Jesus drops by.

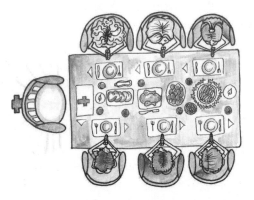

You know what he's like, he never texts beforehand. No matter how many people are squashed around the table, you gotta save a place for Jesus! Don't even try and sit in the spare chair because how much would you kick yourself if right as you pressed your bum into it, DING DONG, naooooo, Jesus is here! He rocks up and is like, whhaaat, you didn't save me a chair? I'm going next door. You'd be proper gutted. So we all sit around the table and make the same old jokes about when he's gonna show up and my mum tells us off for being rude and I'm like, hello, who's being rude, he's the one not eating his fish.

We all had the dinner. I was depressed but dealt with it, then I went upstairs and thought about how I would kill myself if I was going to. I came back down to help my mum with the washing-up.

I finished and went to go and chat to one of my brothers. I passed the room he was sleeping in and from the corner of my eye saw something that didn't seem right. I saw his arm hanging off the side of the bed. So I walked in, his eyes were rolling to the back of his head and he looked ill, all drowsy and out of it. Next to him was a bottle of pills. He had taken an overdose.

We rushed him to A&E and my mum was crying outside the room whilst my brother was getting checked over by a nurse. Two of them were monitoring him and he was slowly getting more and more drowsy.

They give him some stuff and get him stable, they say he needs to just sleep for a bit. I am devastated and gutted and heartbroken. I ask the nurse about when he will see a psychologist or a doctor. She replies, 'Unfortunately, as it's

Christmas Day and because you are here with your brother, you're put down as his primary career so he doesn't need to see anyone. We will monitor him and make sure he's stable.'

'What? But he needs to see a doctor, a psychiatrist; he's just tried to kill himself.'

'I understand but because you are his primary carer, he didn't get enough points to see someone as you are here with him, so we will monitor him and then send him home with you.'

'Points? Well, can't you just pretend I'm not here and then he can get proper attention?'

'I'm afraid it doesn't work like that, I have seen you now. You will have to make an appointment with your GP and go through the system, he will go on a waiting list and hopefully be able to see a psychiatrist in six to eight weeks' time.

Wow. My bro just tried to kill himself and he didn't score enough points to see a psychiatrist. I would hate to know what it takes to score enough to see one.

So picture this, it is Christmas Day, approximately 3 a.m., my mum is outside devastated, my other brothers are crying at home, we didn't call my sister, she was celebrating Christmas at her boyfriend's house and we didn't want to ruin her Christmas as well. I called my dad, I didn't know who else to call. I felt so hurt and desperate, I wanted someone to help. I wanted a man to walk in, for my dad to walk in, for Klaus to walk in and say, 'I got this, everything is gonna be fine, it's gonna be fine because I am going to make it so.'

My dad answered and didn't recognise my voice until I said, 'It's Luisa, your daughter.' I explained to him what had happened and he said he was sad to hear that and to tell my brother to give him a call when he gets out. I say, 'Happy Christmas' and put the phone down.

I look back at my brother. Here we are in the early hours of Christmas Day, sat in this room with harsh bright fluorescent light. And we are here because my beautiful brother wanted to end his beautiful life. My heart is in my stomach and I am numb with sadness and I am looking at him lying on the bed and all I think is, wow, you beat me to it. I wanted to do that.

What do you do in this situation? No one really tells you. Mental health is so taboo and stigmatised, I couldn't put a call out on Facebook, I didn't want to google 'when someone tries to kill themselves'. What do you do? I didn't know. I had no idea. There is no guide in *Cosmo* on how to handle it.

So here is my guide.

What to do when someone you know tries to kill themselves.

1. Be there, just be with them.
2. Don't judge, don't hate, don't be jealous that they beat you to it.
3. Just be there.

That's it. Wow, guides are hard to write, hey?

My brother stirs and whispers that he's tired. He says nothing else, no explanation, no reasoning, just that he is tired. He sounds tired, he sounds exhausted. I look at his beautiful tired face and I am in disbelief. I mean sure, we have all felt that way at some point or another but we never actually do it. And why my family, why does my family have to suffer and feel this worthless, why do we have to be plagued with this mental health bullshit?

This isn't fair, it's not normal! I am looking at my brother and thinking, you are so loved, you could not be more loved. Why? Why would you feel the need to do this? You didn't have to do this! You should never feel like this is the answer! If you ever feel like this again, please please come and talk to me, come and ask me.

My brother stirs again, he looks straight at me and exhales, 'I am so tired, I am just so tired,' and buries his face in the pillow. I wanted to offer him all my comfort and all my love, but my mouth started talking before my heart could catch up.

'You're tired? You're fucking tired?? Its 5 o'clock in the morning, you dickwad! We are all fucking tired, mate! What the fuck were you thinking? An overdose? What a fucking moron! Who takes 12? 12? You couldn't have taken the whole bottle? You can't even do that right, you moron! Here is an idea, you little punk: next time you fancy having a go at killing yourself, why don't you do us all a favour and come and ask me how?!'

I had shouted so loudly a nurse came in. I immediately sat back down. My brother just sat in silence, both of us stubbornly crying.

The nurse leaves and my brother says, 'See what I mean? Nobody loves me, none of you love me.'

With gritted teeth I said, 'Nobody loves you? Nobody loves you? I broke your shit up with a stick!'

I don't know how we all got home; we were nervous and anxious around each other and especially around my brother. We put him in the spare room and wouldn't let him close his door, just kept checking on him every few moments. No one really slept.

It was Christmas morning, and my mum had students over from China, two young girls, so we had to pretend nothing had happened the night before. She was somehow trying to make Christmas dinner as normal as possible. My brother didn't join us. My mum made some excuse that he was hung-over. It was Christmas after all.

I lasted until about 4 p.m. before I screamed and cried at my mother. Why are we pretending nothing is happening? This family is fucked! He just tried to kill himself and you are telling people he's hung-over? We shouldn't be living like this! My mum got upset but said what can she do? She started crying and was defeated, she had no money, no house, no savings, teaching was all she could do, at least these students would cover the bills for January, what else could she do? Send them back to China on Christmas Day? She needed the money.

I resented her for it. I hated that we didn't have money to look after ourselves properly, that my mum had to work and I couldn't get my brother in front of a proper doctor. I hated feeling this stuck by circumstances. If I was rich and famous I would have him in a clinic, he would get taken care of, my mum wouldn't have to work.

We wouldn't have to live in this stress. I hated living like this. Beyoncé does not live like this; Beyoncé would not be living like this at all.

Then it's Boxing Day and my friend Jason Patterson texts me and suggests we meet up. Jason Patterson has a complete heart of gold and is hilarious to boot. It was the last thing I felt like doing but it was good to get out of the house. We met at the South Bank and found this great restaurant in Covent Garden. Jason is one of the kindest, most easy-going, humblest human beings on the planet.

We had dinner and I told him all about Klaus and all about my brother. We talked for hours and Jason made me really laugh and just feel better for having someone to tell it all to.

He had to do a gig and so I went with him, and he suggested I get up and do five minutes. It was the last thing I felt like doing, I didn't want to stand in front of people and try and make them laugh when I felt like I was crumbling underneath my own skin. I was ready to fall, I felt so weak and vulnerable.

Just do a short set, he said. So I got up, and I didn't really know what to say, so I told the audience about my shit Christmas, about Klaus, about how I had seen him with somebody else and how the last two days were some of the most stressful I have ever known.

I told them about the hospital and I told them how loved my brother is, and how I wanted to tell him how loved he is, but instead I called him a dickwad and had a go at him for being selfish.

The weirdest thing happened, there were only about 20 people in the room, and the audience laughed, they really fucking laughed.

Not in a 'laughing at me' way, but in a shit I have been there, I recognise that hardship way. And that did more healing for me and gave me more comfort than I had known in the last three months.

Something about that laughter and recognition and realising that I am not alone and people get it made me feel better. It gave me a break and made me feel at peace and like God or the universe or some higher power was looking after me and saying 'I'm here, you are not alone, there is light.'

I finished my set by talking about Klaus. I told them all about how upset and mental I had been over him. I ended my set with fake crying on the floor singing 'Someone Like You' by Adele. As I got up and said my name, people stood up. I got a standing ovation from about ten people in the audience. I could have cried. I probably did.

Afterwards several people came up and thanked me for talking about a really shitty Christmas. But then again, these were people who spent Boxing Day on their own in a comedy club, so I had found my people! People who wanted hope.

I will never forget that gig; it was the start of me finally listening to what I had always known. That truth is funny, truth is what is precious and valuable and truth is what will connect people. Don't look for jokes, tell the truth. I am funny, funny I have got, but tell the truth. Life is fucking hard, but be honest about how hard it can be, and trust that the funny will follow. Once again comedy was saving me.

15

SENDING THE EX AN EMAIL

Now these emails start with the best of intentions: short, concise, you're just going to get a few things off your chest in a calm and reasonable manner. You are hurting, and it's painful and exhausting not being able to talk to him about it and explain how you are feeling. There is so much left unsaid. Admittedly most of it has been said before but that is not the point. It still hasn't given you your answer. Like U2 said, I still haven't found what I'm looking for. Despite this, despite all this pain, baby girl, don't email him. What would Beyoncé do? Be Yoncé.

Reasons to never send your ex an email

Don't give him the satisfaction of letting him know how much he has hurt you. He does not deserve this attention.

Write it all down and turn those lemons into lemonade, a genius body of art that summarises all your hopes, fears and feelings whilst never directly naming anyone in particular.

I know you are hurting and emotions are high, but this is not the best time to communicate effectively with someone who has seen you naked.

This is just the part of you that is desperate to know why he doesn't love you any more. It's horrible, I know, but his actions are enough to show that he doesn't. Listen to those actions.

It leaves you vulnerable to whether or not he responds. You are already vulnerable. Do not give him more power.

He is not going to suddenly change his mind and think, shit! She is right; I should totally get back together with her.

He will have physical recorded proof of your mental fragility.

You will only be refreshing your laptop or phone waiting for a response.

He might not respond.

If he does, it is never, NEVER the response you want . . . SAID EVERYONE I KNOW!

However, as much as 'I bet it sucks to be you right now' is an anthem, it doesn't quite scratch that unavoidable itch that just won't let you sleep. Sorry Beyoncé, but in this hour of need, you need to step aside. It's time for an intervention, it's time for our ultimate bad bitch alter ego; channel your inner Canadian and ask yourself: What Would Alanis Do?! 'I want you to know that I'm happy for you, I'm not quite as well, I thought you should know' (in an email, phone call, Facebook status, iMessage, WhatsApp).

Reasons to email him

Hello?! *Lemonade* is genius, what's the point in writing genius if you're not going to share it? Why should we care about his satisfaction? Hello, you did that for the whole time you were dating, it's mamma's turn now. Let's talk about *your* satisfaction. You shouldn't be the only one carrying around all this pain. Someone needs to tell him all about himself, and you, my friend, are the perfect, most qualified woman to do it!

This isn't about giving him attention; it's about listening and attending to your own needs. This is about having your voice heard. He is almost irrelevant in this.

Since when did we give a flying fuck about his feelings?! Email him, don't email him, his opinion of you doesn't matter; your opinion of you does.

In this moment of darkness, it's imperative to do whatever you can to make yourself feel better. PS Alcohol helps.

Yes, you are vulnerable, but this is taking control and fighting back. This is your fight song, take back your rights song. You are not a doormat, you are a woman, let him hear you roar!

Of course emotions are running high, yours would too if you were dropped like this. But in the same way that when you are drunk you tell the truth, I have learnt that it is only when you are truly crying that you can really articulate what is actually hurting you.

Of course you will be hoping for a reply that you may not get. The likelihood of him turning around and realising that he has made a mistake is 0.001 per cent. HELLO?! Someone has to be that 0.001 per cent! Be the exception, not the rule. Do you think Beyoncé is the rule? No. Exactly!

So he will think you are mental or an idiot . . . GOOD! He probably thought that anyway, that's why he dated you. Let him. In a few years' time he will be so insignificant that you genuinely won't care, and he will wish fondly that he had someone who had mad love for him and paid him the same attention.

How do we get strong? We get strong by fighting, by fighting and losing and falling and learning. This is all learning. Maybe it is a mistake, maybe it's not; either way, mistakes are important. In fact, they are imperative to your growth. You already feel like crap. You regret everything anyway and have lost most of your dignity, what's a little more for the drain pipes? If you're going to fail, fail hard.

Listen babe, go big or go home. You are home and you are crying. So what's that say? That says you have reached rock bottom. Well done, you are here. And it's only when you have reached rock bottom that you can rise and soar, like a phoenix, like a hot, sexy, covered-in-motherfucking-ash phoenix. So you light that fire, baby girl, send that mental, hurting email. Go on *insert name*, you can do it! I believe in you.

And does she know how you told me you'd hold me until you die, till you die, but you're still alive, and I'm here to remind you, of the mess you left when you went away.

And most importantly above all else, fuck him, we need him to know, with absolute certainty, that we know for sure, that he knows, without doubt, that we think, fuck him. Fuck him, fuck him. Fuck him.

Now my only rule for all of the above, and I mean only rule, this is the only one you cannot cheat on, is that if you are going to send an email, for the love of God show it to your best friend first. Yes, send a mental email, but for the love of God let her proofread the grammar first. There is nothing worse than trying to make someone feel guilty by writing 'Ijst donet know why you made me feel like you lveod me whn the whole time it just felels lkike tyiou were totally lying ebout everything you ever said to me.' Babe, if you had sent me this, I too would have left you.

So I sent Klaus an email, a concise, to-the-point four-page double-sided email (I know you can't send double-sided emails, OK so it was eight pages, and what?). On 31 December 2011 at 7 p.m. Listing everything I had ever wanted to say, I think I read it back about twelve times and sent it to two of my friends. Both approved it (well technically both of my friends said no don't send it but they knew that would make me send it, so they took the bullet for me and edited my grammar) and then, at 7.03 p.m., I got the following reply to my four/eight-page email:

'Hi Luisa, sorry to hear you are feeling like this, we could talk but I don't think it would help.'

Oh. Well. That's not the response I was hoping for. What does that even mean? What does he mean, 'wouldn't help'? You don't know me, you don't know what would help me.

And breathe.

He was done. Just like that, done. My family were done, my ex was done, I was done. And it's time I allowed myself to let it go. My friends were left to pick up the pieces.

The following few months were long. Everything took ages and people told me it would take me months to feel better, if not years. I started seeing a therapist. Every day felt like an effort. I would cry all the time, every day, most nights, just cry. I hate goodbyes, I find them so traumatic, and here I am in the storm of my Achilles heel. My once-a-week therapist was helpful, but that was only temporary relief. Even though I was keeping myself busy, I would often not want to get out of bed. I just didn't feel good, I don't know why. I just felt heavy and I couldn't stop crying.

I went to the doctor, crying for the third time in a week. She suggested that alongside therapy perhaps I should go on antidepressants. This made me cry again. Great, now even my doctor thinks I'm mental.

She was so lovely and did her best to make out like it was no big deal. How was it not a big deal? I am mental, clearly, I felt like the outsider again, the freaky Polish kid. I didn't belong in the world and I hated it. She said, 'Luisa, its fine, one in four people are on them.'

One in four? I didn't believe that. I took the prescription and left.

I hid my face when the pharmacist called out my name on the prescription, quickly threw the packet into my bag and ran home. I was embarrassed walking down the street with antidepressants in my handbag. It would be just my luck someone would come and steal it and they would see the citalopram and hand the bag back to me. Well maybe not, but I still held on to it tightly. I didn't want anyone to know.

One in four people were on antidepressants. One in four, that was huge. I had no idea it was that many. I didn't know anyone who was on them. I kept thinking, if I am on a bus, and the bus is full, likelihood is that the person I'm sat next to is also on them. It can't be that many, surely? That statistic has got to be wrong. One in four?

Why is it in my face every day of the week, my physical health, what I can do to look fitter, younger, slimmer, sexier? Why is the notion of a thigh gap something that is part of my vocabulary?

Why am I aware that I need to be skinny but not too skinny, because no one likes them when they are too skinny do they, babe? And if it's not skinny its 'don't age'. Every face cream I buy is anti-ageing cream. My mum is 64 years old, she has the most beautiful face I have ever seen, I love my mum's face. I love every one of her wrinkles, I don't want to buy my mum anti-wrinkle cream, I want to buy my mum 'fuck me, you're amazing, thank you for being a legend' cream, that's the kinda cream I want to buy my mother!

Why is my sex, my shape, my age used as a currency to value me every day of the week, so much so that the messages for me to change are part of my daily peripheral vision and set as 'the norm'. But it's not on my radar, that if I am feeling sad, desperate or vunerable, that too is actually very normal.

And there might not be a particular reason why I am feeling sad, because no one has died and life is seemingly good. And yet there is this heaviness in me that won't shift, and it has come from trying to cope for too long without respite and no matter how much I try to avoid this feeling of drowning, each time I avoid it, it comes back harder to bring me down.

Why is it not in my face, that one in four people have experienced mental health problems? So if I am feeling that sad and desperate and vulnerable and I am sat on a bus and the bus is full, the likelihood is that the person next to me or the person behind me has felt just as sad, just as desperate, just as vulnerable. And actually there is some comfort in knowing that, because that connects us to another human being, and all we ever want to do is connect to another human being. So why is that message not in my face, that it is very normal and very human, and very much a symptom of our modern life existence to suffer from depression?

It is OK for you to not feel OK. It is good for you to reach out and get the help that is out there because you, my darling child, deserve it.

I started looking at people differently. I would be shopping in Sainsbury's and wondering if the person serving me was on antidepressants, and if they were, how would I know?

I met up with my friend Ellie, who was amazing. She told me that one of her best friends had been on antidepressants for years. That really took the sting off. Then I told another friend. 'Yeah girl, my mum takes them, has done for ages, it's fine.'

I slowly became more confident in asking people about them. It became clear that most people I knew were on them or knew someone who was taking them.

So I literally swallowed the pill and started taking them. I was worried about how they were going to change me. I was worried I had somehow failed at life. I felt guilty for swallowing the first one.

As soon as I started taking them, the weirdest thing happened. I stopped crying. I couldn't cry. What? I love crying. Why can't I cry? I hated that I couldn't let tears out. Forget what other people thought of me; now I felt like I was mental because I had absolutely no control over my emotions; sure, I'd been crying too much, but now not being able to cry at all felt horrible.

I tried everything I could think of to make myself cry. It's my party. Launch 'Operation Cry'. John Lewis Christmas adverts . . . nope. The big one, Adele on repeat, 'Someone Like You' . . . not a flinch, not even a drop. The bit in *The Lion King* where Simba dies . . . nada, not a single tear.

I even tried cutting onions, but nothing was working.

It took a couple of weeks but eventually I started to feel better. Not even better; I just didn't feel shit. I felt normal. And normal felt good. I could cry, I was able to cry, but nothing made me feel like crying, and that was kinda nice.

I can't really describe the difference they made, but by removing the self-loathing I could get out of bed and start doing things with my day. I still had to teach and didn't want to let my kids down. Antidepressants aren't for everyone but they definitely helped me.

The main difference I noticed was how I would react to disappointment. Say for example I have a friend who I'm meeting for coffee on Friday and she texts me on Thursday saying, *Sorry I can't make tomorrow's coffee any more.* Before I started taking antidepressants my response to that situation would be 'WHY DOES EVERYONE ALWAYS REJECT ME IN MY LIFE?' *WAILS UNCONTROLLABLY*

Whereas after I started taking the tablets, the same situation would happen but instead my response would change to 'Hey, they're busy . . . and that's all right!' *high-fives the universe and skips off*

A few months passed and then I got an email from Klaus. It had been a while and he asked if I wanted to meet up. I didn't really want to see him, plus a recent Twitter stalk revealed that he was still dating the singer.

Rules when meeting your ex:

1. You have to look better than him.
2. Hide the fact that you may have grown a tache/piled on half a stone.
3. No crying. If you feel the need to cry, stay away from the cocktail menu. Nothing turns an ex-boyfriend off more than your tear-stained, cosmo-dribbling face.
4. Keep it short, plan a time, and stick to it. None of this 'ah we spoke for hours' bullshit. Make it an hour max and leave politely. If you really both want to, you can arrange to meet up another time.
5. For the love of God, don't fake a new boyfriend. He knows, babe. He's also seen your Twitter, don't you worry.

To be honest, I was exhausted by the whole relationship with Klaus; I didn't really care what I looked like. I dressed casually and did my make-up nice and I met him in a café; it was the same but different. He didn't have the same warmth towards me. Even though he was there in the flesh. Here is the man I had been crying over for months. Here he is.

I don't get it, he's in front of me and I am OK. I started to think maybe Klaus wasn't the problem, maybe Klaus was never the problem, maybe it's what Klaus represented. I stayed for about half an hour. I told him about my comedy club for kids, Musical Bingo and the gigs; I didn't mention Christmas or the antidepressants. When I left, I went to hug him but he reached out his hand for me to shake, so we ended up doing this weird fist bump exchange to say goodbye. There was no synchronicity left.

I called Katerina immediately afterwards. If only I had recorded the meeting with Klaus (I hate it when you forget to record your conversations with an ex) (I have never recorded a conversation in my life). Like you want to explain verbatim what happened but you keep forgetting the details so you just do a general low-down. Problem with that is then you spend the rest of the day calling back every few hours with updates as you remember. 'Hi, me again, I forgot to mention, when he ordered a latte and I ordered a cappuccino, I asked the girl to stir in two sugars first, and he kinda smiled, what do you think that means? Do you think it's because he knew that's how I have my cappuccino? So like he remembers that? Do you think he's missed me ordering cappuccino? Do you think that's why he smiled? Because he misses me? Well he can't be that happy if he's missing me. I hope he misses me, I must have meant something to him. Or do you think it was a "My new girlfriend doesn't order coffee, she only drinks only juices, oh yay, thank God I am with my juicy girlfriend" smile? OK, great chat, thanks, bye.'

That night, on my fifth phone call, Katerina said, 'Luisa, I have noticed something, and I wanna ask you, now brace yourself, listen carefully, you know when you saw him, did you cry?'

'No.'

She laughed so hard,

'Er, what's so funny?'

'Those drugs are gooooooooood!!!'

16

GETTING IN FORMATION

If you are not feeling good, please go and seek the help that is out there, because there *is* help and you deserve to feel better in your own mind, body and skin. Happiness is a baseline we should be setting our lives from. It's not a privilege, it's not something that is found in the right job, clothes, partner. It is an inner knowing, an inner strength and peace that comes from understanding the relationship we have with ourselves. It is so valuable and worth investing in.

You would not think twice about going to the gym and spending £30–75 a month on gym membership. If you had a constant tummy ache you would go to the doctor. Mental health is the same. I want to see that same kind of value and investment in our mental health because it is just as important.

My mental health was tiring, it was making me feel physically tired and vice versa. I was learning how easily my physical health affected my mental. I was run down and exhausted with emotional stress. I needed to put my mental health first and stop dismissing it as something that was not a priority.

The antidepressants were helping me. The gigs were also helpful, really helpful, and talking about Klaus made it feel easier. People were laughing, really laughing.

Stand-up gave me something to focus on that was good for me. I was beginning to think about the next Edinburgh Festival. I had done kids' shows, two-handers, improv shows; the next obvious challenge was to do a solo show. My debut solo show. But was I capable of doing that for an hour? Who would want to listen to me for an hour? What would I have to say that's funny for an hour?

I started preparing my solo show. I wrote to several agents but didn't get a response from any. Some comedians will tell you that in order to do well in Edinburgh, you need a good agent, a good PR and a good venue. At the time, I believed this to be true. I didn't have £12k to pay for a venue, so my only option was to stick with the free fringe.

So how would Beyoncé approach a free debut show? I have to work like Beyoncé. What would Beyoncé do? If I did have a big agent and a PR, what would they do for me? That was it! I decided to work on the premise that I *was* my own agent and PR; whatever I imagined they would do, I had to do for myself.

First I needed a title. That was important, as I needed to attract an audience who wouldn't know me from Adam, so a title is the first step. Lots of comics use their name in the title, usually within a pun, which I think is useless. No one cares about a pun on your name apart from you. Unless you are famous, or your show is all puns, in which case knock yourself out.

I needed a title that would get people in and tell them who I am. No one is going to come to the 'Luisa Omielan' show, nobody knows who I am. Plus Omielan is really hard to say. Christina Aquillera never had this problem. Yes I intentionally spelt 'Aguilera' wrong just to prove my point. Guys, it's my book. Although I don't know why people struggle with Luisa, hello there is no 'O' in Luisa. Beyoncé doesn't have this problem.

I love Beyoncé. I have always loved Beyoncé especially from her DC days. I had motivational Post-it notes on my wall, one of them said 'You have the same amount of hours in a day as Whoopi G and Beyoncé.'

It's obvious, call it 'What Would Beyoncé Do?!' And it needs the question mark followed by the exclamation mark because it's a question and a statement. AMAZING!

No brainer. 'What Would Beyoncé Do?!' Yay, this meant that I could make it feel more like a Musical Bingo gig. So whenever I got bored of my own jokes, I could play a Beyoncé song, perfect, my kind of show. And it means that it immediately attracts the right kinda audience, because if you like Beyoncé, you are gonna like me, and if you don't like Beyoncé, well then I'm probably not going to like you either. Perfect!

Now I needed previews. Previews are show rehearsals in front of an audience. You can go see someone like Michael McIntyre, for example, do a preview and it's basically a chance to workshop new jokes and material. I wrote to all the comedy clubs, all the bookers I knew to see if I could put on a preview of my show. This is where having an agent would help as they could book you lots of previews.

Now most comedians do anything between three and ten previews before they take their show to Edinburgh, and then often they continue to workshop the show throughout the festival. I did not want to be one of those people. I wanted to go to Edinburgh with the show as strong on day 1 as it would be on day 26. I wasn't in a position to be lazy or to wing it. I needed to make an impact from day 1.

I tried booking previews with the clubs – the Stand, the Comedy Café, the 99 Club, the Comedy Pub, the Boat Show – but none of the big clubs would give me a spot. Very few gave me the chance to 20 minutes, let alone a whole hour. I got a few ten-minute slots at clubs, but people didn't take me seriously enough and without an agent it was difficult. So when it came to booking previews, I had to get creative.

Eventually a guy called Mark who runs the Top Secret Comedy Club in central London offered something. He ran his club from 8 to 11 p.m. and suggested that if I wanted to, I could do a spot before or after the main show – at 6 or 11.30 p.m. Afterwards was out of the question as I would have no way of getting back to Farnborough, so 6 p.m. it was. From then on, every Tuesday at 4 p.m. I would be in Covent Garden flyering office workers, trying to get them to come in and see my work-in-progress show. I couldn't afford proper flyers so I just printed it out on A4 on the HP all-in-one printer at my mum's (I knew it would come in handy sleeping on that photocopier). I got four on one piece of paper and chopped it up.

I wrote all the jokes I had ever told out on Post-it notes and put them in front of me. Somewhere in amongst all these notes was my solo show.

My first couple of previews I played to approximately four people. Nevertheless I persevered and was there every Tuesday like clockwork, and my title really helped. It was a free show and people could watch it after work and before meeting their friends for a drink. By my last preview I had 100 people.

For the rest of the week I decided to go outside of London. I went to the Brighton Fringe Festival and performed the show ten times. The audience loved it, especially girls and the gays. This was fast becoming my USP when I was flyering: *What Would Beyoncé Do?! A stand-up comedy show for girls and the gays!* I wanted to perform in different cities and not just play to a London audience, so I started getting in touch with gay bars around the country. It worked; I ended up booking previews in Manchester, Liverpool, Sheffield, Newcastle and Birmingham. I would arrive early and flyer outside, the bar would make money from audiences buying drinks and I would perform my show for free in their function room. I'd record the whole thing on my cheap little Canon camera and make notes on the train home.

I bought a radio alarm that had an iPhone dock and a little remote control and used it as my speaker; I would plug it in near the stage, dock the iPhone and then use the remote to play the music. Plus I could keep an eye on the time; at the moment the show was running to 40 minutes, it needed to be 55.

Initially the format of my show went as follows. Pick up a Post-it note, tell the joke, and if I got stuck, put my iPhone on shuffle and see which Destiny's Child song played next. For example, I would talk about getting dumped and then press play on the remote and 'Girl' would come on. That was it. It was an ambitious and unique way of working and it wasn't until 'Bootylicious' came on during my suicide section that I thought perhaps my format needed reviewing.

It wasn't until after about ten or so previews that my friend Suzi suggested the obvious. She had been picked up by a massive agent and had a director helping her with her show, so she would often give me tips from what they discussed.

'Why don't you structure the show into sections? For example put all your bits about body image together, then put all your jokes about love in another section ... Then when you have your sections, you can match the songs to them.'

Genius! Why didn't I think of that? Well the answer is pretty obvious: I don't have an agent and I can't afford a director. Lucky for me I have friends that can. As I started to put my Post-it notes in order of theme, I genuinely believed my show was meant to be, because as soon as I wrote down all the sections, the rest took care of itself ...

Falling in love jokes CRAZY IN LOVE
Body image jokes BOOTYLICIOUS
Being unemployed jokes INDEPENDENT WOMEN
Being depressed jokes HAPPY FACE
Getting dumped jokes SINGLE LADIES

It was as if Beyoncé had written the lyrics knowing that I wanted to make a stand-up show about them. It was effortless, like it was meant to be. Beyoncé is my spirit animal. This was genius, plus it made so much more sense than hitting shuffle.

I took the show up to Sheffield and got there early to check in to the Travelodge and walk up the high street. I needed a new look as I hated the short bob; so I walked into a salon and got my hair permed. I had always wanted one, and if not now then when? I'd only heard horrible things about perms, but as luck would have it, it totally suited me. It was gorgeous and perfect, Whitney Houston 1980 eat your heart out.

I walked past a charity shop in Sheffield where they had a clothing rail outside and something glittery caught my eye. Among the items of clothing was this really loose, glittery gold shirt. It was like a size 16 old granny's shirt but it was pure gold glitter, and I loved it. It cost £6. I thought, this is very Beyoncé and bought it then and there. Half in jest and half because it made me happy to look at it.

As I headed back to the Travelodge, I ended up in this fancy expensive clothes shop, where all the dresses were like £40, so I started looking on the sales rails and found these black and white woolly ski trousers. They were high-waisted, thick, warm and just ridiculous. I rushed to try them on and they just fit like a glove. Something about them made me really happy; they were fun trousers. And I loved them. At that moment in the changing room, I had a brainwave. I grabbed the charity shop glitter top, tied it around my midriff to accentuate my boobs and teamed it with the woolly trousers. I don't know how and I don't know why but to this day, it is one of my favourite outfits of all time; it just worked.

Here in the middle of Sheffield, wearing something that really shouldn't go but totally did, I had found my show outfit. A perm, woolly trousers and a second-hand granny shirt. For some people, this is just another day in the life of a middle-aged Yorkshire woman. For me, this is my Beyoncé alter ego. Hello Luisa Fierce. Perfect. (See the front cover of the book.)

Things were just falling into place. It felt like it was meant to be. I was loving the journey I was on; it felt like the universe was rewarding me at every step and saying, 'Yes, keep going, do more of this.' I liked that.

A few years ago in Edinburgh I had seen a kid graffiti-ing one of the main strips in the city centre. It looked amazing. To try and get official posters up in the city cost a fortune, a couple of grand at least, so I'd paid this kid a fiver and asked him to graffiti the title and time of my two-hander show. The graffiti lasted about a week and was great cheap advertising. At the time, I took a picture of myself posing next to the graffiti with a can, pretending it was me that had done it. The picture got a lot of likes and lots of comics commented on how cool it was.

I had always remembered that picture. I loved the image and wanted to recreate something similar for my solo show artwork. I googled a few graffiti places and called around, eventually getting in touch with a lad who had seen me at Musical Bingo. He met me at the South Bank in London with his cans and even brought a camera with him. He spraypainted the wall with 'What Would Beyoncé Do?!' Then I put on my show costume – woolly trousers and gold top – and sat underneath the title with a can. He took the shot.

Bingo. The first shot we took we nailed it. This was the poster image. Bright, colourful attitude, and Beyoncé would be proud. I paid him £75 and got excited about ordering my new posters.

I sent out press releases with my new image and tried to get journalists to come and see the work in progress; often newspapers would run features on shows to look out for in Edinburgh. But again I didn't get a response.

I emailed agents but heard nothing. I emailed PR companies saying I had this show called 'What Would Beyoncé Do?!' that I thought was really going to do well in Edinburgh and would be an easy sell with that title. I emailed one PR 13 times. What can I say? I was very persistent. I wasn't disheartened, as my audiences were loving it. And what's that expression? Beyoncé wasn't built in a day? No, not that one . . . To Bey or not to Bey? No, not that one either . . . Build it and they will come. That's the one.

I kept previewing and previewing and previewing. I even found a place for my cow impressions, which surprisingly worked and helped give the show light relief after my sad Christmas story. I liked that the snow was developing moments where I could make people cry and then laugh immediately afterwards. I loved creating this emotional rollercoaster. It's good to cleanse the audience's palate.

Now in the early days, I would finish my show by crying on the floor to Adele, and then I would say, 'Guys, I know we love Beyoncé, but my true hero is Cher.' I would then disappear behind a curtain and pretend to get Cher.

She was never there. But the audience didn't know that. I did, because I would be devastated every time. Hoping she would miraculously appear. I saw her do it at a concert once. 'Follow This Bitches' then she disappeared behind a curtain. It was epic and worked really well. But that curtain wasn't upstairs in the Caroline of Brunswick. So instead the conversation behind that curtain went like this:

Me: Hello Cher! Cher? Cher, are you there?

Me: Oh hi Luisa, it's me, Cher.

Me: Hi Cher, the audience are desperate for you to come out and sing your classic hit.

Me: 'Turn Back Time'?

Me: Not that one.

Me: 'Heart of Stone'?

Me: Not that one either, Cher.

Me: 'Main Man'?

Me: That's on the B-side, Cher, only your true fans know that song. *Pumps fist out from behind the curtain in celebration of being a true Cher fan*

Me: OK Luisa, what song do they want?

Me: They want your smash hit . . .

At this point, I would come out and ask the audience what they wanted a song about; it had to be something everyday, like a spatula or a flannel or buying milk or having a wash. They would shout out random suggestions and I would quickly pick one then head back behind the curtain to carry out the illusion and prep the best-selling female all time.

Me: OK Luisa, I guess I will come out and sing my hit single for you, 'Why Don't You Have a Bath?!'

I would then improvise a song whilst doing a Cher impression and make up lyrics to 'Why Don't You Have a Bath'. I thought this was genius and most importantly, it made me laugh. Unfortunately it was only ever me laughing. Well, me and Cher.

By the way, Cher, if you are reading this, I love you and have many rivers to cross, you give me such emotional fire, and I would make love on a rooftop for you. Hopefully this proves I am a true fan and you and I both know that I *should* have called my show 'What Would Cher Do?!' But someone told me if I did that I would only be playing to middle-aged gay men. Hey, I love the pink pound but I just can't pull off a leotard or straddle a canon.

People would come up to me afterwards and say, 'Luisa, I love your show, but it does seem a bit weird you end on a Cher song, you can't do that.' Er yes I can. And I continued to end on a Cher song until the 35th person told me it didn't make sense to end it on a Cher song. So time to go back to the drawing board for a finale.

I was going over my show notes again; I couldn't afford a director, like I said, so I just kept asking audiences for notes. I think this helped mould the show so all kinds of people would like it, it wasn't just for girls and gays. People of all ages were seeing it and I was getting their feedback. I knew I was on to a good thing because I would have audiences come back again and again. In Brighton, the bar manager of the Caroline of Brunswick (my venue), a guy called Cliff, was a middle-aged white punk-rocker with blue dreads, and he watched every single preview of mine in Brighton. He said he hadn't done that with any other act and that it was his favourite show. So I knew I was doing something right as I was appealing to more people than I thought I would.

One comic saw the preview and said it was fine, but at the moment a three-star show: 'Yeah, the ending is just really bad.' Three stars? I wanted it to be five, it had to be five. I had worked so hard at it.

I stayed up all night in my mum's living room watching Beyoncé and Destiny's Child music videos and trying to come up with some inspiration. 'Cater 2 U', no, nothing; 'Crazy in Love', no, that didn't work, and then 'Survivor' came on. Bingo. Oh my God, oh my God, oh my God, what if . . . wait a minute . . . how about if I just . . . I practised my ending, crying on the floor to Adele, then whilst I am on the floor, literally and figuratively (still need to check with my editor on that one), slumped as if I have given up, what if, what if at this moment I say, 'What, what, what would Beyoncé do?!'

Then I reached up and pressed play on the 'Survivor' video, when Beyoncé starts by crawling on the sand. Oh. My. Fucking. God. I had it. My last line would be both the title and the punchline to the whole show. What Would Beyoncé Do?! I had goose bumps.

Every now and then there are very rare moments in your life where you feel something magical is tangibly happening. You feel so excited and alive and in the moment, in this very moment, you are in the middle of experiencing magic.

As I lay on the floor and howled, I was so excited, then called my mum to show her. She didn't get it, she didn't have to, I was over the moon. I really felt so excited and so proud and so pleased to be alive. I had figured it out, after 33 previews and endless rewrites, the finale to my solo show. I couldn't wait to show people.

There are two reviewers in Edinburgh that everybody cares about. Number one is Kate Copstick; she works for *The Scotsman* and every comedian wants a review from her, she can make or break you. The second is Steve Bennett from *Chortle*. A strong review from either of them guarantees you an audience and industry attention. Kate had previously advocated free fringe shows and Steve was the guy who said I was a *Britain's Got Talent* reject. So my money was on trying to get Kate down.

After emailing *The Scotsman* to no avail, I eventually wrote to her on Facebook. My message went like this.

Hi Kate

I hope you don't mind me contacting you on here, I have been umming and ahhing whether or not to get in touch but I would love your advice!

My name is Luisa, I am a comedian taking my debut solo show to the Edinburgh Fringe, I am a newcomer and I have performed in nine shows at the festival but this is my debut solo show.

I haven't got the finances or the backing to perform in the paid venues yet so I am doing my show for free. I am doing my own PR and have been working really hard at putting together the best show I can!

I have been taking previews to venues up and down the country; I play weekends at the Stand and have been putting the show together since November.

I know you are a big supporter of the free fringe, how could I get someone like yourself down to do a review? I would love you to come and see it, I love the free fringe, it enables people like myself the chance to perform and connect with a wide audience. My friend Lewis Schaffer speaks very highly of you, Lewis is an act I really admire. I would love it if you could give me your insight, could I email you a press release?

I look forward to hearing what you think; once again apologies if Facebook is too intrusive,

I hope you have had a wonderful Jubilee weekend.

Best,

Luisa xx

She replied.

Dear Luisa

Well done you!! You are doing exactly the right thing. Send me the press release and I will put you on my wish list!

All best

Cop

I cried, I was so happy.

Wednesday 1 August and I leave for Edinburgh. I packed and dragged my heavy suitcase halfway across London feeling sick, stressed and sweaty but so anxious to just get up there. I got to King's Cross and sat on the train in my seat. I had treated myself to first class. I took a deep breath, ready to embark on an adventure, and checked my ticket.

Fuck fuck fuck, my ticket was for 2 August. Fuck. In all my anxiety, I'd boarded the wrong fucking train on the wrong fucking day and I'm in first class and no way can I afford the standard fare, I can't afford any fare right now, I've spent everything I have on this festival.

Fuck. What do I do? There is no way I am dragging my suitcase halfway back across London, it's taken me an hour to get here. I could move into standard and hide in a toilet. No. I prayed, and I prayed hard. I was going today! The inspector came round, stamped the ticket. Phew. See, I told you the universe was looking out for me.

I arrived in Edinburgh, got to my room and dumped my stuff. Accommodation at the festival is ridiculous; a room that would normally cost £320 a month in rent would suddenly be going for £2,000 for the month of August. When you don't have much cash but like your lifestyle nice, you get savvy very quickly. I couldn't afford to pay £2k for a standard bedroom so instead I put up ads in Gumtree aimed at students, offering to pay their summer rent. Often university students would have to take out 12-month contracts for a place but they would want to go home for the summer, so this way, I offered to cover their whole summer rent, they were happy and I could live in a nice place for a not extortionate amount.

I'd found a student house about 20 minutes' walk from the Meadow Bar, and I was sharing with two other comics, Jason Patterson, my friend who took me out at Christmas. Jason is amazing; he is what I would describe as a true gentleman, in his attitude, his values, just the way he is. He is the kind of person I would hope to marry one day and wish nothing but the best of everything for him. And Marc Burrows. Marc taught me how to ask for money after shows in Edinburgh; I call him Marc 'best bucket speech in the 'burgh' Burrows. He's the biggest indie-kid raver softie you could ever hope to meet; he wears guy-liner and plays in a hard-core rock band but gives the sweetest hugs and always buys me caramel wafer bars. He is the Meat Loaf to my Cher.

I was in Edinburgh a day early and the boys were yet to arrive. I dropped off my suitcase and went out to all the free venues to put up my posters. I loved the Meadow Bar. It felt so familiar and I had so many good memories of performing with Rachel here that I knew that this was where I wanted to have my debut solo show. Plus Zac the chef was still there. The team welcomed me back and remembered my veggie burger with a fried egg, no salsa, cheesy wedges instead of chips. As a congratulations on my debut show they added a 'Luisa' button to the till! So every day I would come in and get my special burger. Bet Beyoncé doesn't have a burger with her name.

I liked that, I liked that I got my own button on the till, I liked that I didn't get thrown off the train for having the wrong ticket. I liked the way things were working out for me. But I was feeling exhausted. I didn't want to worry about flyering for my first solo show so decided I would pay flyerers. I needed the best, most beautiful flyerers in town, I didn't care about type-casting, I wanted gorgeous, bubbly, lovable flyerers, and I found them. These two girls were amazing, they knew the single ladies dance and everything! I gave them my flyers and the first day's pay and went home to collapse.

I woke up the following morning with a fever and couldn't breathe. I went to the emergency doctor, who said I had developed a chest infection probably due to stress; she prescribed two days' rest and antibiotics.

It was opening night; I couldn't afford a chest infection. I received a message from *The Scotsman* that Kate Copstick wanted to get into my show and could I reserve her a seat. I was heartbroken. Here I was finally having the chance to impress someone that could help me and I had two choices. Do the show and potentially kill myself or pull the first two shows and then go back stronger for the rest of the run. I pulled the first two shows.

I opened on the Saturday. I was still disheartened over missing Copstick, who said she would come at a later date. As I walked up to the Meadow Bar, there was a queue forming outside the front door of the venue.

'Excuse me?' I asked. 'What are you queuing for?'

'The Beyoncé show.'

17

SHE WORKS HARD FOR THE MONEY

It was amazing, they laughed in all the right places, they even cried in all the right places. The audience loved it, I had a full house and made over £100 in donations. The feedback was amazing, people were saying how honest and funny it was. I was worried that they might not get on board, but they totally did, and I was so relieved. I was very lucky and this is pretty much how every single show at the festival carried on.

I developed pre-show rituals. Every night in my flat, I would play my favourite party songs, have a shower and do my make-up. I loved doing make-up and beginning the transformational process, from bedtime Luisa to showtime Luisa. I wore the same outfit every day, the gold top with the woolly trousers. Big gold hoop earrings, spray of perfume and a grey hoodie so I wouldn't get cold walking to the venue.

Every night there was a queue coming out of the venue. I felt so proud and excited; these people were here to see me. It was only a small room, approx. 60-seater, but the excitement of seeing people waiting outside felt like such a privilege. Plus nothing sells a show out like a queue outside the door.

With free shows, you have to wait for the previous show to come out and then you have 15 minutes to clear the floor and get your audience in. My slot was 10.45 p.m., so by the time I got into the room, it would be really hot and sweaty from a day's worth of shows. I would rearrange the chairs, clear the glasses and put my playlist on. Upbeat songs that would get the audience ready for a party. No Beyoncé songs though; they weren't allowed to hear Beyoncé until the show started.

My playlist is vital to the show. For me, it's always about the pre-show jams. My last song before the show was Rudimental, 'Feel the Love'. This song meant show time. My pre-pre-show song was 'The Fighter' by Gym Class Heroes.

Here comes the fighter
That's what they'll say to me, say to me, say to me; this one's a fighter

That's what I was. A fighter, trying my best, fighting hard right now to make my dreams come true. I wanted the audience to come in and hear that song and on a sub-conscious level see that I was fighting. Maybe they didn't think about it that deeply, but I did. I never started my show without those songs.

The room was tiny and next to the toilets; there would be people sat on the floor right up to the stage. It was sweltering. Once 'Feel the Love' kicked in, I would ask an audience member to go on stage and say 'Welcome to Luisa Omielan, What Would Beyoncé Do?!' and I would come on stage.

These pre-show rituals developed to become very much part of the show. One day early in the run, I was setting up the room in my hoodie as the audience were coming in, and as I asked an audience member to introduce me, I took the hoodie off to reveal my gold sparkly top and someone wolf-whistled. Of course. How obvious. Make taking off the hoodie part of the show. This is like clowning in Chicago: always know that you are interesting to watch. Make everything you do interesting.

This mantra started becoming a vital part of the show. As soon as my audience were in the room, I knew they were watching me. So every action I did needed purpose. My audience member would introduce me, I would hit play on my radio, 'Crazy in Love' would kick in, I would strut to the tiny stage, unzip the hoodie and throw it into the crowd. It really got them going!

Now the speech at the end of a free show is impera-tive. You have to nail it. My regular Edinburgh Festival flatmate Marc told me how to do it. So often audiences leave free shows and they don't expect to pay anything. WRONG, it's free to get in, it's going to cost you to get out. This is how we change the game . . .

Start with 'Hi guys, now I think this show is just as good as any of the other shows you have paid to see at the festival.' Say 'I' to personalise it and 'other shows you have paid to see' to get them to create a comparative in their head, so hopefully if they have paid £15 for another show, that gets them ready for what you are about to ask.

'Now I think this show is worth at least a fiver.' Set the expected donation. 'If you haven't got a fiver, two or three pounds would be lovely.' Set the average. 'And if you haven't got that, keep it, you need it more than I do, thanks so much for coming.' In other words, you tight bastard, how dare you take up a seat where someone would pay, look me in the eyes as you walk out, your tweeting of my show better be priceless.

This speech hopefully stops the audience from just dropping their loose 20ps and 2ps into your bucket.

I would also ask my audience to tweet about the show with the hashtag #WhatWouldBeyonceDo; I would then retweet their praise and compliments. I knew people wouldn't remember how to spell Luisa Omielan, but they would know how to spell Beyoncé.

I'd finish the show, wait at the door to collect the donations, say goodbye to the staff and go straight home. I didn't care about getting drunk and partying this festival. I had no interest in getting wasted or

having sex with another comedian. I just wanted to perform my show. I hadn't come this far to fuck it all up.
When I got home, I'd wash my glittery top in the sink,
count my coins on the bed and then Twitter-search my
hashtag.

I loved seeing what people were saying.

@luisaomielan's show is life. Go see and it's free. #WhatWouldBeyonceDo!!

#WhatWouldBeyonceDo Best show I have seen of the fringe, do yourself a favour and get there early!

OH MY GOD go and see @LuisaOmielan's show, so funny I cried!

Such a rollercoaster, I laughed, I cried, go see @luisaomielan. EPIC.

Go and see #WhatWouldBeyonceDo?! IT'S THE BEST THING I HAVE SEEN!

I retweeted all of them. Comics didn't really do that at the time. I had to. It was the only way my audience was going to find me. If papers weren't going to write about me and say it was worth seeing, I needed my audience to. Having a 25-year-old from Edinburgh tweet to her network of thousands that I was amazing was worth everything. If I RT'd all the comments, that meant in a Google search I would come up at the top. I needed social media; I needed my audience to know I existed.

With paid shows and PRs, they organise industry to come for you and then afterwards might say, oh we had this journalist in yesterday, or we had blah blah from this production company. Because I was a one-man band and being a free show, I would have no idea who would be coming in and who was watching. In a way it made it easier as I couldn't get stressed out by the anticipation, but at the same time I was hopeful that industry would find me.

On the third day, a representative from a big agency came. They had heard about the show and were keen to work with me. I could have cried. I was beside myself that people were noticing. I started waking up and feeling really excited. Proud that audiences were loving it as much as they were.

I was feeling good for the first time in ages, not just after the show, but during the day as well, and it was a real feeling, not because of the antidepressants, not because of the adrenaline, but because I had worked at something and I was seeing the fruits of my labour. It gave me self-esteem to have my work recognised and enjoyed. I liked it. It had nothing to do with a boy. Some people complain about Edinburgh, some comics hate it for the pressure, but I was having the Edinburgh of dreams. Getting up every day to perform a show I loved, having cash in my pocket afterwards and love from people who said it was their favourite show, eating my favourite meal and sleeping in a comfortable warm bed. That's a pretty cool life.

On my fifth night, my friend came and showed me a copy of *The Scotsman*. Kate Copstick had sent along a colleague, and here in black and white was a four-star review of my show. Lord did I dance. I was elated and proud and happy. To get four stars from *The Scotsman* is really prestigious. As I said, in Edinburgh it's pretty much them and *Chortle*. Now *Chortle* have several reviewers, but nobody counts any of the reviews unless they are from Steve.

'What did you get? Five stars? Who from? Not Steve. Oh, never mind.'

'What did you get? Two stars? Who from? Steve. OUCH!'

You knew if *Chortle* were coming in, you could hear it a mile off. If you didn't hear it from other comics, then a PR would let you know pretty quickly. I didn't have a PR, but thanks to my RT'ing and audience reviews, publications started getting in touch. I got my first five-star review from *The Skinny*. I was over the moon! I ran to the local printing shop, printed off 100 sheets of paper with ***** all over them and then sellotaped them over every single one of my posters.

More and more people started coming to the show; they were queuing for like half an hour before it started. It was a free show, so people got in on a first come, first served basis. I wanted to keep it as fair as possible. I was turning people away and that felt ridiculous and amazing.

There was talk about the nominations for the Edinburgh awards, and because of the buzz my show was getting, people kept telling me I would be a shoo-in. I got a phone call from someone from the awards panel who said one of their judges had tried to come in but had been turned away. They must have got there late then. Normally with a paid show, the judges get a ticket and show up as it starts, but they hadn't thought it through with free shows.

You see, at the time, there was snobbery around doing free shows, and industry didn't take it too seriously. The previous year two acts were nominated from the free shows. This was a first, acts were proving themselves to be good enough, bypassing the paid-venue system. These nominations started to shift the balance, but bias towards free shows still existed, agents were always telling their clients to avoid it. I would hear it all the time, 'Only shit shows are free.'

Fuck them. I loved being part of the movement that was showing off the free festival in all its richness, its all-inclusive, salt-of-the-earth, underdog, accessible, grass-roots, talented, heart-of-gold richness. And I was killing it.

It didn't really surprise me that the judges couldn't get in; typical that they just assumed they could show up. To arrive for a popular free show at the last minute and just hope to get a seat is short-sighted. Of course they may have been running across town from other shows, but I actually found it quite funny that they got turned away, even if it was at the risk of a nomination.

The lady from the panel asked me to reserve some-one a seat for the following day, so from then on I started managing the queue a bit more. I would arrive at 10 p.m. and walk up and down the waiting queue shouting, 'Press and industry, any press and industry?' People would reply and say, 'Er, I'm here.' And I would be like 'And who are you?!' And they would say, 'Oh we are from blah blah blah' and I would be like 'OK, wait there.' They were shocked that it was me – they didn't expect me to perform the show and also be my own bouncer/ticket master.

The show was fast becoming a runaway hit. Ten days in, guess who walked in. The PR who had ignored all 13 of my emails. 'Listen Luisa, your show is good, and I have contacts. I'll do you a deal if you promise to sign to me and no one else. I will send my contact in but only if you do a handshake now, because listen, there are a few things you are doing wrong. First off, you don't need the music, and the title, it's not good, you should have your name, like a pun. Luisa the Teaser? I don't know, you think of something, you're the comedian.'

I laughed. Probably a bit too hard, as she didn't get what was funny. But I didn't have much choice and this was someone offering to help, so I skimmed over removing the two elements that were intrinsic to making my show the success it was becoming and I shook her hand. Sometimes you gotta play the game, so I shook it and waited to see what she came back with.

Give her her due, over the following days, more and more agents came along. I met with a woman called Debi Allen, who punched the air for the whole show, she loved it. She waited around afterwards to grab me and we spoke for about an hour, she wanted to sign me. I hadn't heard of Debi before, but then I hadn't heard of most agents apart from the really massive ones. But I hadn't met an agent before who was this excited about my show.

I met with Debi a few times and really got on with her. She's down-to-earth and such a hustler. The first time I met her, we went and sat in a bar and Beyoncé was playing in the background and I took that as a sign. Debi wasn't the most powerful agent and she had a massive roster of clients, but she really seemed to get me. Debi hadn't come from money, she had built her company up from scratch, nothing was handed to her. I liked her and she seemed to like me. She started coming to every show.

Day 20 of the festival, I'd come to the Meadow Bar to check in, and as I went to get my pint of Coke and blackcurrant (it was my signature stage drink, it's delicious, you should totally try it, and yes, it all goes in the same glass, you donkey), that was when I saw her. A woman I had never met but who I recognised instantly, and she looked at me with the same 'Oh I recognise you from social media but shit just realised we have never met and so I shouldn't have recognised you' face.

We said hello at the same time, but the air caught in my chest and my hello came out a bit swallowed and so to make up for it, I got friendly.

'Oh hi!! You're Klaus's girlfriend, aren't you?'

'Hello Luisa.'

'Yeah! That's me! So what are you doing here?'

'Oh I just came with my friend for a drink, but he's not here. We wanted to go for a quiet drink.' *Gets jostled by people at the bar*

'Oh great, well my show's upstairs.'

'Is it here? I didn't know.'

'Yeah, the er poster's outside.'

'Good.'

'Yeah, well, I guess you can come if you want, I er I'm starting in ten minutes.'

'Great I will get a glass of wine and come.'

Fuck fuck fuck fuck. Why the fuck did I just invite Klaus's new girlfriend to come and see my show all about Klaus and his new girlfriend? Fuck. This was possibly the most nerve-racking gig of my entire life. The girlfriend, the new girlfriend that I talk about in my beautiful, artistic, heart-breaking show, is here and she is coming to watch. Hey, here are my jokes about how he left me because he wasn't ready and now he is dating you. And worst of all? I have a packed room, the queue is going around the corner of the pub, so now I have to let her in first with industry to make sure she gets a seat. FFS.

This is so embarrassing. Imagine writing your diary after a break-up, imagine pouring out your heartache and depression and how your brother tried to kill himself and you were jealous. Now imagine reading that diary entry out loud to the woman who is dating your ex-boyfriend. Then imagine doing that whilst wearing a second-hand sequinned top and thick woolly ski trousers, badly replicating the single ladies dance whilst standing on a crate in a room above a pub next to the toilets where the hand dryers go off every 10 minutes. Imagine having to do that. Fuck. What do you do? If only there was some kind of uplifting, empowering mantra that could help a person at such a moment . . .

As I was about to open house I quickly caught a moment with my back up against the door and I prayed: 'Please, please God, please, I beg you Jesus, of all the gigs I die at, please do not let it be this one, please, you can have me die at every other gig for the rest of the year, every one, I don't mind, but not tonight, please, please, please, don't let me die tonight.' Then I let the audience in.

I did it, I did the show, I didn't cry, I held my own and I did it. I actually had a great show, well the audience did. My show carried me through on autopilot. And she was kind, and laughed and clapped and cheered in all the right places. She was actually rather lovely.

There is a moment in the show where, after talking about Klaus and his new singer girlfriend, I sing Alanis Morissette's 'You Oughta Know' and get the audience to join in with the chorus. As I was singing it, she joined in, and I thought, ahh that's really nice of you, and at the same time, mate you are killing me.

I came off stage and stood at the door waiting for people to come out. I could not have felt more depleted, but the adrenaline high was keeping me standing. She came past and put a tenner in the bucket, more than most people put in, then she hugged me and said I deserved to win all the awards. She was lovely and pretty and not like Paint Dries at all. I actually kinda liked her, or at least, I liked her as much as I could, only now I guess I just didn't hate her. She was nice, really nice, just a nice, regular girl. We were quite similar in a way, the sort of girl who in any other situation you go shit, we would be really good friends.

After the rest of the room cleared and I came downstairs, she came over all excited.

'Oh goodness, I tell Klaus I saw your show, he was so surprised!'

'Great!'

'Honestly babe, it was amazing.'

'What did he say?'

'Just asked if you were weird with me. I said no, you are nice.'

The compliment was weird coming from her, but rather than listening to the fact that she'd called me nice, I just thought 'Aww, she spoke to Klaus.'

I had made myself proud, I'd taken a hit and I'd done my best, and now as I walked home, I just felt numb.

The next day I slept until 3 p.m., then ordered Chinese food and got ready. I hadn't wanted to go out all day and was still in a state of shock from the night before but amazed it hadn't affected me. That evening Katerina rocked up to help me with the queue. She wasn't doing a show in Edinburgh that year so she'd come up to visit for a week. Thank God she did, her timing was perfect.

Now have you ever suppressed frustration so much that you act completely fine but then will randomly punch a wall if you can't find your keys, even though they were in your pocket the whole time? Well the night after Klaus's new girlfriend came to see me, I was feeling this level of misplaced frustration. I went on stage. My audience were quieter than usual, and didn't laugh particularly loudly at the jokes. Rather than just going with it and trying to adapt my energy to their level, I found myself taking what I can only call the road of no return.

'So you didn't like that joke either, eh? I have an idea. You know what you could do, come to a fucking free comedy show and just sit there in fucking silence. And here's a better idea, why don't you all fuck yourselves, bucket's there, pay what you want, I don't care, you're all dicks.'

And I stormed off stage. Amazing, completely unsalvageable, unforgivable, amazing. As I flew past Katerina she gave me a look that said 'Oh you're doing this, are you? Yep, yes she's doing it! OK! OK! OK? I am here!' She took the bucket for donations and I ran downstairs and slumped at the bar, heart pounding and out of breath.

The audience came out and one by one apologised for being quiet and hugged me, and I felt awful and thanked them for being so nice. Katerina walked me home. I told her all about the night before and how it hadn't bothered me the whole day, and then the tears came. I cried and cried and cried. I cried for the first time since being on antidepressants. I cried and wailed for the first time in months and it was exactly what I needed. It felt good.

Katerina just held me and listened and was amazing. I love Katerina, she is so funny and smart and insightful and she drops these truth bombs that are pretty epic. As I sobbed into her lap, she started laughing. 'It's not funny,' I moaned like a five-year-old.

'Luisa, his girlfriend came to see you do a solo show about her current boyfriend. You literally sang one of the best break-up songs in history to her face and despite this, despite you writing a whole show about their relationship, she still comes out and calls him to tell him how amazing the show is. Don't you get it Luisa, his girlfriend thinks you are brilliant even when you slag her off on stage and vent about her boyfriend. You have won, well done, take it!'

And I had won, because that girl did me a massive favour. If I could do that show at that time in front of her, I could do it in front of anyone. To this day whenever I go on stage and am particularly nervous about who is watching, I just think to myself, remember when Klaus's girlfriend came to see What Would Beyoncé Do?! in Edinburgh and she loved it and you nailed it, if you can do that, you can do this. Even when I die at the gig I'm nervous at, it doesn't matter, I can die and I can get up and do it again.

I was feeling really excited about what was happening. I was getting a lot of buzz from the festival. A comic stopped me on the street and said, 'Oh my gosh Luisa, congratulations, I hear your show is like the best of the festival, and I overheard an agent talking about it, saying that this show could be bigger than *Mamma Mia*.' My heart sang.

One morning I was in the living room chatting jokes with Jason, and Marc came running in. 'Luisa, Luisa! Have you seen *Chortle*?! You got four stars!!!' Steve Bennett had given me the best review: 'Only one word for it, Bootylicious!' Yes Steve! Icing on cake! I was done, Edinburgh was officially perfect. I'd got four stars from *Chortle*. I mean it reads like a five-star, but fuck it, I got four stars!!!

18

ALMA . . . *FOOT STOMP TWICE* . . . CHECK YOUR BATTERY

It's night 23, and I meet this suave-looking older dude at the bottom of the stairs. He stood out like a sore thumb in Edinburgh so I asked if he was industry. He nodded, and so I brought him upstairs. On the way out, he threw £20 and his card into my bucket, said 'You girl are phenomenal, let me take you for lunch, we can talk' and left. Ahh he seems nice, I thought.

That night as I did my ritual of counting my money out, I told Katerina about the guy. 'Yeah, he gave me his card, hang on.' I took the card out of my bag of coins and notes. 'His name is Mick Perrin, for Just for Laughs.'

'Shut the fuck up!'

'What? Is that good?!'

'Mick fucking Perrin?! You got Mick fucking Perrin?!!'

'Yeah, who is he?'

'He is Eddie Izzard's tour promoter, one of the biggest promoters in the country and a fucking legend!!'

'Ahh!' I squealed. 'And he said I was phenomenal! Wahooo!!' I slept very well that night.

The next morning the nominations came out, and I wasn't nominated. I was really disheartened. I'd thought with all the heat and love I was getting from the audiences, I might get a nod. But it didn't happen.

My show went on to become one of the most successful solo shows to ever come out of Edinburgh, so who needs awards? (Apart from my ego.) For a moment I was upset, as I thought it would mean something. But it didn't knock me for long, as the love I was getting for the show was overwhelming. Powerful even. I took Mick's card and went to meet him for lunch. I apologised for not getting nominated. I felt like a nomination would have given me the gravitas I needed to meet him. He laughed so hard and told me they were idiots. I warmed to Mick immediately. In fact it's pretty safe to say I loved him.

In a weird way I felt like I had won Edinburgh. I had my choice of agents, four- and five-star reviews and was performing the show of my dreams. It had only taken me till the age of 28, but I finally felt like I was being me and fulfilling my destiny. Destiny's Child.

After Edinburgh, I went back home and everything had changed – my new plot point. I moved out of my mum's house and found a room in London, living with two Polish girls in a two-bed house in Lambeth North.

We turned the living room into a bedroom, and the living room faced the front door, so it meant every time you came in, you walked into this girl's bedroom. But it was central, £550 a month and I could walk home after gigs. It wasn't perfect, but it was perfect for now.

I stopped teaching my comedy classes as I started doing more and more shows. I went to meetings with different agents. I was in love with Mick and signed with him as my promoter, and as I walked around Debi's central London office, I fell a little bit in love with her too. She has this amazing three-floor central London office space. She has worked hard, hustled and built herself an empire. And that's the kind of person I wanted on my team, someone to help me build my empire.

It was a bit confusing for me having several agents, but it's the way it works. I got my mate Della, to help me get little stand-up gigs in clubs, while Debi and Mick looked after the big stuff. My own mini team.

I decided to put on a six-week run of my show. Mick wanted me to do a paid theatre, but I didn't want to. I rang around venues and the Comedy Café were the first to offer a midweek slot. Amazing how a good festival can turn things around. I couldn't get booked at the Comedy Café before August, and now they were trusting me with their club every Tuesday for six weeks. Against everyone's suggestion, I put it on for free. The club would make money from drinks at the bar and I could do my bucket donations at the end.

I have this weird tradition before I go on stage. I hate it when people say to you, 'Mate, you're going to be amazing, you're going to smash it.' I feel like that immediately puts me under pressure, so I prefer if they say something like 'You're awful, I don't know why you are doing comedy, the audience are so disappointed already.' Sounds odd, but it takes the pressure off. Maybe it's coming back to that 'have to win' feeling from dance classes and competitions. This way there's no pressure. In fact whenever people do say 'You will kill it and be amazing!!!' I always find I have the worst gigs.

The first Tuesday of the Comedy Café, my mum was coming to watch. I had gathered a mailing list from my previews and had used social media to get 140 names on the guest list. I was hoping at least half would show up. It was a Tuesday after all. Katerina was on the door marking the names off and then she was on the DJ decks doing my sound check. I'd cried on the train there, and I bit everyone's head off then cried again. Katerina said, 'I don't know why you are doing comedy, they all think you're shit, hugs, now get up there.'

I had the best show. It was oversubscribed and a packed house. They laughed and clapped and cheered. The show still worked out of Edinburgh. I said my goodbye speech and people at the side stood up, then people in the middle, then the whole room. I got my first standing ovation. It was epic. And humbling and amazing and powerful and generous and fucking awesome. I never get tired of them. I love standing ovations.

I caught the bus home, sneaked in through my roommate's bedroom and got into bed. It was freezing outside and the heating didn't work, we only had old single-pane windows. So I put on my coat and hat and slept in them.

I felt so proud and delighted, I got a standing ovation. I was sleeping in a coat and hat but I didn't care. I got a standing ovation, baby.

Whilst at the café, I met a guy called Lee Griffith who worked at the Soho Theatre. He said he loved the show and would I be interested in coming to perform? I nearly wet myself. Soho Theatre, Soho Theatre!!!! One of the most prestigious venues in London, where all the award-nominated comedy shows go, and they were offering me the chance to come and play.

They booked me in for ten nights in the main house. Ten nights in the main house. This time I nearly shat myself. People were going to pay for tickets to see me; £15 a ticket, 160 seats in the main house, to see me. My little free show. Tickets went on sale and I sold out. I went on to have five sell-out runs of What Would Beyoncé Do?! in the main house. Standing ovations every night, playing to packed rooms. My tech, Eve, who I loved, would be up in the balcony in the tech box every night, singing and dancing along. This was not the free festival any more. I had proper lighting, sound, a tech, but still my wonderful audience. I was living my dreams.

There is something about being on stage and having my audience in the room with me, women of all ages, all backgrounds, black, white, Chinese, headscarves, shaved, braided, all women. The energy is electric. There were nights when they would run and join me on stage. Nights when they would shout stuff out from the crowd and everyone would join in. I never got heckled, only in the good sense. I remember one time doing this bit about

Klaus and it's a breakdown crying bit where I do a big finale, and one girl shouted out, 'Forget him babe, he's not good enough for you! Come out with us!' It totally broke the tension I was trying to build. Er OK, just let me have this finale and I'll be right with you!

I loved performing at Soho. I'd liked how in Edinburgh I had my playlist and I was in the room as the audience were coming in. I wanted to continue that tradition. So I'd go through my ritual of doing my hair and make-up in the dressing room and then I would start the show. My playlist would play, the doors would open and the audience would come in as I was on stage.

This pre-show thing of mine, being on stage as the audience come in, actually calms me, I love it. I hate being off stage waiting to be announced, I get too nervous. My audience transformed my show, they would start dancing to the songs, so as I grew in confidence I would start dancing and joking around as they came in. Doing little one-woman plays to the song lyrics and messing with them by throwing in a power ballad after a proper raga tune. I could tell how much fun the show was going to be by how hyped up the audience were.

My ritual of getting somebody to announce me transformed into a warm-up act. I would get the most nervous-looking human being up on stage, build them up like a hero, with everyone cheering them, then give them a cuddle and get them to repeat my name several times, Luisa Omielan, Omielan, Omielan – it was important to get the audience familiar with it. Then I would disappear behind the curtain in my grey hoodie, ready to unveil. As

I left, I would tell my warm-up, 'Don't be nervous, just think of yourself as er Kelly or Michelle . . .' and then point at myself and do a fist pump. The audience would howl. It was showtime.

After the show, I'd run to the exit door as the audience left. Even though it felt weird not having a bucket in my hand, I didn't like not being there to say goodbye. It became my house, my party, I'd invite my audience in and wave goodbye as they left. This became a brilliant time to take selfies with my audience. I love selfies! But for the love of the Lord, take it from above and put a filter on it babe!

One night I got a standing ovation for ten minutes. I was so fricking elated, and amazed. The next day there was a review in the *Evening Standard*: '3 stars, female-friendly, urban pocket rocket.' Urban? Pocket rocket? Female-friendly? I don't know why these words were used in the sense that it was a bad thing. The reviewer (male) went on to mention 'white wine spritzer audiences'. What's that supposed to mean? I didn't understand why this critic would reduce me and my audience to a box like that. My show made me feel empowered and excited about the world. This review reflected none of that.

I had never known sexism in comedy. I was born funny, I am funny, women I know are hilarious. But people love to tell you what you are. What you do, how and why you do it. I feel sorry for these people. Why can't they just let themselves go and love the emotions and the comedy? We make it all for them to enjoy. You have to take it on the chin, though, because sometimes they write amazing things and other times they write things you wish they hadn't. But my audience had my back, they wrote to the critic disagreeing with his review; he later retracted it and changed it to four stars. But I didn't care after that; my audience loved me anyway.

I started getting a few pieces in the paper, and was so excited getting listed in online events as a show to go and see. It was fun but I felt like ha! My audience already know it's the show to go and see, my audiences were somehow finding me.

Here is how shows work. When a performer puts on a show, they pay for everything through the ticket sales. A promoter will front the upfront cost and the good ones, someone like Mick, will swallow the debt if the ticket prices don't cover the costs. This took a long time for me to get my head around. This whole time I thought agents or promoters would pay for things, but it's always the artist. So out of my ticket sales I would pay for the venue hire, ticket printing, venue staff, insurance, music licensing, poster design, poster printing, advertising, PR, travel, sound equipment, etc. Once that was paid, I would give my agents their percentage and then after that I would get the rest. I always struggled with this, as pound for pound I made more money with the free shows.

I was desperate to make more money. I'd seen guys come out of the fringe and get invited on *Live at the Apollo* or Jonathan Ross and then star in their own series. I had a better show but was making just enough to cover my rent and not much more, plus the whole sleeping in a coat thing was getting annoying. Going from earning cash from my workshops and knowing my monthly income to suddenly not earning anything for three months and then getting paid a lump sum of £2k.

I begged Mick to let me tour. He kept advising against it as I didn't have a TV profile. Who needs a TV profile? I said. Let's just repeat what I've done with Edinburgh but in the major cities. I want to go to Manchester, Sheffield, Newcastle, Glasgow, let's do it!! In the same way as when it comes to food my eyes are bigger than my belly, when it comes to my career, I want everything and hated that I couldn't have it all at once. Eventually he caved in and got me a 12-date tour.

I won't lie. I hated it. It wasn't like the fringe in the provinces. I would rock up in the middle of nowhere, in venues where the tech would stare at me and I would feel out of my depth and isolated. Once you're a bigger name on tour you can afford a tour manager; they pick you up, get you to the venue and then do all your music cues for you so you don't have to worry about it. But they come at a daily cost of around £300, fine if you are taking home a couple of grand per show, but not when you are playing small theatres.

At the end of my tour, I received my budget break-down. My show had generated £12k in ticket sales. Oh my goodness, I was over the moon. But I got paid £800. £800 for 12 shows. I had made more money at the free festival. This was why Mick didn't want me to tour yet.

I could see that my shows were successful and that people went crazy for them, but those ticket sales didn't cover my heating. I came back off tour and caught pneumonia. I was sleeping in a coat and hat and shivering every night. It was horrendous. I tried every heating trick I could google, bought a cheap heater, but that made the bills extortionate. I just wanted to be paid well for the work I did and have a warm room to come home to.

I was working my arse off; I felt like I had been working until I got sick and then working again. I was meeting with TV people who seemed really excited about the potential of a TV format based on my live show. I was meeting lots of people behind the scenes, some really talented and driven individuals, but there were a lot of dudes. In writing, in production, there isn't much diversity. I kept finding myself sat around the table with the same old faces. These people were lovely, but they didn't represent my audiences or the people buying tickets to my shows. Their suggestions were things like 'Hey, maybe the TV show could open with you walking down the street in gold glittery hot pants and be like, bitch, I'm Beyoncé.' It just didn't sit right with me.

August quickly came around again and I went up to Edinburgh with 'Beyoncé' for ten nights. I ended up selling out all ten so added extra dates and ended up playing for the month. This year was different. I had a promoter behind me and I was in the Gilded Balloon, a paid-for venue run by Edinburgh legend Karen Koren. My tickets were £15 and I had people on the street working for me.

Technically it should have been easier, but I didn't enjoy it. I loved Karen and Mick Perrin but hated performing on the paid fringe. My show was cut to an hour time slot, even though it had become a fully fledged 75-minute show, Edinburgh is a long festival, venue staff would be tired and overworked, I felt rushed in and rushed out, and even though I was paying for the room, I had none of the control or freedom I had learnt to love in the free venues. I was missing being in change of every detail of my show.

I wanted to regain control and figure out what I wanted, so I decided to try it without a promoter – I left Mick shortly after finishing Edinburgh. I was heartbroken, cried for about a week and couldn't sleep for about a month. I hate endings.

One night in Edinburgh, I finish my show and go upstairs to one of the industry bars, where I see Aunt Hilda from *Sabrina the Teenage Witch*. Holy shit I was excited. She looked at me and said, 'You are amazing, I just watched your Beyoncé show, you speak to my girls. Come here, why is your shirt inside out?!'

I look down and it is. Before I can say anything, Aunt Hilda is unbuttoning my shirt, turning it the right way and putting it back on for me. This is brilliant. She says, 'Look at me, do you know who I am?'

'Er yes, you are Caroline Rhea, Aunt Hilda from *Sabrina the Teenage Wi*—'

'NO!' she interrupts. 'I am your Christmas Future, and what I'm looking at is my Christmas Past. I want to help you, you need to come to New York. Have you been to New York?'

'Er no ma'am.'

'What's with the ma'am?! OK, have you got a producer? No? Do you know who would be great to produce your show? My friend Whoopi.'

SHUT THE FRONT DOOR!! At this point, I lost my shit.

'Oh my God!' I told her. 'I have to show you something.' I went on my phone and desperately tried to upload my website page. Why oh why in your hour of need to show a website page does your stupid mobile service provider decide to go for a dump and work like it's running on dial-up? I was so embarrassed, but it finally loaded and there on my website in black and bright blue was *Hi. My name is Luisa Omielan and I want to be the white Whoopi Goldberg.*

Caroline laughed, took a screen grab and there and then typed an email to Whoopi Goldberg with my name in the subject box. Remember those moments I told you about where you feel like magic is happening? This was one of them.

I slept with the biggest smile on my face and didn't care about the shows after that. Let them tell me off, I was so happy.

One show I was waiting outside to go in and 15 hens dressed up as nurses were outside and I ran and asked for a photo. Normally the sight of a hen party puts the fear of God into a comedian; for me, it means party time! They were the best audience ever and every time I said a song lyric, they would take over. Normally I did a bit about Klaus saying goodbye to me and saying 'I hope life treats you kind.' For the first time, some-one from the party piped up 'And I hope you have all you've dreamed of.' A few more joined in with 'And I wish you joy and happiness,' and then the rest of them 'But above all this I wish you looooove.' I was giddy with excitement as the whole room launched into 'AND I . . .'

Magic. I love my audiences.

So the next day I go back to the bar and Caroline sees me and calls me over, saying, 'I have someone on the phone that wants to talk to you.'

I take the phone, shaking. 'Hello?'

'Hello Luisa, it's Whoopi.'

'Oh my gosh, hello.'

'Hi, how's it going?'

'Oh my gosh, I am literally your biggest fan, I can't believe it, like you made me so happy growing up, I was just so happy . . .' WTF, who says this shit?! Someone on the phone to their hero, that's who.

'Well for my friend to call me all the way from Edinburgh must mean you are pretty special, and she knows what's good, so why don't you bring your show to New York and maybe myself and Caroline could produce it for you?'

'Oh my gosh, er yes, that would be fantastic.'

'OK, great, let's do it.'

Caroline: 'OK Luisa, get off the phone.'

'OK, thank you so much, that's so very kind, thank you, have a wonderful day.'

I was screaming in delight. I just got off the phone to Whoopi fucking Goldberg. This really is my show of dreams. I couldn't sleep that night. It was like a dream come true.

It gets to my last night in Edinburgh, I have a ball with the show, it runs over and I don't care. As I stand by the door and do my ritual of saying goodbye to my audience, this American dude comes over. 'Hi, I'm Max, loved your show, I wanna talk to you but I gotta leave now.' He gives me his card and walks off.

That night was the infamous Mick Perrin party; it's a pretty legendary party in Edinburgh with a free bar, but having only been part of the free festival and stealing drinks vouchers to get wasted, I'd never had a chance of getting in. This time I was on the guest list, no blagging required. I go to the bar and 'Feel the Love' comes on and I smile because that is my show song. I see Max again and he says, 'Look, I don't like a lot of people, but I like you!' I laugh at his Americanness, keep his card and go and get drunk.

Turns out Max is Eddie Izzard and Tim Minchin's agent. So Edinburgh yet again is as magical as ever.

When I got back to London, I decided now would be a good time to head to the States. I knew Max and I knew Caroline. That was all I needed!

Caroline called and invited me to come and stay at hers, and said she would bring Whoopi to a show. I called up a few venues in New York, and with Caroline's help got booked in at the UCB comedy club for 18 October. I sent off an application for a visa, so that I could legally perform the show; it cost £3k, but I was now in a position to apply to be an extraordinary alien.

That was at the beginning of September; by 10 October, still no visa. I went to the passport office and queued up for four hours, and they took my passport for fast-tracking, telling me it should be back with me in three to four days. Jesus, this was tight but it was worth it. I just wanted to do my show for Whoopi!

It was getting closer to my flight date of the 16th, and still no passport. It got to the morning of my flight, still no passport. I rang the airline, who said I could change my ticket and would only have to pay a couple of hundred pounds. I was more worried about losing my show slot. It got to the 18th and still no passport. It finally arrived at 9 a.m. on the 19th. I could have cried,

I had missed my show at the UCB and missed my chance to perform in front of Whoopi. All the stress, and the sleepless nights, and now the worst had happened and strangely I felt calm. Caroline suggested I come out anyway; I may as well since I had the flight voucher, so as soon as I picked up my passport, my friend dropped me off at the airport and I flew to New York.

Caroline had confirmed the arrangement in an email, but on the day itself I couldn't get through on the phone and I arrived in New York not totally sure of where I was going. Luckily I had her address in a previous email, so I just got in a taxi and asked to head to the Upper West Side.

So I am in a yellow New York cab at 2 a.m., with some old Indian dude driving me to a place I don't know. I have my bag, my passport and my show in my head, and all I can think about is the American dream, the story of how Madonna rocked up broke with $5 and made it in the city. OK, so I am rocking up with $200, about to stay for free in a famous woman's apartment in one of the best areas of New York, and even though it's all laid out for me, I still feel like I am taking a risk. I struggle with new environments, I always have done.

When I go to a new place I lay my belongings out in the same way, so it feels more familiar. I read a story about a famous woman who unpacks candles and pictures and photographs in every hotel she goes to, so they all look and smell the same. I like that dedication to comfort and that sense of showing yourself love. Do what you can to be comfortable.

I arrive at Caroline's apartment building and the door guy sends me up in the lift. I have no idea if she will be expecting me. I knock.

'Oh my Gawd, hello, come in, I'm asleep, take the couch, I was expecting you next week – get in here, I'll take you for breakfast in the morning.'

The next morning she did just that, eggs sunny side up! It was so lovely to see her, she said to not worry about a thing, she would help organise another show in a comedy club and still get Whoopi along at some point to come and see it.

Caroline calls New York City Comedy Club and arranges a show for me that night.

I rocked up to the club at 4 p.m. to do a sound check. As I walked in, I was so excited, the room looked great. That was when the manager came and told me, 'Oh no, you're upstairs' and took me to a shoebox that would fit maybe 15 people. He said, 'Sure, do a show tonight; I don't know if you'll get anyone, but Caroline will get some numbers in off the street, this is New York!'

Three thousand pounds for a visa, £800 for a flight, sleepless nights for two weeks, to come and play a shoebox to 15 people, but this is a New YOORKK shoebox!!

I performed that night to eight people. They liked it. They nodded and smiled and clapped at the end, and it was nice. As they came out I got 'Great job! You should pursue that!' Thank you, thank you so much, wow, I must have impressed them with my well-worn comedy show if their response was 'You should keep going.'

I had gone from selling out London dates, standing ovations, huge love and applause and accolades to eight people in a shoe cupboard saying 'You should pursue that.' Who said stand-up is stable?

Over the course of a career you have to give shows to people who don't know or like you; that's part of comedy, comedy is the house, you don't get to win or lose, you just get to play. I put way too much pressure on myself to deliver and felt like because Caroline had supported me, I had to prove that I was as good as she said I was, when in actual fact I was kinda like a fish out of water. Just a giant flapping fish. I was relieved Whoopi didn't see it.

After a few nights, Caroline got a call. Whoopi had a film, and since she doesn't fly, she had to get a bus to her next job and would be out of town for the rest of the week. Obviously it wasn't meant to be.

BTW, I have a feeling Whoopi rides a very different bus to the one I do. I can't imagine her with an Oyster card in one hand and a kebab in the other, getting the night bus. I waved goodbye to Caroline, my fairy godmanager, got my flight back to London and caught the C10 home.

19

BODY'S TOO BOOTYLICIOUS FOR YOU, MATE

Back in England I organised myself a couple of tour dates up and down the country with the venues directly. They shows were nice enough, but nothing like my London crowds, I hadn't had the chance to develop my relationship with the crowds like I had in London. My London audiences were in a league of their own. All girls, all colours, all backgrounds, all shapes, sizes and looks coming to my shows. I had women in hijabs, women in pencil skirts, tattooed lesbian bikers, African queens and jogger-wearing white women all whooping and hollering and ready to party from the off! They even started coming twice and bringing their mums. What a complete joy. I felt so lucky to have found this crowd, the atmosphere was like nothing I had ever experienced. The universe is really cool like that: whenever I have gone abroad and struggled with shows, even though I find them painful at the time I feel like I grow, because when I come back to London to play, I have the show of dreams. I believe this is what they call 'learning'.

It came around to Valentine's Day. Now the best Valentine's I had ever had was a few years ago with Pas when we met up in Sheffield, got blind drunk, ate a Subway, prank-called our exs from each other's phones and spent the whole night congratulating ourselves on being fucking hilarious. The night ended with a sing-song and an improvised rap battle in bed. The perfect Valentine's. Every Valentine's Day after that was wack in comparison. I would just find myself moping around, depressed that I hadn't got a boyfriend or depressed because I was missing a boy who wasn't my boyfriend or depressed because I had no one to practice rap battling with. Either way I was pining.

I wanted to make this Valentine's special, for me, for my audiences. I had an idea. My show is a bit of a party any-way, so what if I hired a room and did my Beyoncé show, but afterwards, instead of everyone going home, I played music, and turned it into an event like a club night?

I called my lovely Musical Bingo DJ Olly Stock, or Stockeroller as I liked to call him, and asked him if he would be up for it. He was well up for it! He would do my sound cues in my show and then afterwards play RnB all night! Perfect!

I was looking after my own live work and I knew I didn't want it in a theatre, so I called Concrete, a club basement in London, my Musical Bingo home, and they let me have the room for free as long as I could guarantee the audience would come and spend at the bar. I was hopeful they would, but was still unsure how many people would turn up. Wouldn't they all be having sex on Valentine's Day?

I booked it and advertised it. It sold out within a week! 200 people at £10 a ticket, a room full of single women for Valentine's. Pas and Katerina came down and joined me, and we decorated the venue, put Love Heart sweets in the toilets. I hired two door girls to help me with people coming in, and boom! The event was amazing! Everyone had so much fun! We all danced until three in the morning, I loved it; my Valentine's party was a success!

I paid the staff who helped me, paid my DJ and still managed to take home 50 percent of ticket sales. That was the first time I had ever taken home that kind of split and I liked it!

My mum had just sold the family home and had moved up to the Midlands as she couldn't afford to live down south any more. Five-beds in Farnborough were now really expensive, and as her mortgage was all tied up, she said she would have found it harder to stay in the area in a little flat, so instead we encouraged her to buy a gorgeous house in the Midlands.

My sister is based in Birmingham, my brothers live in Manchester and with me being based in London, the Midlands were the centre of everyone. I wanted to help my mum somehow with the move.

As I had been paid for my V-Day gig, I wanted to get her something as a thank-you for all her love and support plus a house-warming gift to help her with the change (as in the house change not the menopausal one, she went through that years ago lol, #SorryMum). So, I bought her a Smeg fridge.

Yes babe, a Smeg fridge, she had always wanted one, I say she, I have always told her that she definitely needs one. So I bought her a gorgeous duck-egg blue Smeg fridge and it is stunning. I mean I couldn't pay my own rent for the next two months (hello overdraft!), but she deserved it.

I feel like me buying her a fridge is a bit of a parable.
Because get this, my mum is Polish. She grew up on a
farm and used to milk cows. Then she had me, I go on
stage and go 'moo' and I get the money to buy my mum
a fridge to put the milk in! It's a modern-day Jesus and
the five fish. It's like the great circle of life, but the great
circle of Smeg. One day I want to get her the whole col-
lection, kettle, dishwasher, everything! (I say her, I think
we all know, I still mean me).

It was now the summer and I was going back to
America again, this time to LA, and Debi came with me.
We booked a theatre ourselves and put on a week-long
run. Debi was amazing. She made a list of industry people to invite. We got Max down; I had kept in touch with
him. I thought, I am OK, I have done this before, I know
America will be quieter but I will get them!

The venue was perfect, a black-box, red-velvet-chair
space off Broadway in LA. The ideal place to cause a
storm. Or a very British bit of drizzle. The first night I
had 22 people buying tickets; this was totally doable.

Eager to prove a point and not be discouraged if they
were quiet, I decided to open the show the way I always
did: get someone that looked shy up on stage to be
my warm-up act. This whole skit is very universal;
the idea is to set the tone with the audience, level
the playing field and get them invested early on by
supporting one of their comrades. I just needed to pick
someone who looked a little bit timid or embarrassed
and the humour would come in them being nervous
introducing me.

Word to the wise, never, I repeat never, expect an audience member to be shy and retiring in LA. I had only got as far as 'I can't introduce myself . . .' when this woman jumped up, WITHOUT SEEKING PERMISSION. She had a shaved head and no arms, and opened with 'I'm a performer, I got this, actually you guys, you wanna see my party trick?!' Without a beat, she jumped up on stage, was addressing the audience like a pro and took a can of beer from her bag.

Sorry, what? I am stood in shock, going what the fuck, Luisa, regain the status, regain the status, remember clowning, regain the status, this woman is on stage running shit, what the fuck are you going to do? I wanted to do something, but I didn't know what, so I thought, just be nice, she has no arms, let's see what she is about to do. Now I don't know how she did it as I was in too much pain watching this unfold, but this woman with no arms opened the can of beer and put it on her head, literally no idea how, then started to dance. With a can of beer on her head. Without spilling it.

This took four and a half minutes. I could not believe this bitch; I wanted to punch her but didn't want to be head-butted. And admittedly it was a pretty cool trick. However this completely threw me, I did not know how to start after that. She sat back down, WITHOUT INTRODUCING ME, and shouted out her email in case anyone wanted to get in touch.

Her email. My opening night in LA and an armless beer woman is shouting out her email. These American bitches. This was no oh-I'm-disabled-give-me-a-free-pass shit, no, this bitch knew what she was doing, coming on to my stage, eating into my show time. But obviously I couldn't be a dick, because I was trying my whole be-nice-to-people-and-act-more-grateful thing. FFS. I did the show and performed to silence. Afterwards I did my usual stand at the door, saying goodbye to people. The first person came out and said, 'Hey Lucy, that beer can trick was amazing.'

I ended up doing five shows in LA; after the third I knew I definitely wanted to kill myself. I would play an all-singing, all-dancing show, face, heart and soul on the floor, to people who would just look at me. They wouldn't laugh, they wouldn't engage or sing along when there was a clear chorus to join in, unless it was at the beginning of the show and they wanted a shot at performing their showreel. They would just look at me.

Have you ever been crying on public transport and people either avoid eye contact or, if they do look at you, suck in their lips for a toothless smile and furrow their eyebrows in an 'I'm sorry you're sad' way? Well that may be the correct and appropriate response when someone is crying, but not when I am doing my genius art form and sweating like a pig on stage. I felt like I was the emperor in 'The Emperor's New Clothes' but going, 'No, don't you get it, I'm not the one that's naked, you all are, honestly, it's definitely you.'

I would see women who were performers, all acne-scarred and lips pumped on stretched-out faces, wearing cheap clothes with designer shoes. And as I performed, they would lower their sunglasses and look me up and down and up again, and then reattach their sunglasses. I guess it is important to protect your eyes FROM THE LIGHT GLARING OFF YOUR PHONE!! (In other words, please turn your phone off when you are in a show, especially one with only 12 other people in the room.)

They would sit and stare and after the show they would clap and come up to me at the door, where I wanted the ground to swallow me whole. It's fun to wait at the door and say goodbye to the audience when you have just had a standing ovation. It's not when you have just died on your hole, but I'll be damned if I don't do it. I have to stand by my work whether I smash or die. Just gotta take it on the chin. What Would Beyoncé Do?! She would stand by the bloody door. SO I stood at the door and smiled. And they would come out and be like 'Oh my gosh, that was awesome, you are really brave' and I would have to bite my tongue and graciously say thank you without punching them. And I would hold a clenched smile as they said 'I really enjoyed it' and try not to scream 'YOU COULD HAVE TOLD YOUR FUCKING FACE THAT!!!!'

I can't remember who it was, but somebody said to me that if I am struggling in my show, don't tell the audience, because they might actually be enjoying it. Just because they haven't experienced the show when people run down the aisles and lose their tiny little minds doesn't mean that the room of eight people who aren't laughing aren't enjoying it. It's really hard to be gracious. I wonder what Beyoncé does in these situations. JOKES. Beyoncé's never been in these situations.

I saw it with Dolly Parton once. The whole crowd were sat down for the first half, except for me and my friend who were up on our feet dancing and cheering along, getting shouted at to sit down. I was like 'What is wrong with you idiots? It's Dolly frickin' Parton.' She must have known people were being reserved, but she just carried on singing and being amazing and then after about 45 minutes, the crowd finally stood up and joined in and she said, 'I knew you had it in you! I was worried you might be too quiet but no, you were just waiting to join the party! Well now you have let's get it started!'

That's how I should learn to behave, more like Dolly, although I still think I would want to punch everyone. Maybe I need anger therapy. What would Dolly do?!

I was asked to meet an American manager who was interested in representing me. I was so excited, like oh my gosh, here I am in the Hollywood Hills, in Soho House, this private members' bar, with a manager who potentially wants to look after my career in the States. This is amazing, look how my life has turned around. Only this time a year ago I was living at my mum's house, having a nice lie-in after eating too much Chinese food the night before, when I went to have a cheeky little fart and it became clear that I had shat myself in a onesie. And now here I am in Hollywood, you guys! Reading *The Secret* really does work!

The conversation with the manager went like this. (NB: Manager must be read in an American accent, without moving your lips and like you're running out of air; also look surprised and no other facial expression.)

Manager: OK, so here's the thing Lisa.

Me: Sorry, it's Luisa, Luisa Omielan.

Manager: OK, so here's the thing Lucy, I really like you, like I really really like you and I think you could be amazing and do really well out here. I just have a couple of concerns. So how old are you?

Me: I'm 31.

Manager: Oh no, no, that needs to go, that's too old.

Me: Old? It's taken me this long to get good enough at comedy to just be in the same room as you. I have been working towards this my entire life, like from the age of—

Manager: OK, that's great Lucy, but in Hollywood you need to be like 21 or 22, otherwise you're dead.

Me: OK.

Manager: The only other thing that I could see that would stop you from doing really well in the States, Lucy—

Me: It's Luisa.

Manager: OK Charlotte, stop talking. The only thing stopping you from doing really well in the States is this, this whole erm 'figure' *fake vomits* that you have. I'm sure in the UK it's adorable *does a head tilt and a two-second hand clap* but here in Hollywood the women are really skinny and glamorous and that's not really you, no. So all I need you to do is not eat for like a year. OK?

Wow. I'd never had that before, so brazen, to my face, someone telling me, Luisa, you are too old and you are too fat.

I felt so disheartened. What about my comedy, what about my beautifully crafted material that I have trekked across the United Kingdom, playing up and down the country to empty bars and full rooms? What about all the years that I have begged and dreamed and wished and prayed to work in comedy, all the nights of crying and talking to my mum, when will it happen, when will it happen? Then to finally craft a body of work where no breath is wasted and every line is carefully placed, that has its own beat and rhythm, my show, my baby, my soul laid bare on stage, my show that was the most successful debut solo show to come out of the Edinburgh festival, my money that I borrowed to pay for the flight to LA, the gamble of spending £3k on a visa and hiring a theatre to play and then to finally get a meeting with someone with power and for them to turn around and say, 'Yeah, but you are too old and too fat.' That's really difficult to take on the chin, even if you do have two of them.

It was my last show in LA and I was feeling deflated after my meeting. I spoke to Debi, my agent; I said I can't do this, they don't laugh, I am playing to silence, it's so hard.

'Look Luisa, I had Sarah Silverman's old manager come in yesterday. She said you're too fat and you haven't got enough jokes, but I've got other managers in there tonight and they haven't seen you and they are excited!'

'Too fat? Another one? What? And not enough jokes?' I started crying.

'Do not do this to me Luisa, not now, you gotta go out there and prove 'em all wrong. Besides, you're not Sarah Silverman, you're Luisa fucking Omielan, it's fine.'

I went on stage and couldn't be bothered to get anyone up to introduce me. Instead I opened with 'Be clear, I don't like you, I don't want to be here. You know, every night I have come and performed and delivered my masterpiece and none of you bitches have shown me the appreciation I deserve. Normally I let someone introduce me, but I forgot we are in LA and you're all fucking performers. Well I'm sorry LA but I paid for this theatre and you paid to come and see me – well you didn't pay, you all got in free because I'm a nobody in America . . . So I have just been told that I am apparently too fat for you bitches. Too fat. You know what . . .' Now I don't know what came over me, but at this point I pulled my trousers down, grabbed my stomach and said, 'Bite me.'

And here is why the world and the universe are wonderful. And hilarious. And giving. And beautiful in every sweet way possible. For some reason, for some unknown reason, the second I pulled my trousers down, they all started laughing. Really LA?! Really?! That's all I needed to do all week? All I could hear were cheers from Americans, from people from LA; with chants of 'Oh my Gawd, I totally love her.' I pulled up my trousers and got on with the show. That night I killed, and they laughed throughout.

Fuck you LA, fuck you. But I did finally sleep like a baby.

I didn't realise, but that night I had a manager come to my show. She was this white chick with long hair, big booty and earrings and I liked her as soon as she walked in. We met up and went for a cocktail. She was called Tatiana Sarah and she worked for the same company that managed Tina Fey and Amy Poehler. Tatiana is awesome and we swapped numbers. Shit, America, maybe you ain't so bad after all.

I signed to Max who got me some gigs in New York. I went back out and stayed with Caroline. I ended up playing five nights in a venue called SubCulture on Bleecker Street. The first night I played to an old lady with a beard and a cat on her lap; the last night I played to 80 and they rocked out. America you are amazing; just when I think I hate you, you go ahead and make me love you again.

20

FLAWLESS

I wish more women liked themselves, especially naked. Nothing wrong with a naked selfie. You don't have to post it online if you don't want to, equally kudos to you if you want to, but I think it is important to look at yourself naked. I think a woman should know what she looks like. I know I look at myself and think I need to look fitter and eat healthier and be stronger. But I certainly don't look in the mirror and hate myself. I love the female form, it is perfect.

I read this thing once which totally resonated with me. In advertising we like women being sexy. If it's for porn we like women being sexy because it's for the pleasure of the man. But if a woman ever just wants to admire herself and be sexy and own her own body, she is vilified, because there is nothing more powerful than a woman who likes herself. We need to stop it with the vitriol.

When I was younger, I had a slamming body. I grew up skinny. Like proper skinny frickin' minnie. I would walk through the town centre and see market stalls of Spanx and think, duh, why would women buy that? Just lose the fat, weirdos. At school I was called Twig Face. While all my friends would be in the toilet cubicle at break time sticking two fingers down their throats after devouring a pack of Space Invaders, I would be on my second helping of iced bun.

If I was eating ice cream in the street and an old man walked past and with a cheeky wink said, 'Careful, you'll get fat,' I'd think, what an idiot.

a) Why would you be so rude and interrupt my happy eating time and

b) Fat? As if . . . knobhead. Little did I know that by 28, back fat would be a thing.

Luckily though, given the plethora of issues that the world has bestowed on me, body issues isn't one of them. I've never felt body-conscious. I always had a big butt but since it was behind me I never bothered to do anything about it. In my eyes I have always had an amazing shape. Only now I have what you might call the opposite of body dysmorphia, where I walk into New Look, try on a size 8 pair of jeans that don't fit around my left big toe and think, well this is very strange . . . obviously New Look has done something to their sizes.

I'm a size 14 now, a SIZE 14!! I have cellulite on the back of my knees. I mean I have always had cellulite, but it's spreading. I remember being really young, about four or five, and getting out of the bath and running around naked, wiggling my bum at my mum and laughing like a hyena about how I could make it feel all dimply. Cellulite at the age of four brought me great joy. It brought my family great joy/humiliation.

Now being older and on the other side of skinny, I find it so upsetting when other people put their own body insecurities on me. I have never had these issues; I've got plenty of issues bitches, I don't need yours as well.

My experience in America was a real eye-opener. Of course the Hollywood industry looks at you like you are a product, a weight, a height, a colour. And they are shameless with it. I came back to the UK and signed up for the gym.

The thing is, I do love going to the gym. When I was 19, I fancied the guy who worked in my local gym, so started going every day just to impress him. It's amazing how sometimes all you need for that dangling carrot is a penis. Carrot is also the wrong word here; it should be doughnut, saying that maybe if I was led by a carrot then I wouldn't need to go to the gym in the first place, but you catch my drift. My plan worked. I was a size 10 when I joined but had no muscle. Fast forward six weeks of hard-core rowing and sit-ups, and mamma has a four-pack, my gym guy clearly liked it and we would fuck in the middle of the gym after he locked up.

On a couple of occasions he would drive me to his house in his sports car, but he would always make me wait outside while he went in to clean up. I would think, wow, what a guy, cleaning his flat, he is so sweet trying to impress me. After three months, one of the other personal trainers couldn't hold it in any longer and said, 'Luisa, you are such a nice girl, why are you sleeping with that idiot? He's not good enough for you, it's bad enough he is cheating on his girlfriend.'

SAYYY WHAT?!!! Oh yes, he had a girlfriend, who he lived with. And every time I went to his flat unplanned, he would go in first to take down the pictures of them together. And here was me thinking that he just liked cleaning the flat before fucking on the couch. I mean it should have been obvious that the carpet hadn't been hoovered, but how was I to know? I was blinded by his 5ft 2 frame (I know he was tiny but I am a sucker for a chiselled jaw). I stopped going to the gym after that.

Don't get me wrong, I like looking fly, but I also like Greggs (insert sausage and egg McMuffin meal for my non-UK friends *waves*); for me, it's a healthy balance. So I find myself back from LA and going for lunch with a TV producer, who sits me down in a private members' bar and says, 'So Luisa, would you like to order a starter and a main course or a main course and a dessert?'

Me: Er, sorry bitch, what the fuck makes you think I am not going to eat the fuck out of all three, er bring the bread back *calls waiter*, bring the frickin' bread back!

When I am about to sit down and enjoy my mother-fucking food is not the time to tell me how many calories are on my plate or how long you went for a run that day; it's called a happy meal for a reason bitches, stop raining on my parade.

I don't like hearing my friends calling themselves disgusting, fat, horrendous, ugly, and grabbing and pulling their skin. I don't like seeing my beautiful size 8 friend picking around the salad on her plate and not using any dressing and only drinking vodka with diet tonic water. I don't like seeing my friends not realising how utterly beautiful and gorgeous they are and not living their lives and enjoying their food.

My belly can look pregnant on some days and skinny on others, depends what I've eaten. My size 12 waist and 14 butt, do you know what it means; it means I go out for dinner with friends. It means yes, I will have another mojito, let's get shit-faced and have a kebab on the way home. It means I am someone who knows how to have fun.

I know some bitches that save up all month and don't eat properly so they can afford to pay their rent and buy a Prada designer handbag, and I am thinking, I'm sorry bitches, do you have any idea how much this figure cost me? This isn't Lidl shit; this is Marks and Spencer's finest!!!

I like my life, I like going to dance classes, I like going out, I like having a cocktail, please don't waste my time with am I the right body shape. Am I skinny enough, make sure I am skinny, guys love skinny, no they don't, not too skinny, they like curvy like a woman, not too curvy, be less curvy, skinny with curves but curvy who is skinny. Also the most important thing is to not let your thighs touch.

Sorry, what? My thighs?

Yeah, your thighs can't touch.

What? Of course they touch; my legs are next to each other.

Yeah, but when you stand with your legs together you wanna make sure there is a gap at the top, so the thighs don't touch.

Really? Well I've never heard such nonsense in my . . . Oh hang on, mine touch, oh shit, oh my God, is that bad? That's bad, isn't it, I never noticed it, oh God, like I didn't even know that was a thing, that is so embarrassing, they totally touch, that's horrific, oh my God, that is disgusting, hide me, take me away, someone needs to send me home, quick, wrap me up and send me away to the circus, be like 'Roll up, roll up, come check out the freak-show bitch whose thighs are touching each other! You've never seen anything like it, freak-show bitch whose thighs are touching each other . . .'

Yes, my thighs might be touching each other, but I'm sorry bitches, if you were this close to my vagina, wouldn't you start touching yourself? *Drops mic exits stage*

(Actually it's one of my opening jokes so I stay on stage for another hour or so, but for the sake of impact in the book . . . totally has left the stage.)

21

I'D DO ANYTHING FOR LOVE, AND I PROBABLY WOULD DO THAT AS WELL

Things that most people struggle with I find easy, e.g. dropping my pants in front of a room full of people. But things other people find really easy I find really hard. Like change. I hate change, like I really struggle with it. That's why I hate goodbyes and break-ups, I don't like anything that doesn't feel safe or familiar. This can be exhausting. I can travel to different places but then need to eat food that is familiar and set up my room the same in every place I go to. I have even started buying candles and bringing photos with me, even if it's just for a night.

I am worse with people. When I love you and you have gone, I hate it. It had been over a year since Klaus and my Beyoncé show was keeping me busy, but it was difficult to move on as I was talking about him on stage every day.

My friends encouraged me to meet someone else, but it just didn't seem to work. I couldn't, I wouldn't meet anyone at my shows, I think guys found me intimidating and any guy who did show interest I didn't want to date. Especially if he had just seen me on stage, I felt like that was weird, because he would know everything about me and I would know nothing about him. After my shows I would just catch the bus home. I wasn't ready to have sex with anyone but everyone told me that to get over someone you gotta get under someone else.

So I called my bisexual mate Dave. He's a comedian but when he married his partner, they decided to adopt so Dave stopped working and stayed at home with the baby whilst Michael kept working in graphic design. They had recently split up and Michael had taken the baby to his mum's house.

Dave was a mess so we would meet up and get really drunk and be self-destructive together. Then one night, the weirdest thing happened. We went out, got blind drunk and we thought as an experiment we should have sex.

I know the alarm bells should have rung, but I can't tell you how close we were. He said it would be good for me to get over Klaus, as I needed to get back on the horse, and he wanted to do it because he hadn't had sex with a woman in years. So we did it, we had sex. I don't know how he got it up, I just kept throwing my bum in his face.

It was awkward and weird, we liked each other, so we were nice to each other but I don't think either of us was at all into it. This was the first guy I was having sex with since Klaus and it was nothing like with Klaus. It's 2 a.m. in the morning and Dave is trying to thrust me in this really weird friendship sex when all of a sudden he stops.

'What's wrong?!' I ask him.

'Er, I think I miss Michael.'

'Oh, ermm OK, you're still inside me.'

Oh how superb. We were both missing a penis we couldn't have. I gave him a cuddle and left. That's right; I gave him a cuddle, because I am not emotionally devoid.

I cried afterwards, I don't know why, I don't know if it was over Klaus or because I had failed at successfully moving on. Even though it had been nearly a year, I didn't want to have sex with Dave; I didn't wanna have sex with anybody, let alone my married best friend. But all my mates were like 'You have to move on, you have to just fuck someone, you'll feel better.'

As I found myself crawling out of his flat, empowerment was not what I was feeling. If anything I felt worse, because now I had had sex with someone different, and worse, it was crap sex. This was awful.

Plus having sex with me made a grown man think of his husband. I don't know what I was thinking. When will I meet someone who on having sex with someone else will stop pounding halfway through and say 'I miss Luisa'? Yeah, that's the dream. My dream guy to be fucking someone else and missing me. FFS. Can you write that on a Valentine's card: *If I ever fuck anyone else, I will call out your name.*

Oh why am I such a loser? I bet Klaus isn't doing this, Klaus is happily in love with his girlfriend, bet he holds her after they have sex and says 'Luisa who?!'

Don't be ridiculous; they don't even mention your name. It's so unfair; it's the one who is heartbroken who needs the love more. When it comes to my career I feel so inspired and excited, but in my downtime, in my personal life, why is this ghost still not shifting?

I start crying at a random bus stop in east London. I sit down next to an old lady and want to ask her for advice. 'Have you ever felt so heartbroken over someone that you have sex with a friend who then says they miss their husband whilst they are still inside you?' But I decided against it. She didn't look like a talker.

I felt like shit for about a month but me and Dave kept in touch. It was a bit weird but we still tried to be friends, I think we represented the other person's worst fears though. That neither of us was ready. He missed his husband, it wasn't his fault. He was having a really hard time but so was I. I didn't want to be a bad friend and drop him, so we stayed in touch.

New Year's Eve and I get a call offering me to MC a gig. I wanted to take it as Dave was back on the comedy horse and he was going to be closing the show. Gigging together on New Year's Eve, maybe someone would happen? You would think I would learn after the last time, but I still hadn't had sex and maybe trying to have sex with Dave a second time would be easier? This is how bipolar my life is, career-wise I was having shows of dreams and love from audiences, love-life-wise I was so desperate I was willing to try and have sex with a man who was still in love with another man. Nailing life Luisa, nailing life.

I spent three hours getting ready. Curling my hair, and not just rush-curling it, I mean curling it in small sections so it's really tight and curly. Washing, shaving, fake-tanning everything. I looked super hot. Like proper smoking. There was a problem on the tube, and by the time I walked to the venue in heels, I had sweated off any sense of clean.

I arrived to find a queue around the door and the open-mic'er panicking: people had paid £45 for a three-course meal and London's best comics. The reality was the restaurant was never told to provide food; there was no three courses. They started panicking and tried to appease the angry customers with plates of hummus. The comedians booked were all open spots. It's New Year's Eve in central London. Everywhere was rammed and people had already made their plans.

I had people complaining and shouting at me all night demanding their money back. I just gave as many refunds as possible. It was their New Year, I wanted them to try and catch a good night. Just because mine was ruined didn't mean theirs had to be. The promoter was running three nights simultaneously. He had arranged for Dave to open at one venue, middle at another and close at mine; the rest of the acts were all open spots and all on rotation.

I did my best to appease people, rearranged the room, gave refunds where I could and tried my best to entertain the rest. All three gigs were poorly organised so all my acts were late. I would have to MC longer than usual until finally an act would arrive, sweaty and out of breath, I could see the glee from arriving slowly drain from their faces as they saw the audience and what they would had to contend with.

Do you have any idea how hard it is to MC to a room full of people who are already pissed off and hate you, all whilst you are dressed up to the nines, wearing heels?

My patience ended by about 11.35. Dave was meant to be on at 11.30 and I was MC'ing the gig into the ground. At 11.58 he ran through the door, grabbed the mic and we all sang the New Year's Eve countdown, you know the one, 10, 9, 8, 7 . . . it's a classic. Dave kissed me on the cheek and started doing his set at 12.01. I don't think anyone was in the mood for more comedy at 12.01, but the audience seemed happy enough so I just let him get on with it. I was standing at the back of the room patiently waiting for him when I got a tap on my shoulder from a guy in corduroy trousers and a bow tie.

'Are you Luisa?'

'Yes.'

'I've heard so much about you, Dave just won't shut up about you! Your dress is lush.'

'Thanks Michael, Dave's husband.' Here I was on New Year's Day, not even ten minutes into 2014, and I had managed to orchestrate a situation where I would feel like shit. I was happy for Dave, of course, this is where he should be, with his husband. I was disappointed with myself. I thought of Klaus, I thought of all the guys I had ever loved, imagined them all kissing and slow-dancing.

I looked around me and saw everyone in slow motion, laughing and embracing each other. Cheers Luisa, happy fucking New Year. Why do I keep trying to fall in love with men who are completely unavailable? Why am I unavailable? And what are the rest of the words to 'Auld Lang Syne'? So many questions.

22

ROMEO, WHEREFORE ART THOU? 'COS YOU AIN'T IN SINGAPORE

There is a famous expression that life will keep throwing the same lesson at you until you finally decide to learn it. I always felt and maybe still do that this is a load of bullshit. If I am always getting hurt in relationships, why can't the universe cut me some slack and give me some love and happiness instead? And here is what I noticed.

I give my career so much love, care and attention; the attention to detail is amazing. I don't let anyone else run or control it and can be viciously protective of my work. I am not like that with my love life. I throw myself at anyone who is nice to me and pray they catch me.

My career made me feel strong and I came off the anti-depressants and was still feeling good, I felt genuinely happy. I was worried that coming off them would mean that the happiness and high I had felt were false, but they weren't. I still got just as high from doing my shows. I felt stronger and like myself. I felt happy and much better than I was; my work had given me that satisfaction. The sense of achievement filled me with confidence.

I got invited out to Singapore to do Beyoncé as part of the Magners comedy festival. (PS I know I now use 'Beyoncé' as synonymous with my show and not necessarily the artist.) The festival was the first of its kind in Singapore, and the sponsor was paying for the flights. I booked to go out a week early and bought a direct flight from Singapore to Thailand. Take a few days of holiday before the festival started.

I found an island called Bottle Beach – pure sand, clear blue water, everything I wanted. I spent hours imagining what it would be like if I was here with a man. It was perfect. I could have sex with him in the sea, I could have sex with him on the beach, I could have sex with him in the hotel. Basically I could have a lot of sex. I'd found a cheap hotel app and got booked into the honeymoon suite of this beautiful resort. I ordered champagne with strawberries, a three-course meal and watched *Bridget Jones's Diary* in bed. My kinda honeymoon. The wedding to myself.

A comedian I half knew called Juice had also been invited to play Singapore and had had the same thoughts about a holiday beforehand. (Remember Juice, he was the one who was nice to me after I got my bad review a few years back.) He was going to Thailand but he didn't wanna spend the money on a nice hotel, and because I didn't really know him, I decided it would be better if I just stayed on my own and left him to it. I had four days in the honeymoon suite, by myself. I think Beyoncé would do that.

I think it's really important to take time out by yourself, give yourself a chance to reflect on what you are doing and how far you have come. I am used to being on my own but I love company. By the time I got to Singapore I had been on my own for a week, so it was nice to see a familiar face.

I'd never really warmed to Juice before. I'd known him for a few years on the open mic circuit when I first started and hadn't thought much of him. Katerina said he'd got really good recently, but I just remembered him as a rudeboy who spoke in this stupid accent and did jokes about poo.

He was staying at the same hotel as me in Singapore and we shared our experiences of Thailand. I told him about my amazing open-air shower and honeymoon suite for one. And he told me about how he did magic mushrooms and saw ladyboys. We were so different, but actually he was refreshing. I was kinda grateful for the relief. It was either hang with him or be on my own.

He basically has no filter, he puts his foot in it and always says the wrong things and people sometimes mistake him for a child. I'd had training in working with children, I liked it.

Juice quickly got himself fired from the festival. On the opening night there was a big gig in front of the promoters, lots of reps from Magners were there and Juice decided to open his set with 'I love Bulmers.' The promoter dragged him off stage and they got into a punch-up. He's an idiot, and for some reason I felt sorry for him and reached out.

As he got kicked off the festival, he had to move into a mate's room, two grown men sharing a small bed. I called up and offered Juice some respite by coming with me to get my nails done instead.

I met this five-year-old man in the lobby and he came with me to town.

'Why do they drive on this side of the road?'

'Because they do.'

'Yeah but why?'

'I don't know.'

'Why do they have trees like that in the pavement?'

'To swallow up the rain.'

'But why?'

'I don't know. Jesus you're annoying.'

We walked into the local shopping centre and found a nail salon.

Me: Hello, can I get a shellac please?

Nail lady: Shellac for two?

Me: Er no, just for me please.

Juice: Yeah, I want shellac.

Me: No you don't.

Juice: Yeah I do, what is it? I wanna see what she does with the shellac. So what is this shellac?

Me: It's just like a manicure but it's paint that doesn't budge.

Juice (to the nail technician): So what else is there to do in Singapore that's a must-see tourist destination?

Nail lady: Shellac?

Juice: Yes, the shellac is very nice but I have not travelled across the globe to see shellac nails.

Nail lady: You want shellac nails?

Juice: Yes they are very nice but I don't recall going on the tourist-board website and seeing shellac nails. My dad owns kebab shops . . .

I howled. I don't know why; in hindsight, it wasn't even that funny. But I liked him and felt very comfortable viewing the world with him.

I had a ball performing my show in Singapore. The audiences were quiet and it was weird playing to a crowd who would be eating or getting up and ordering food halfway through, but I liked it. I had learnt after my American experiences to just run with it.

My stepbrother Paul was living in Singapore with his wife. They came and saw my show and were really proud. Last time I'd seen them I was a spotty teenager with dreams of being an actress, and here I was getting flown out to Singapore to perform. It was a nice moment.

Nela, Paul's wife, invited me to this private members' bar in Singapore. So after the show, I changed my sweaty, humid top and got a cab over to this hotel. The club was amazing, like a boat that went across these two large high-rises. Nela had put my name at the door, and as I walked through the club, I came out on to the balcony and there was a VIP section and a VVIP section. Holy shit, I'd never seen anything like it.

Nela called me over. She was with her Singapore friends and they were gorgeous. This was a Tuesday night; they were dressed up to the nines, slammin' figures, big hair, stilettos and designer handbags. I rocked up in my woolly trousers, fake Isabel Marant hi-tops and an 'I ♥ New York' ripped T-shirt. I could see as Nela introduced me that her friends were judging me; they looked at my cheap clothes and ratty sneakers and I didn't belong with them in the VVIP section. But I didn't care, I was like, well let them judge. I'd been flown out to Singapore to go 'Moo', I was in a pretty good place, but at the same time, I wished Juice or someone was out there with me to enjoy the spectacle of being in a bar where they clearly think I don't belong.

One of the women ordered a bottle of vodka. A small Filipino woman came over with a bottle half the size of her. It cost $6,000. $6,000!!! That's like six fridges, bitches. I was in complete shock. But also ecstatic: look how my life has changed, here I am, wearing fake Isabel Marant trainers, at a rooftop bar overlooking the whole of Singapore with a $6,000 bottle of vodka. I don't know how I sneaked in, but I liked it.

The next night it was the closing night of the festival. Before the end-of-festival party, I'd had a gig called Joke Thieves. I love Joke Thieves, it's where you do a five-minute set and then you swap with another comedian. They do your material and you do theirs. I have a knack for it. I love mimicry and essentially that's what you do with this. I always play safe and easy and physical on my material, making me easy to mimic.

The other comics on the night hadn't seen me before and only knew about my Beyoncé show. You see, as I started playing these festivals, I was put on the bill with much more experienced comics, who hadn't seen me come up through the club circuit. I just came out of nowhere with a solo show. I constantly felt the need to prove myself. I wasn't feeling part of the circuit I'd started on as I was travelling with gigs, but I hadn't earned my place with my peers on these circuits either. I got a guy called Alan Anderson, an unabashedly shame-less comic who other comedians either love or hate. He can be a knob but I like him.

I did my set and Alan went up and just took the piss out of me calling me some dumb bitch. Everyone laughed and applauded his piss-take of my accent and material; he made me sound really common and stupid, basically playground mocking me being a girl. It was almost hurtful. The audience would look over to see how I was responding. And normally I would laugh along and they'd see that it was all in jest. But this didn't feel like jest. This one was taking the piss, so when people looked over to see my response, I just didn't look impressed. I was too stubborn to laugh; besides, I wasn't going to give them the satisfaction of me laughing at a man who was mocking me.

It got to my turn to do Alan. I took his material and ripped it to shreds, mocked his jokes, mocked his accent, mocked his attitude. Annihilated him, annihilated the room, got the best response of the night. After that Alan shook my hand and has been nice to me ever since. We get on really well now. It's like that as a woman in comedy. Sometimes dudes will use that you're a girl as a way to patronise or belittle you, but when you prove yourself, you're part of the team.

Later, at the party, I saw the promoter, who came and chewed my ear off about how he hated Juice and what an obnoxious arse he was. I said that was unfair and Juice was just doing his job. He'd told a joke that was funny and it was unfair how the festival had treated him. I was sticking up for my new best friend.

The promoter didn't like me sticking up for Juice, but he wasn't in a position to be horrible to me. I had one of the most popular shows at the festival, so he kinda listened to me and nodded but I could see he completely disagreed. It was weird seeing someone bite their tongue around me. Who would have thought, a fully grown man biting his tongue and respecting my opinion. What a difference a good show makes.

I met Juice and he asked me if I had ever been in love, as he was worried because he hadn't. He had started seeing two girls he liked, both at the same time, and now he couldn't decide which one to drop. He had inadvertently got into a situation where two women think he is their boyfriend and now doesn't know what to do. It was possibly the first time he had opened up. I laughed so hard: 'You're a fucking idiot!'

'I know, but it's not my fault.'

Then the promoter came in. I got all protective over Juice, but Juice stood up and walked over to the promoter. I saw him offer his hand and they chatted, shook hands and Juice came back. Wow, I thought, that was impressive, he acted like a complete adult. No fighting, no punch-up, no drama, just a good man. What a beautiful quality.

The bar asked everyone to come in from inside or leave. I went to leave but Juice said let's dance for one more song. OK, I said, whatever the next song is, that's our song. (You know how much I love this game!) The band played 'Free Fallin''. I was like, what the fuck is this song? Juice was like, oh my God, this is my favourite song ever! And sang all the words at me.

We walked home in the humidity, and as we got to the lift and I pressed the button for my floor, I was really tempted to ask him to come and stay with me and we could just talk, but I panicked and just barked, 'See you tomorrow, dickhead.' I'm really quite charming.

As I went to my room, I was annoyed that I didn't have him to talk to. I had a shower, put on my knickers and admired myself half naked. I wondered whether he'd like me naked. Eurgh, quickly get rid of that thought, why would I want an emotionally sturted, immature guy like Juice to see me naked? Gross. I convinced myself I had done the right thing. I didn't want Juice; besides, he can't decide between two girls. I went to sleep alone, again.

At 4 a.m. my phone rang.

'Hello.'

'Why are you still awake?'

'Oh my God, yes; because you called me. What do you want?'

'Can I come and stay with you please?!'

'What? No. Go away, it's four a.m.'

'I know and I'm sorry but my mate has brought a girl back and they are having sex in the bed and it's really awkward for me sat here watching them.'

'Haha, you're unwanted in a threesome,' I sang at him, and then hated myself because I'd clearly spent too much time with this man child and was now regressing myself.

He knocked on my door and I answered topless, holding my boobs, wearing nothing but a pair of pants. I had been dying to show someone my tan. I go golden. He came in and got into my bed. I was nervous and needed a wee but didn't want him to hear me weeing so I made him sing really loudly whilst I weed with the tap on. That's the thing about idiots, they will do whatever you ask them to. That's kinda nice.

I got into bed and marked his side of the bed and mine, he ignored it, grabbed me and spooned me. A storm kicked off outside and the thunder made me jump. He held me tighter, and we lay there laughing at how weird it was that of all the people we would find ourselves with, it was me and him in a thunderstorm in a hotel in Singapore. We put on my iPhone and played 'Free Fallin'' and that song 'Devil Went Down to Georgia'.

I was conscious that he had his arms around me and I didn't want to breathe in, just be natural Luisa, never apologise for your body. I couldn't help myself and said, 'I'm sorry for my fatness.' Now people have different ways of complimenting you. Juice went with 'I don't think you are fat at all, I think you feel really nice and soft, you are like a Premiership footballer . . . who's retired.'

Awww, I thought. He said Premiership.

As I tried to sleep, Juice held on to me but kept his waist away from me. I said, 'That's cute. You're not pushing your penis into me.'

He said, 'Well I haven't got an erection now, but if you needed me to have one, I could get one for you.'

Charming. Shakespeare must be shitting himself.

The following morning Juice had to get an early-morning flight; I was still in bed when I got a phone call.

'Hi, did I leave my Rolex in your room last night?'

'No.'

'Did my mate leave his wallet or his Ray-Bans or his Rolex?'

'No, why?'

'Oh because he brought a prostitute back to the hotel last night and I think she robbed us.'

23

IF I WERE A BOY . . . I'D BE BETTER AT IT THAN YOU

Time came around for me to start working on a second show. I had a title, 'Am I Right Ladies?!' It's a follow-on from 'WWBD' and it's a line in Beyoncé that audiences would always quote back at me, so it made sense. The only problem now I was writing it was that I didn't know how anything was going to top the magic of the first one. Beyoncé was so incredible and everything was changing and I really felt excited about my life. But the pressure of writing a new show felt quite overwhelming. 'WWBD' had been touring for three years; how was I going to deliver something as good? The by-product of travelling so much and doing my solo show meant that I had lost touch with the community spirit of the gigging comedy circuit. I wasn't gigging with other people and was on my own a lot. I had my gorgeous friends outside of comedy, Delia, Pas, Zoe, but they all had regular jobs or didn't live in the city. Suzi and I would always miss each other because of touring and Katerina had moved back to Greece, and I found my new timetable quite lonely.

Turns out Juice actually lived ten minutes down the road from me. With him being unemployed, I had a new friend to hang out with. He was impressed with what I had achieved in my career, he wasn't at all competitive or jealous, he was really supportive. I got asked to do an interview in the *Guardian*. I read the comments when it came out online. Readers, men, commenting things like 'Dumb bitch, why don't you try and work on being funny, women aren't funny.' I got really upset and clicked on the replies. There from KebabJuice81: 'Go fuck yourself, she's amazing, and funny, hilarious, go back and work in Tesco you sad little closed-minded twat of a human being.'

Ahh, he did it on every negative one. Any bad comment, there was a reply from Juice telling them to go fuck themselves. He not only read my interview, but he stuck up for me in the *Guardian*. Yes, he had two girlfriends, but he stuck up for me. I'd not had that before. I liked it. I liked hanging out with Juice. He became a good friend. I got all the attention of a man without the pressure of a relationship, all the fun without any of the potential disaster. *Cue haunting music*

He would talk to me about his girl problems and I had someone to call my friend. I liked him. I also liked his comedy, which was weird because I never laugh at comedians – well I do, but not often.

I started coming up with material for my new show and I would run it past him; he never berated or judged me for it. And I needed that freedom. I mean, I had an audience that was coming to my shows and I needed to work on something to give them. Something that would make them want to stand up at the end. The test of my new show was making it good enough to receive a standing ovation.

What I love about my audiences is their loyalty. I know my audiences and I knew what I wanted to talk to them about. I wanted to say to them everything I wanted to say to myself. I wanted to tackle body image, not being over an ex, having one-night stands and going on antidepressants. Beyoncé was all about being depressed and hopeless in a narrative; this time I was stronger, happier and wanted to write a manifesto. A manifesto with jokes.

I booked in my first preview in the tunnels at Waterloo. I felt so much pressure to deliver; I didn't want to let my audience down. Katerina was over from Greece, so I got her over a few hours beforehand and we started coming up with a rough running order. I knew I wanted to open with my thigh gap joke and be like, look, here is my body, deal with it. Also Spanx are funny, what if I added a layer and as I took my trousers down, I had Spanx on first and then took them off. This would all be more fun if I did it to a song, so Katerina pressed shuffle on my iPhone and we agreed that whatever song came up was the one I was going to strip to. It was Mariah Carey, 'All I Want for Christmas Is You'. Perfect!

I arrived at the tunnels and to my amazement the show was sold out. I could have shat myself. But my audiences being as gorgeous as they are, they were so supportive. I did the show and got a standing ovation, on my first preview of my second show. Phew, I felt good, the comedy gods were smiling on me.

The show evolved really quickly. I liked incorporating music into my shows, and the second was no different, but instead of a particular artist I decided to use more movie references and quotes. I also started talking about my desire for a boyfriend.

I was bored of always getting asked about women in comedy and what it was like to be a woman in comedy. There is the cliché that female comedians dress frumpily, and I'm not frumpy, I'm glamorous. I wanted to be myself on stage.

In the previews, my difficulty was that by taking all my clothes off at the beginning, I had created a real high. Then it becomes how do you top that high? Where do you go from there? Some comics suggested I should end on the stripping. But that felt so wrong and why should me being half naked be the punchline, why is my body the punchline to a joke? No, this was about more than just being stripped back on stage; it's metaphorical, stripping down to my bra and Spanx and being like, look, I am a woman, here are my boobs, this is my body, can we get over it and on with the jokes now please? And then I'd strip bare my soul on stage. Why should nudity be the climax? I am smarter than that. I set myself a high bar, a hill if you like, then previewed the life out of the show as a means to figure out how to climb it.

Eventually I found my finale and it's brilliant – but I don't wanna ruin the surprise for you.

As I got more confident with the show and booked in more previews, I asked Juice if he wanted to come along and be my support act. Basically someone to go on first and do ten minutes of material just to warm them up a little bit. I would go on first, say hello and then introduce my support act as my guest. I liked doing it like that, because my audiences had come to see my show but by me introducing Juice, it showed that he was my guest and I wanted my audience to love him. Sounds like a long way round to do it, but it works.

Now normally when I do new material I say something along the lines of 'Guys, this is going to be new material. Now you know when you get a newborn baby and it tries to walk, just a little baby, trying to walk, and sometimes it might fall over and hurt itself. When that happens you don't go "Ahh you're a shit baby, I'm gonna throw you into the river" . . . no, you go "Ahh don't worry baby, just try again, keep going, keep going!!!" I just want you to think of that analogy when I do my jokes!'

The audience like it and it settles me into their expectations. I opened with that joke, then introduced Juice to do a short set before I tried the new show. He did his set, my audience loved him, and that's hard because they don't love everyone. Afterwards he said, 'Now, don't listen to Luisa and her "just a little baby" crap, she's phenomenal and I know she is going to kill it.' The whole room went awwwww and looked over at me. I mimed a humping-the-air action.

I did my preview and got a standing ovation. After that I booked Juice for most of my previews. I felt more confident that I had something to talk about beyond Beyoncé. Not all of the previews went well, but that's part of the process.

I remember doing one particular preview in Brighton. A woman came up and said, 'I saw Beyoncé and have brought six of my friends! We are so excited to see you!' They left the room at the end of the preview and avoided all eye contact. It felt like shit, that feeling. I had to work harder.

Valentine's came round again and I booked in another party show. I'd had my confidence knocked a bit because of the 'Am I Right Ladies?!' previews, so I booked in to do Beyoncé again. I love doing Beyoncé; nothing gives me greater joy. I wanted 'Am I Right' to feel like that. I booked out Concrete again and we just had a ball, I loved my Valentine's parties.

In the day, no TV stuff was happening and if I wasn't doing shows or previews I didn't have much else going on so, Juice encouraged me to go to the gym. He said I could watch him work out. Joy.

We're in the gym, riding next to each other on the bikes:

Juice: You see, I know what my drawbacks are, and that's empowering, always know your own weaknesses.

Luisa: (trying not to sound out of breath): Yeah, weaknesses.

Juice: So like my only faults are a) I still live with my mum and b) I haven't got a job, but apart from that, I am a catch.

Luisa: (laughs really hard, too hard): Well what do you think my flaws are?

Juice: Well first off, I think you're too fussy.

Luisa: I'm not fussy. I love having sex with guys who are unemployed or still live at their mum's house. *Winks*

Juice: And secondly, I think you might be too clingy to guys when they first meet you.

Luisa: (goes quiet): Really.

Juice: Yeah, like last week, every day texting 'Juice can we go to the gym, Juice can we go to the gym.'

Luisa: (welling up, embarrassed and avoiding eye contact): Yeah, but that's because I really wanted to train.

Juice: Yeah, but you don't ring at like one in the morning.

Luisa: But that's because I had just done a gig. *Starts crying*

Juice: Oh my days, what are you crying for?

Luisa: (clearly crying): I'm not crying, I'm just sweating really hard.

Juice: Come here. *Gives her a one-armed cuddle*

Luisa: It's just I haven't really got anyone to hang out with at the moment and you kinda became the highlight of my week.

Juice: OK, see this bottle of water? I'm gonna pour it over your head.

Luisa: OK.

(Juice slowly pours bottle of water over Luisa's crying sweaty head. She just lets him, and then smiles feebly.)

Luisa: I knew you liked me.

Juice threatening to pour water over my head became a thing.

In the time I was previewing 'Am I Right Ladies?!' I got invited out to Montreal to the Just for Laughs festival, one of the most prestigious comedy festivals in the entire world. When I got the news, my friends were elated and other comics were jealous. Just for Laughs is where people get discovered; you get famous if you get invited on Just for Laughs.

I thought it was best to move out of my London pad as I couldn't afford the rent for the time I would be away, plus the lease was nearly up. So Juice helped me pack, loaded it all into the car for me and moved it to a storage unit. That was the kinda stuff we did, hung out, went to the gym, packed my things, he drove me places. Maybe I did want a boyfriend; I don't know what is so wrong with saying that. It felt nice to have a guy around, but not Juice? No, he was an idiot, he had two girlfriends. He kept suggesting I do online dating, that I needed to put myself out there but the thought of Tinder or Guardian Soulmates filled me with dread. Plus the last guy I had sex with had a husband. It would probably be best if I avoided love altogether. Why couldn't dating be easier, like old-school, wear a miniskirt, drink a few Smirnoff Ices and pull someone on the dance floor? Where was this penis-offering dance floor?

I don't know, even once you catch a dick, there's more issues to contend with. Here's something that annoys me about the whole sex thing.

You know when you meet a guy and you bring him back to your place and you're about to make love for the first time and you're a little bit nervous, you're a bit like

'Ooh, I hope it fits!' It does, it's fine, I am actually surprisingly accommodating, apart from with Egor, that took ages . . . I digress. You have a mad night of passionate, headboard-banging, back-arching, body-wriggling sex. And to be honest, you don't even know his name, so you are just calling him 'hun' but he keeps calling you 'babe', so fuck it, you're playing the same console.

The sex is amazing and he leaves first thing in the morning; well someone's got to drive the bus, oi oi! You run downstairs to your flatmates or your mum, whoever you live with. 'Oh my God!! I had the most amazing time!' And after a night of intimacy with someone, especially if it was good, if you are anything like me you are going to want to feel close to that person, maybe to see them again, so you say to your flatmate 'I think I'm gonna text him.'

Cue tumbleweed.

Flatmate: Text him? You can't text him.

Me: Course I can, I'm just gonna text him and say hi.

Flatmate: Are you fucking mental, that is way too keen and desperate, he will think you are a psycho.

Me: If I text him, he'll think I'm a psycho?

Flatmate: Yes, he's a dude remember, let him chase you, you got to let him feel like the alpha male.

Me: Alpha male? Why does he get to be the alpha? What does that make me? Omega 3? I am not a fish!

Flatmate: Look, if you text him now, it will just come across as too forward and you'll make it really awkward. Don't be such a whore, just let him chase you.

Too awkward? The guy fucked me so hard my vagina farted, yet sending him a text message is where it gets awkward? I have never understood this rationale. In bed I am encouraged to be sexual and in control (or submissive depending on the role play), yet when it comes to the next morning, it's like we're back to 1812.

How come in every other aspect of my life I am encouraged to get everything I want – strive for my education, strive for my career, buy my own car, buy my own house, it's the year of Beyoncé, bitches, go get it – but when it comes to the morning after sex, oh hell no, bitch, sit down and know your place, You'll scare the man.

I have never nailed this sex game. I am rubbish at games, I don't like lies and I like being frank and upfront. Some people think it's mental, I just think it's honest. Hey, like showing up outside your house with your favourite Five Guys and leaving it on the doorstep when you're not in. I like coming round whilst you are at work and cleaning your flat and rearranging your room for you. I like sucking your dick dry and being really enthusiastic when you are fucking me. These are the things I like to do with someone I like. Why does that make me mental? Deal with it, dickhead!

I hate these bullshit games. I have had sex with you but now I can't text you? I have to wait for you to text me? Just wait, sit on your hands, I don't care how long it takes, don't give in to temptation to say 'Hi, How r u?!' No, no, fight it Luisa, fight it, let the man be the alpha, let the man be the alpha!!! Be the strong independent woman you are and just sit wide awake until your eyes start bleeding. Never text the man, let the man text you.

Jog on dickhead, if we are close enough for you to rim me, we are close enough for me to text you first.

Anyway I digress . . . So I am avoiding love and continue making love to my career. I arrive in Montreal. It's the Just For Laughs comedy festival, and I had been booked not for a showcase but for a ten-night run of my whole solo show. This was huge. It's an invitation-only festival; people's careers have been made in Montreal. Well at least in the '80s they had. Oh my goodness, this is it. If I can nail these shows maybe they would invite me to America, maybe I could get on *The View*! My dream of meeting Whoopi would be realised!

I was on so early, 6.30 p.m., but I was going to give it my all. On opening night I played to 12 people. I did my usual spiel of 'I need a warm-up act . . .' and a young woman jumped on stage and said 'I'm a comic, it's OK' and pushed me to the side. Oh God, it's like LA all over again. Why, America, why?! Shit, I am in Canada, OK this isn't helping me. I watched in shock as she started doing jokes, then said 'Oh here is something about Beyoncé' and gestured at me.

The most awkward start to a show ever. I continued and had just got to the sad part of the show, where I talk about my brother and Christmas. I did the punchline and they didn't laugh. They did not like my depression section at all, this was not funny. They didn't get the irony, at which point the warm-up woman jumped up on stage, wrapped her arms around me whilst simultaneously taking off my head mic, then whispering in to it . . . 'Your sense of humour is awful but it's all going to be OK.'

Looks like *The View* will have to wait. I did find a relationship in Montreal though, just not a sexy one, well I mean, it's kinda sexy. Tatiana was out there, remember Tat? The manager from LA? She came to see me perform to 12 people; it was the night after I played to a school of 29 French kids. She still wanted to sign me. I was like, shit, well if you can handle me in my room of 12 people eating a Subway, then I want you on board for when I have my sold-out stadium.

I rocked up to her room one afternoon and asked her to call my phone, which was on her bed; her number came up as 'Tatiana My Manager' and that is the most romantic commitment I had ever made.

That night I had a late-night spot to practise a five-minute set for a gala I was doing. I went on stage and didn't do great, then came back to the green room and sat feeling awkward whilst all the big comics were coming in and high-fiving each other and I just felt like a twat who had bombed trying to do cow impressions. What idiot does cow impressions?! I felt such a fraud being in that room. These guys were all pros, ahead of their game, the best of the best and I can't even moo properly. SMH. My eyes were starting to well up when Adam Hills came over and introduced himself. I knew who he was; I told him there was no point in him knowing my name as I was awful and had just died. He patted me on the arm and said not to worry about dying and it happens to all of us. He said he would love to chat longer afterwards but he had to go and do his spot.

I watched him walk on stage and he bombed. And oh it made me so happy. He came running up to me and gave me the biggest hug and said, 'I can't believe I just gave you advice about dying and then just died so hard, God that's painful!' We both laughed and in that moment we became great friends. I love him. That's the thing about stand-up, no matter how big or great you get, every now and then comedy can always remind you who is in charge.

Thankfully my bad luck didn't continue. The following night I performed at the gala and got to do a late-night set for a night hosted by the girls from *Broad City*. I was so nervous. I was wearing a pink dress which I didn't realise was see-through from the back so you could see my black thong and my cellulite. I went out and did my five minutes and the crowd were whooping and cheering. I was so relieved. I looked up and guess who was stood in the balcony. I recognised him in the shadows and almost did a double take. It was Klaus, he was leaning against the pillar and smiling down at me. I hadn't realised he had also been invited out to the festival. Ha, how things had come full circle, here he was watching me kill it and he was smiling and I, well I didn't care. I didn't care one single bit. I didn't have time to. I didn't look at him or acknowledge him, this was no time to concentrate on boys, I had to concentrate on the audience in front of me and I did and I killed it. So once again, hello comedy, reminding me how beautiful and magical you truly are.

24

BAT-SHIT CRAY (CRAY)

Back in London and sleeping on my friend's couch, the universe was looking out for me, and my gorgeous friend who has a place in north London, a room with an ensuite, is like 'Luisa, it's yours, move in and have it for cheap.'

I move in with two hoots, Kat and Sophie, and we have so much fun dancing around in our pants. I have finally found somewhere that feels like a real home in central London and it makes all the difference. I have girls to hang out with!

Only thing is, the flat is amazing, but my room is at the back and on a corner, so I have all outside walls, and three massive windows, all single-glazed. The room soaks up heat in the summer but I feel absolutely freezing in the winter. The flat is perfect in every other way, I'm not moving out and try to find a solution. I got a standalone heater but in one month it cost me an extra £260 in electricity. Oh FFS.

I read up online and buy shitloads of cling film and cover my windows with it. Yes I have sell-out shows, yes I have performed in New York, Montreal, LA, but I am still just a normal girl with £800 in her bank account and doing a budget double-glazing job with cling film on the windows.

Who needs a guy around when I have cling film? I just wanted to keep focusing on being on my own for a bit. OK, so I hadn't had sex more than once in two years, but my career was taking off: in the last year I had travelled to LA, New York, Singapore, Montreal, Thailand. It was incredible. I read in a book once about how if you want to succeed, you have to put all your energy into something, and that includes your sexual energy. You know like how footballers can't have sex the night before a game to improve their per- formance? Well it's kinda the same for me, but instead of me kicking a ball, my audience were having a ball, and instead of not having sex the day before a show, I hadn't seen a dick in months. But I was fucking my audiences' brains out. That's where my sexual energy was going.

It's my biggest fear or regret, not having more sex. It feels like everyone I know goes home to someone, gets it regularly and has that partner to lean on. I can go for years without. When I have it, I love it, like I love to taste it, smell it, enjoy every second of it. I love teabagging; teabagging is one of my favourite things. Can. Not. Get. Enough. So can you imagine my pain when I haven't had any balls in my mouth for over two years? Two years!

'But Luisa, that just shows what great self-discipline you have.' Babe, none of this is by choice, I have no self-discipline. I tried low carb once; three days later I was eating ice cream with a fork.

I miss sex. I love sex. But every time I had sex, it always seemed to go wrong and I would go mental. Let's set the scene. You meet a guy, you go out for some drinks, you have a great evening, he is being charming and calling you beautiful, you are being charming and laughing at all his jokes. Even though you write better ones, hello cows?! Don't turn your nose up at cows; cow jokes bought my mum a Smeg fridge, remember?

One cosmo leads to another and you end up fucking him. Or not; maybe you just get fingered, it's your prerogative babe, whatever you wanna do. He leaves first thing and you go about your day with a spring in your step. You didn't even get his number, doesn't matter if you don't see him again, the sex was amazing. Like it felt good to remember what your cunt feels like from the inside. And to have naked skin on naked skin, and to be kissed, touched and held. It was just nice. But you don't *need* to see him again.

You are walking round feeling confident, attractive, oozing an air of positivity and glow. It's nice to be fucked sometimes, it's healing.

You go to meet your friends in a bar to tell them all the details about how you didn't even cry. Before or after. You are a legend. Oh yes, they are going to high-five the shit out of you, but then you remember they have proper jobs so you have to wait a couple of hours. So you prop up the bar and order a cosmo. 'What do you mean you don't do cocktails? What kind of establishment is this?! Fine, I'll have a Smirnoff Ice, with a straw, yes I am 33, and make it a pink one.'

Then who do you see at the side of the bar? ONLY THE GUY YOU FUCKED THIS MORNING! And this is where it starts. The conversation. Not with someone else. The one in your brain. The internal monologue that you should never ever say out loud: the one where on the inside you are on fire but on the outside you try to make sure the straw from the Smirnoff Ice goes in your mouth and not in your eye.

Fuck fuck fuck, act natural.

Fuck, thank God I have my face on, just play it cool.

Pretend you have not seen him.

Don't be ridiculous, why would you do that?

Why don't you just say hi?

Don't be ridiculous, why would you say hi?

Because it's normal to say hi?

That such a stupid idea.

It's not that stupid, I mean you said hello to the postman this morning and well, you didn't suck him off, so maybe it wouldn't be so weird??

OK, good point!

Just say hi.

But be breezy, breezy and casual.

Wait. Practise it first. Is 'hi' good? Come on, you are creative. You can do way better than hi.

Think!

Hi.

Hey.

Hello.

Hey you!

Top of the morning to ya.

Hey guv'nor (the comedians from Chicago would love that).

Areet (he's not a Geordie, but I'm good with accents, right?).

Moo? The audiences love moo. Smegs love moo.

Fine. Just say hi, Luisa.

So you saddle up next to him at the bar and tap him on the shoulder and go for it.

'Hi.'

He looks at you, nearly spits his drink out and says 'All right?' before walking off, away from you, in the opposite direction to where you are sat, he could not get away quicker. Literally pounced, a bit like Simba did in *The Lion King* when he was practising with his dad. Only this pounce is in the opposite direction to wherever you are. No thanks mate, I had zebra last night. Well, you didn't, technically you had vagina, am I right ladies?! I'm digressing, abort the situation, the man has walked away.

You feel like your stomach has just sunk. All that confidence from this morning is slowly draining from your body, leaving you with flushed cheeks, but this time for all the wrong reasons.

And it's fine, obviously it's fine, because you were an idiot for saying hi. Should have gone with the guv'nor line! Shut up brain. It's your fault. I don't know why you thought it would even be OK to say anything, that was a really dumb move, you should have just played it cool, but that is your problem, you are never cool. Why couldn't you be like last night when you were reverse cowgirl and totally in control? But no, instead here you are holding a Smirnoff Ice with a pink straw and your eyes feel like they are welling up. Fuck this shit, if you are going to cry, go to the toilets, Luisa, go to the fucking toilets. Oh, remember when you were on antidepressants and you couldn't cry, ha, what you would give to be on then now, eh? Shut up, brain.

So you swig your Smirnoff and make your way to the ladies' and lock yourself in a cubicle and could kick yourself that your eyes nearly watered, though you did not let a teardrop fall. Hell no, you don't know this man, you don't owe him anything, he certainly doesn't get to make you cry, so you wipe that nearly smudged mascara and you think fuck this, go back out there, prop up that bar and fuck him (not in the literal sense again), show him and all the world that you don't need his validation and he will not ruin your night now or spoil what was your conscious choice of a great night of sex.

So you come out of the toilet and bam, you walk straight into him and you think this is ridiculous, I am 33 years old, I am just going to say hi.

Luisa: Hey, how's it going? I didn't expect to see you so soon after this morning. *Shy laugh*

Man child: Er yeah, all right. *Walks off into the gents*

Say what? What just happened there? Did I just see him and immediately forget my plan of screw him and instead some mature adult 33-year-old normal person butted in with 'Hey, how's it going? I didn't expect to see you so soon after this morning'?

How weird.

On some subconscious level, part of me assumed that because I had his balls in my mouth the night before we are no longer strangers and I should treat him as such. It was instinctive, I didn't even plan it, it just blurted out.

And yet now here we are dealing with *his* subconscious. A 12-year-old man child.

Now your instinct, every fibre of your being is telling you to run after the little prick, head into the gents' toilets, bang on the cubicle door and shout, 'Come out here and face me, fucktard, come out here and face me. Say hello to my face, just come out and say hello to my fucking face. Cat got your tongue? That's funny, because last night you were cupping my face and calling me beautiful, you were calling me beautiful all night long, you couldn't stop waxing lyrical, I was getting a running commentary, and now you can't even manage a hello? What's changed, dickwad? Oh, the sex! Because you fucked me so you win, so you don't need to make an effort with me any more. I get it, it's a status thing. You fucked me, so I am dismissed; there is no reason for you to be nice to be now. Let's talk about status, shall we fucktard, let's talk about fucking status when it comes to sex. Technically, technically, my body let you in, I decided to open myself to you, I had the power. Technically my body ate you, fucktard, my body ate you! In the animal-kingdom scheme of things, I win, you lose! So if anyone is technically spitting anyone out here, it's me spitting you. Jesus, why are you so emotionally stunted? I don't wanna marry you, fucktard, I don't wanna have your babies. I just want you to show me a little bit of R.E.S.P.E.C.T. and say hello to me properly when it's been less than eight hours since I sucked your dick dry.' *Hair flick* *Walks off*

But alas, sigh, no. You can't do that. You can't run after him, you can't say any of that because if you do, well that would make you a CRAZY BITCH.

So instead when he says 'Er yeah, all right' you smile politely and let him go. You don't want to kick up a fuss, no, shhh Luisa you gotta play nice, you gotta tiptoe around the alpha. Because hey ladies, maybe if you play your cards right and don't kick up a fuss now, then he will text you on some random Tuesday in two and a half weeks' time at 1 a.m. asking to come over for a blow job, or whatever he feels like he needs. And well, you would sure hate to miss out on that opportunity, all because you went crazy bitch on him now, so no, say nothing, just smile politely and say thank you. 'Thank you for the opportunity.'

As if you should be fucking grateful.

Sex is fun, sex is good, it takes two to tango and the guilt felt by women is depressing. I don't want to teach my daughter that. For too long I have felt shit about relationships and shit about the sex I have been having. It's best if I just avoid it all for now, I would rather have nothing than be tired of feeling grateful for breadcrumbs.

25

HOT SAUCE IN MY BAG . . . SWAG (I JUST WANT SOME)

You have to smile politely and say thank you a lot in life, not just in love. Especially if you work in entertainment. You have to play the game. Most of the people who run production companies and work as writers on TV shows are male. As I've said before, for every five men I met, I would meet one woman.

All the TV people I was meeting were excited about me, but it wasn't translating into cold, hard offers. They all kept asking, 'Great, what else have you got?!' And I would feel bewildered; you think a show like that just gets spat out? My show was what I had. I want adverts on the underground already! Come on, spend £10k on the advertising and I promise a West End musical of 'What Would Beyoncé Do?!' It's what the Spice Girls musical should have been, I'm telling you; well, me and *ArtsEd Review Online*, December 2012: 'It's what the Spice Girls musical should have been.' I was frustrated. I can see my shows work. Audiences were losing their shit and were excited about what I had to say, and yet the only room there was for me in television was 'Can you write topical jokes about the *Daily Mail* for a really exciting new panel show that's an exact replica of every other panel show?' It was really depressing.

ITV2 asked for a pilot version of my stage show. So Debi set me up with a production company. We started coming up with TV formats that would fit my show. It would be my own show and I could have a live audience and it was finding a way to make it feel like I was presenting. I didn't want my debut to be TV presenting. I want to be a comedian and capture what I do in my live shows on TV. One day I came in for a meeting with my producer who had two guys with him.

'Now Luisa, don't panic, these are going to be your co-presenters.'

What? But I'm not a presenter.

'Yes, but look, women don't like women, they will feel better if you have two guys. And you are not a presenter, just the three of you are "presenting" a show together, but you are still the star.'

But I don't want to do a show with two dudes.

'Listen Luisa, you're not famous enough for that right now, just do what you're told and when you are bigger you can start behaving like a little diva. For now, let's just make this work for the pilot.'

We shot the pilot, I hated it. It was me sitting on a couch and saying, 'Join us after the break when we will be speaking to Mary who wants to try anal sex for the first time, oooh cheeky! See you in three.' But Debi and the producers all said it would be good practice.

We did a live show version of the pilot, which was filmed but not to go out on telly. ITV2 loved it and wanted to commission a transmittable version. I said no. They called me in for a meeting and literally were like 'Who do you think you are? Do you have any idea how many people would bite our hand off to have this opportunity?' And they weren't wrong, but I didn't want to attach my name to something I didn't believe in. They didn't know my audiences; my audiences would hate this.

So I just focused on what my audiences would like. I had previewed my new show 'Am I Right Ladies?!' about 34 times and now it was ready for Edinburgh. Simultaneously doing Beyoncé made it very difficult to compare the two; one had been well oiled and performed for three years, the other was seven months old.

For Edinburgh this year, I was still looking after my own live work, so I went back and did 'Am I Right Ladies?!' on the Laughing Horse Free Festival. I could have easily done a paid venue, they would all accept my show, but I felt like I would enjoy it more if I could oversee everything. So once again I hired my own team, auditioned flyerers, got a PA on board and asked a friend to come and help me with the tech.

The room held 120 people and I was turning away the same number. It was amazing seeing the queue form around the block. I was so excited and pleased to see how far I had come from playing a 50-seater at the Meadow Bar.

I was getting four- and five-star reviews across the board, and then the big one: I got a five-star review from Steve Bennett at *Chortle*. They tweeted me, 'Sound the klaxon, it's another rare five-star review.' I was one of three people at that point who had got five stars, fantastic! I was delighted. I'd see other comics and they would be like 'Heard about your review, he's not seen my show yet.' They wouldn't say, 'Hey, huge congrats on the review, he hasn't come to mine yet.'

And this is what I mean about the pressure during Edinburgh. The industry makes comedy feel like there is only room for 'one chosen person' at a time. It's so difficult not to constantly compare what everyone else is doing to what you're doing and get lost in your own head. It makes it difficult to enjoy other people's successes because in this kind of environment, someone else's success can feel like your failure. I know I've been like that myself. Anyone who has done Edinburgh has been like that.

I would then make a point of asking comics about themselves and about their shows. All comics will tell you not to buy into the awards and review nonsense, but we all do. It surrounds you. Sometimes I feel like the industry acts like a bunch of sheep. I saw it with my own Beyoncé show, as soon as one industry person came, they all started coming. Which is lovely but sometimes it's as if a lot of the individuals involved are too scared to make their own decision about what is good. So they wait and see who is getting a buzz or some heat and then everyone jumps on the hot one. This hesitance to take a leap of faith on a variety of talent breeds an environment of jealousy and unhealthy competition.

I wish my industry took more risks and showed more faith in talent. That's why I love my audiences so much, they have found me through good old-fashioned word of mouth, and their friends told them about me. Social media has been amazing in helping me build a following. My new show was getting just as much love as my last one.

I was feeling proud and really chuffed that once again I had proved myself. Maybe this would make the difference and help me finally secure some TV. I had a follow-up show that was as solid as my first. I felt so excited!

I spent most of my evenings with either Katerina or Juice. If I didn't see Juice out, he would drop in for a cup of tea on his way home. One week one of his girlfriends came up and he didn't speak to me for four days, and as soon as she got on the train he called me. I was annoyed with him for going AWOL. 'If we are just friends you would have introduced me to your girlfriend!' He said he was sorry and that he didn't know how to act; he'd never had a best friend that was a girl before and he'd panicked. But he would make it up to me by coming to my show that night.

I caught him as he walked in and I performed so hard. I had a killer show and afterwards he was waiting outside with Katerina and another girl. Katerina whispered to me, 'Er I think that is Juice's other girlfriend.' What the actual fuck? SMH.

'Are you fucking joking? You brought your other girlfriend? You haven't spoken to me for a week and you knew I was upset and now you brought your other girlfriend?'

'Yeah, I know, because you said I acted weird and I should have treated you as a friend and then she arrived just as the other one left and I didn't want to let you down so I thought I would bring her with me.'

What the fuck am I doing? Why am I shouting at Juice for bringing his other girlfriend to my show? He kinda clicked that something had changed in me; I don't think either of us expected me to be as upset as I was. Fuck. I got my stuff and went home.

I didn't speak to him for a few days and just got on with doing my show. I was embarrassed as I knew now that I liked him and what's more, now I knew that he knew that I liked him, and that was mortifying. He was meant to be my friend. He had two girlfriends; why, when I was nailing my career, did I feel like I was back at square one with Mr Unavailable? I deleted his number. I needed to leave him alone.

The nominations came out and once again I wasn't nominated. I didn't get it. I kept feeling like the comedy elite did not want to let me in. I don't know why I cared or wanted their approval.

My work is accessible, it's pop culture, it's mainstream but it also goes deep. Sure, some press would comment on what I wear, on my accent or what my audiences are drinking. But that's all superficial, I talk about power-ful things; I talk about body image, antidepressants, sex, mental health, relationships, a woman's sense of self. And yet all they care to mention is 'Scantily clad female comedian performs in a bra for Bacardi Breezer hen par-ties.' I feel like sometimes there is a class issue at play. It's frustrating.

In many ways I am part of a really exciting movement in comedy. Free festival fringe acts are breaking through, so many agents are now booking their acts to do the free shows because they get it! Social media is giving artists direct con-tact with fans like never before, yet here I am looking for validation from the old-school system. Fuck 'em, fuck all of them. I worked harder at every show after that.

I was upset and called my mum; I couldn't really speak to other comedians about it. Everyone who wasn't nominated would be upset that they weren't nominated. I really felt like I deserved it though, that I had proved that I belonged at the festival and that my shows had an impact on audiences there. My phone rang from a num-ber I didn't recognise and I answered.

'What a bunch of motherfuckers, what a bunch of cock-sucking, classist, sexist, up-their-own-arse twat scum, they should be sucking your dick. I cannot believe, let me say this again, I was in shock, utter shock that you haven't been nominated, it's a travesty. This just proves Edinburgh is a sham. The awards are a sham. I used to think that maybe after Beyoncé they kicked themselves and they would repay you this year, but what a bunch of cock-sucking twats. A fucking insult to you and an insult to comedy. I have no time for them. Edinburgh is a sham and the awards are rigged, they will fucking rue the day, you watch, you watch your career, one day you will make them all look like fucking idiots.'

'Hi Juice.'

Roll on September and Soho had booked me for a two-week run in the main house, which sold out! It got to Christmas time and I was on my second two-week sold-out run. The theatre then asked if I would like to come back and do another week in January. London audiences were coming in their hundreds and I loved them!

Debi got me a job doing TV warm-up for Mel and Sue. They had a lunchtime show and it would be my job to come and speak to the audience beforehand. I got to meet lots of exciting guests like Alan Davies and Dermot O'Leary, who were both lovely, and of course Mel and Sue were hilarious. I loved being part of the show, but I was feeling anxious in general with the direction of my career. I still didn't have much money and because there is no set wage or salary, it can feel stressful. I wasn't seeing financial clarity or consistency and yet I was working all the time.

I started distancing myself from Juice. He sensed it and so started contacting me more (I swear boys have like a siren for this shit . . . Quick, she's moving on, call her!) He asked me to come and meet him at a gig one night but I politely declined. It was good; I was starting to take care of myself and do the right thing by me. So I washed all my make-up off and went to bed. Forty-five minutes later, I was fully dressed, fully made up and on my way to go find Juice. Fuck it, YOLO.

I walked into the bar he was in and all the comics were sat around a table. I saw him and asked if we could have a chat in private, and he went all Danny Zuko on me.

'We can talk here in front of my friends.'

I started crying.

'Why have you come here to cry?'

'I'm not crying, I just wanted to talk to you.'

'Luisa, I'm not your boyfriend, you can't just come here and cry on me.'

'I'm not crying!'

'See this pint of water, I am gonna pour it over your head in three . . . two . . . one . . .'

'Oh fuck off then.'

I caught sight of myself, a 33-year-old woman chasing a man child with two girlfriends. Could I have any lower self-esteem? I was an independent woman, last year I earned enough to buy my mum a Smeg fridge. And here I was struggling to catch a dick, disobeying every rule in *How to Get Laid for Dummies*.

1. Smile nicely and question nothing.
2. Don't fucking cry.

We left the bar and he offered to drive me home, but first we stopped at Sainsbury's as he had to get some Tabasco sauce. This seemed like the perfect time to talk about my feelings.

'Look, I don't know what you want because you say I treat you like a boyfriend.'

'I just want hot sauce.'

'Why won't you talk to me? This whole thing is getting really stressful for me.'

'I am talking to you. I am sorry you feel stressed, but it's your own doing, all I can focus on right now is hot sauce.'

'It wasn't all my doing. What about my feelings?'

'I feel you will be happier once I find hot sauce.'

'Juice, fuck off, what do you want from me?'

'I just want hot sauce, don't bust my balls and we are fine.'

'OK, OK, I'm sorry.'

'It's fine, so should I get chilli or Mexican spice?'

'Mexican spice.'

He paid, we walked to the car and he dropped me home. He got out of the car and came round and opened the door for me. It was a clear night, a full moon and the stars were super bright. We were stood underneath the lamp post, both of us in leather jackets.

'Look Luisa, I have told you, I do love you as a friend, but I'm not ready. I have two girlfriends and I miss both of them.'

I started crying again. He went to get back in the car and I stepped in front of him.

'I'm sorry, I know I'm a mess, I've been behaving like an idiot and I hate myself for being this needy and desperate but I've got confused with what I want and where I am at, and I didn't expect to develop feelings for you, like you have been my best friend and I have loved having you in my life and I don't want to lose that. But then I think it's weird so I try not to talk to you, and then you call me, no, no, wait, let me finish. I know you are in a weird space and I am sorry if you feel I am putting more pressure on you, that's the last thing I want to do. Look, I love you, I really do, and I don't want to keep feeling upset or confused, no let me finish, so I think it's probably for the best if I just let you go for a bit and we don't hang out for a while. I probably just need to give you some space and to give me some space.'

'Awww.' He patted me on the head. 'That's really beautiful, but look around, this is not a movie, there are no cameras anywhere, so you can stop all this *mocking my voice* "then I looked at him under the stars and I said I have to let you go". There will be no letting go, there are no cameras, this is not a film. I am your friend, it's fine, I have my hot sauce. I'll call you tomorrow.'

26

SINGLE LADIES' BALL

And that was that. The next day I got a call from the *Sunday Times*. They were doing a front-page centre-fold feature on female comedians and they wanted me in it!

'See,' said Debi. 'It's changing, be patient!'

I arrived at the photo shoot and there was a team of people waiting. I had people doing my hair, make-up and nails all at the same time. Beyoncé eat your heart out. There was even someone there whose job it was to hold my water to my mouth whilst I drank it through a straw. It was ridiculous.

I was the first to arrive at the shoot, and so I got to choose from all the dresses. It was either ball gown, sleek and slender or a big fuck-off dress. What would Beyoncé do?! I went for the big fuck-off one of course.

It was a designer dress, baby pink, and had the longest train. I felt amazing. I looked amazing. The journalist then decided to put everyone else in matching themed dresses. Thank God I had got there first; could you imagine if they had gone for sleek and slender? I would have been devo'd.

Juice had just been dumped by his two girlfriends, they'd found out about each other and so made the decision of who to date much easier for him. To . . . er . . . cheer him up I sent him a picture of me in the dress. He said I looked beautiful. He said he showed it to his mum (who I had met, and is awesome) and she thought I looked stunning and couldn't wait to buy the newspaper. I was chuffed.

I was gearing myself up to leave London again as I had been invited out to Australia to do a three-month tour with 'What Would Beyoncé Do?!' This was huge and again I shat myself. Would they get it? Would it be like America? I was feeling nervous about the whole thing and knew I would miss Juice. I'd planned a holiday to Thailand on the way back from Oz and Juice said he might come out and join me.

Before my Australian adventure, it was coming up to Valentine's Day and I wanted to do another party. I had signed up to a new promoter who suggested we hold it in a nicer venue, so we booked Islington Town Hall, which can hold up to 450 people and is really fancy and expensive to hire. It's a gorgeous venue but I could only do it at a higher ticket price, which I really didn't want. It's really important to me to keep my shows accessible but the higher ticket price would be the only way to cover the venue costs. Even if I sold all 450 seats I would be making less money than I had the year before, when I played to 180 people in a dirty basement. But my promoter explained it's all about being seen in the right places, and career progression. I couldn't find another venue in the short amount of time and I really wanted to do the Valentine's show party. So I said yes to the deal. I used the fact that it was more expensive to my advantage and pitched it as a Valentine's Single Ladies' Ball. The dress code was 'ball gowns and trainers'. I wanted women to wear any dress they liked, the dress that they had had in their cupboard that they had worn once in five years, their old bridesmaids dress, their old prom dress, fancy dress, whatever it is, just wear that! I wanted people to feel they had a reason to get dolled up and come and have a good time.

I had only sold 250 tickets and was annoyed that I hadn't organised it all myself, there was not going to be much of a pay-out from this gig but I didn't have time to get stressed, the promoter was all over it and I was flying to Australia in a week. Besides, this is why you have a team, so they can do these things for you.

I called the stylist from the *Sunday Times* shoot and asked if I could borrow the dress for my gig. It didn't fit properly or do up but I was so in love with it, I was desperate to wear it for my show. The designer agreed and it was couriered over! Imagine that, a dress in its own taxi!

I had a killer show and LOVED wearing the dress, even though I had to take it off halfway through. Word to the wise, for your wedding day, get a dress that a) you don't have to hold up and b) that you can breathe in, 'cos the second I had a Prosecco, I just wanted to throw it off.

Juice arrived. He said I looked stunning and I told him I loved him and he said, 'I love you too.' LIKE HELLO?! The DJ was playing tunes and there were about 150 people still left dancing. I got Juice up on stage and introduced him to my audience. I grabbed the mic and said, 'Guys, guys, this is my friend in inverted commas, Juice, say hi Juice, he says we can only be friends.'

The audience started booing, it was hilarious. Juice took the mic and said, 'Look yeah, she is my friend. I love Luisa but I don't wanna ruin the friendship.'

The audience then started chanting, 'Fuck her, fuck her, fuck her!' A hundred and fifty people chanting at Juice to fuck me. Brilliant.

The gig finished and I went to the changing room and he tried to fuck me in the toilet but I wouldn't let him because we were just friends and it didn't feel right to do that to him. Even though I loved him.

We spent the rest of the night in a bar, snogging and holding hands. He told me his mum loved me and she had never responded like that to any of the girls he had brought home but that I needed to know he couldn't date me. Besides, I was going to Australia for three months and he didn't want to miss me.

He walked me home. He said he would only walk me to my door and then he had to leave. We got to my door, I promised him that we could get him a taxi but it was cold outside so probably best if he just come inside for now and wait. He came in and I stripped to my bra and kissed him. He said to stop it and order him a taxi. I said OK, but I am just going to stroke your face.

He grabbed both my arms and pinned me to the bed. 'Luisa, you either get me a taxi now or I'm gonna fuck your brains out, I'm not playing these stupid games, which do you want it to be?!' God I really do have the best audiences in the world. I panicked and went to get my phone to call a taxi and he pulled me back down and kissed me and we had sex. I was so nervous, I couldn't stop talking throughout the whole thing.

'Oh no no no, bad idea, we shouldn't be doing this, we're just friends.'

'Shut up.'

'OK, but are you sure, oh fuck, once you put this in, it's game over.'

'Can you be quiet please?'

'OK, but I am just saying once this goes in *penis goes in*, oh shit oh shit, it's over, it's game over.'

'Can you just shut up and enjoy it please?' *Trying to thrust*

'OK, sorry, I will, I just, fuck, you're my friend. Fine, sorry, I will. *Goes on top* By the way, I'm really sorry, I have put on a lot of weight, just so you know.'

'Shut up, you look great, you are my Premiership footballer remember.'

'I thought you said I had retired.' *Bouncing on top of him*

'Nah, you can still play.'

Stops bouncing 'Awww, thank you.' *Goes in for a cuddle*

'Luisa, concentrate.'

'Sorry.' *Goes back to bouncing*

We had sex all night and again in the morning and then he said no more, back to being friends.

So that was that, I had sex with Juice, I liked it, but I also felt worried. Like I had somehow let my friend down. The next day, we acted normal, just totally normal. He left in the afternoon and I went and got a pizza. He called me that evening and I asked him to come over, but he said he was busy and already had plans.

Plans?

'What plans?'

'A girl.'

'What girl?'

'Just a girl from Facebook, she keeps asking me out so I said I would go meet her for a drink.'

'Are you fucking joking?'

'Look, it's fine, it's just a drink.'

27

KEEP ON RUNNIN' . . . LOSE IT ALL

I flew to Australia the next morning and Juice met me to say goodbye, but I couldn't stop sniping at him. We Skyped a few times for the first couple of weeks and he never mentioned dates, but I knew he was going on them.

I was gutted and found it really difficult to keep talking to him. I couldn't be friends with him any more. I felt so hurt by it. I cut him off and blocked his calls. I was in Australia by myself, crying my eyes out over a man back home. I hadn't had sex in two years, fucked my best friend and then he goes on Facebook dates.

I spent the three months in Australia feeling drained and tired and missing Juice. But I couldn't call him.

It took a few weeks for me to get a handle on Australian audiences. I was playing to rooms of like 12–30 people.

It was tough and my emotional state didn't help, the audiences didn't know me and they didn't know what to expect, and I would feel defeated when they wouldn't jump on board and then get into the party spirit. But then something amazing happened. I got asked to do a short spot for a gala on Australian television.

The day of the filming came and I had stressed myself out into relentless tears and a cold sore. I was doing my Beyoncé show every night to a half-empty room and I was exhausted and heartbroken. I didn't know what material to do but figured my thigh gap joke was pretty short and memorable. Go on stage, drop my pants and done. I wore my woolly trousers from my Beyoncé show because they were my lucky trousers.

When I did my spot, the audience laughed but it was no big deal. Afterwards I went straight back to my hotel to meet Katerina. Thank God for Katerina. She'd flown out and was doing her show 'Feta with the Queen'. Her show was blowing up in Greece so it was great to have her in Australia and hang out with her every day. That's one of the best things about the comedy circuit, you build your comedy friends and then you get to see them at every festival you go to. It's amazing.

Katerina came round the night Channel Ten were airing the gala. I had no idea what my spot was going to look like and just prayed it would be funny. I made a note of my Twitter followers and hoped I would see some movement. Twitter was at 6,790; my Facebook page had 3,433 likes. My gala spot went out on TV and I had like three tweets about it. Oh well, I thought it looked good and was funny, so I ripped it and posted it on my page so my mum and friends at home could see.

As we watched, my clip started getting views: 500, 1,000, 30,000, what the fuck was happening? It was going viral. Holy shit Katerina, I've hit 100,000 views! This is crazy! My thigh gap routine was getting shared and people were loving it. It was insane!

I was so excited. The clip got 4 million views in three days. It had been shared and liked by hundreds of thousands of people. I wished I could tell Juice. I wanted him to like it. Two hundred thousand likes, on my Facebook page, the most I have ever had, and yet I still kept looking to see Juice's name being one of them.

The next few days were really exciting for me. I would see comics and they would just be like 'Hi, saw that clip of yours' and I'm thinking, oh OK, what do I say to that? Great? Did you like it? I hate passive comments. I hated having to downplay how fucking excited I was. I was so grateful to have Katerina and my Greek mate George there to celebrate with me. George is awesome, he is also an idiot. He once missed his flight from Sydney to London whilst being sat at Sydney airport. He's Greek and hilarious but partially deaf in one ear, so he kinda shouts at you with love. PS I don't think his deafness had anything to do with him missing the flight, it was more just him being an idiot.

I had my favourite Greeks with me and once again comedy was being magic for me.

The gala clip started having an impact on sales and I was selling more and more tickets and playing to fuller rooms; audiences were beginning to get it! Seven million views, this is amazing, oh my gosh, surely now I can go on *The View*, and meet Whoopi?! Maybe I could go on *Ellen*! This will get me *Live at the Apollo* in the UK; who else has had 7 million views and counting of a gala spot? It could get me a tour. Maybe this is what we have been waiting for.

Then I got nominated for best show. The Barry Awards are named after Barry Humphries and every year out of all the comedy shows, five or six get nominated for the best comedy show of the festival. And I was nominated. I could have cried! It was Katerina's birthday; we hadn't been getting on that well because I had been going mad over Juice and panicking about going viral and she had been having a rough time with accommodation, where she'd moved in with a crazy woman.

We were eating tapas when I got the call just after midnight. 'Yay! I've been nominated for best show.'

Katerina said 'Cool' and kept eating hummus.

'Cool? You could be a bit happier for me you know, this is really exciting. I know it's your birthday but you could say more than cool.' Oh why was I taking everything out on my friends, my best friends?

'Really? Is this what you're doing to me now? For fuck's sake, I don't care that you got nominated, you should be nominated, you should have won fucking everything, but they don't care about you and I don't care about them. Whether they nominate you or not, you shouldn't care, you are a superstar and you know it.'

I was so stressed. I was burnt out. On the night of the awards, I got dressed up and went along with Katerina to hear the winners. We were sat in a VIP booth, with lots of people crowding around looking at who was on stage making the announcements. My category came up and all I could think about was Juice. I didn't win but it was lovely to be nominated.

I went back to my hotel, got into bed and called my dad. It was the first time I'd spoken to him all year. I didn't mention the nomination but I told him about being in Australia, and he seemed genuinely happy that I was travelling. He suggested I should be looking to settle down soon though, meet a nice man and think about having babies as I am in my thirties, the joker! I didn't have the heart to point out the obvious to him, so I played nice and went along with it: 'It's not for lack of trying.' We both laughed, I said good-bye and we ended the conversation. I plugged Cher into my ears, and she soothed my tears to sleep.

On paper everything looked good, great shows, viral video, nomination. But I didn't feel good, because what do I do with it? I couldn't work any harder and yet I was still struggling to see a game plan. I wasn't secure financially; I was making maybe a grand a month on average, was clearing my old student overdraft and unclearing it again. I am in my thirties FFS. I couldn't enjoy the good things that were happening for panicking about what I thought should be happening. Things were out of my control and my personal life was crap. I was exhausted and burnt out.

I got through the rest of the tour and my video was now on something like 10 million views. I caught a plane to Thailand and booked myself for two nights into the same honeymoon suite hotel as the year before. Here I am in Thailand and I am exhausted and crying in the ocean (have I mentioned how much I love crying?). The adrena-line of three months touring is slowly leaving my body and it is debilitating as it takes my joints with it, my knees give in, I can't walk and I crash and burn in paradise.

How to filter your social media so everyone thinks you are having a really good time:

1. Take everything from above at an angle.
2. Take 100 pictures of yourself until you have one where you are showing boobs, legs and tan but it's

done in such an arty way that people will think it is really about the elephant you are stood next to.

3. Do not post pictures of yourself next to an elephant, even if you are on holiday in Thailand, lying on a beach minding your own business and it happens to walk past, especially if you have just acquired 77,000 new fans who now think you support the elephant trade in Asia.

4. Get really dressed up and ask hotel reception to take a picture and then go back to bed.

5. Don't cry. Or if you are going to have a picture of you crying, use a cool filter and # it.

6. For the love of God, always use a filter. Always.

I moved around Thailand and found a hut on Bottle Beach for £12 a night. I arranged for my mum and my sister to fly out so we could have our first holiday together. Neither of them had ever been to Thailand before and I loved having them there. Thank God for the women in my life who have always come to my rescue, no matter what, no matter where. My mum and my sister totally saved me.

When I got back from Thailand, I met up with Debi, to see what we could do, my clip was on like 15 million views but TV people weren't showing interest. 'Maybe it's because you say bitches a lot?'

I wanted to leave the industry, to leave Debi. I loved comedy and the gigs but just the politics and the business side of it all. I didn't know what more I had to do. I had a joke that was now on 15 million views, and I had £800 in my account. Why is it always £800? That's my go-to number. As long as I have £800 I am all right. That's a lie; I start getting worried when I have minus £800. You got to think rich. Think like you have money. And I do. I'd flown my mum and sister out and we'd had an amazing holiday. But I earned that, I needed that, I want to be able to go on lots of holidays. I want to be able to take my mum on lots of holidays. I don't want money to be an issue.

Off the back of my clip, my promoter booked some live dates around the country, little 150–400-seaters, and they sold really well. People were now coming up to me and asking for selfies. As soon as I came on stage to do my pre-show dancing, they were quoting my thigh joke back to me. I liked touring this time around, it felt so much easier, and I made an effort to book myself in nicer hotels and be more comfortable. It was a last-minute tour though, so one day I would be in Glasgow, the next in Cardiff, the next in Newcastle.

As well as Debi and a promoter, I had another agent called Charlotte who booked my little gigs for me. My little gigs kept clashing with my big gigs and it was tricky trying to honour all of my bookings. So on my day off in Newcastle I would have to go and do 20 minutes in Bristol. It was pretty full-on but at least I was working.

On my Manchester tour date, I got Zoe to come and open for me. It made such a difference having a friend with me there at a tour show. It was so much fun and Zoe is so funny, it was awesome to share a stage with her again.

After one of my shows in Manchester, I got this beautiful message from a guy called Richard.

Hi Luisa,

I brought my girlfriend to come and see your show tonight and was blown away. My girlfriend has been suffering with depression over the last few months. For the last few years she has been working in a really stressful job and it's begun to really take its toll. She struggles with her self-esteem, she is so beautiful but doesn't see it. I have never seen her laugh so hard as she did tonight. She came out so happy and inspired and I have never seen her look more beautiful. Please keep doing what you are doing, thank you for making the woman I love happier than I have seen her in ages.

Messages like that make it all worth it. I feel very lucky and thankful to be able to do my show and do what I do. That right there is why I do comedy.

I heard that *Live at the Apollo* were booking their new season and got really excited, hoping that they would let me try out for it. You do a twenty-minute set and then they show the best ten minutes. The trials were happening over the next few weeks but I wasn't asked to be seen. They didn't think I was ready. Why wouldn't they at least let me try? I swear if I was a guy and my solo shows had the same mass appeal to men, they wouldn't have hesitated to trial me.

Then some good news came. Debi kept hustling and got me booked for *The John Bishop Show*, BBC 1 prime-time Saturday-night TV. It was a four-minute set at the Hackney Empire. I was so excited, I had loved going to the Hackney Empire, the audience were always young, black and totally up for it. The atmosphere at the Empire can be insane! I was so excited and went on stage and did all right. They just looked at me like I was a bit mental. I did the exact routine from Melbourne, the same one that had gone viral, but this lot were not impressed. The audience were not what I expected at all, not young, just older, middle-class, middle-aged white couples who looked bemused. Ahhh. So this is why TV isn't booking me.

But if my Australian gala clip had taught me anything, it was that I knew I had an audience. And sure, I need to be able to play any room, but just because I might not be the BBC's version of mainstream, that doesn't mean I don't have a mainstream audience. What I needed was more online content. I was now on 30 million views, on Facebook, not YouTube (you don't make money off Facebook videos, only YouTube ones. D'oh).

But I don't care about not making money from the clip; I care about using it to my advantage to build my fan base. My new promoters booked in a tour date at the Bloomsbury Theatre in central London. It's a 500-seater and they organised it so I would play the week after *The John Bishop Show* went on air. The idea is that TV sells tour seats. So as soon as the show went to air, I should see my ticket hotline bling.

It got to the airing. The prime-time BBC show made no difference to my ticket sales. This was weird. Instead we just put up my old viral clip as an advert on Facebook and the Bloomsbury show sold out.

This is how I reach my audience; social media is changing the game. This is what I should be focusing on. Well actually what I should be focusing on is writing more jokes, but I'm a business, I have to think about writing jokes and building an audience, and doing more shows, and reaching more people and making enough money to be secure. It's not enough to just write the jokes. My audience go bat-shit over my shows, the shows are not enough. I have to find a way to let people who will love my shows know I exist. How can I reach these people?

So I decided to record my show at the Bloomsbury and release it online as a download. This was the best way to access my fans, it means people can download it all around the world. Now I just needed the filming crew. I got in touch with my friend Rosie, a wonderful new producer who, like me, was super hungry to work in comedy. She had lots of production experience and said she could help me draw up a budget. We worked out that I needed £10,800 for filming alone. That didn't include editing or any post-show stuff, it didn't include the website hosting for the downloads; that was just for filming.

How was I going to raise over £10k? I don't have that kind of money, even though Debi kindly offered a loan if I needed it. I got in touch with my friend Darshan, who runs a start-up company. He said he could build my website for me and help with the downloads, and as for raising money for the filming, why not crowdfund it?

Crowdfunding is utilising social media to get people to help you fulfil your dream. So that's what I did. I set a crowdfunding budget of £10,000. I would offer a pre-order download for £10. Then, if I got enough pre-orders, I could use that money to pay for the crew and the filming. My friends all pitched in to help, my flatmate Kat helped me come up with little video ideas to ask for money, Katerina helped me write my pitch, Delia said she would do my hair and make-up for the shoot, my friend Monica volunteered to be a production assistant, and Pas offered to help out in any way she could. I thought, I can make this happen, I can make a DVD. Now I just needed a director.

I called my friend Sarah Townsend, an amazing director who had worked on several comedy specials. She had seen 'WWBD' and was a fan, and loved 'Am I Right Ladies?!' too. I asked her advice on the best way to shoot the show. She said, 'Luisa, if you can get the budget for the crew, I can help you film it.' Yay, I love the universe.

With crowdfunding, you set prices and perks and then people can pay for the perk they want. Mine were:

£5 – love and luck and a wish to the Good Sex Fairy
£10 – a download of my show
£20 – a download of my show and a signed poster
£100 – a download of my show, a show credit, and
　　　　some 'Mind the Gap' home-made pants
£500 – a producer credit and all of the above

£1,000 – I would come and do my show in your living
   room for you and your friends

I didn't think I would sell any of my £1k perks but I
had nothing to lose by offering it. Then I logged onto my
Facebook page and got a message:

Hi Luisa, it's Beth, I believe my boyfriend wrote to
you after your show in Manchester. Your show was
amazing and has really helped me. We have just
paid £1,000 towards your crowdfunding but have
a request. We would love you to come and do your
show for us as it meant so much to us, but the gig
is an unusual one. Richard proposed and we are
getting married. We have booked a restaurant in
Wilmslow in Manchester, friends and family think
they are coming because we have been together ten
years; actually it's going to be our secret wedding.
Nobody knows yet and it's only a small ceremony,
but we would love you to come and perform your
show as part of our big day.

Wow, wow, wow, wow. What an honour to perform at
their wedding, I mean, sure, I would have to deal with the
day not being all about me, but I think I could manage
that ;P. So that was one of my gigs. I performed my show
at Richard and Beth's wedding, in front of their gorgeous
friends and family. It was amazing. They had a beautiful
ceremony in a family-run restaurant, we had an amazing
dinner, and afterwards they cleared all the tables aside,

set up a stage by the window and I did my show. Such a privelege. I did the whole show in front of the window, as in all of it, including the bits where I pull my trousers down and do my thigh gap joke. I did that. At a wedding ceremony, in a restaurant, by the window, facing Wilmslow Road, with people walking past. I love my job.

After the wedding party I went back to my hotel. As I checked in I saw Larry, my old mate from my stand-up class at uni. We got chatting and went for a drink. We reminisced about Salford, our stand-up classes. He had lost touch with everyone at uni and so I filled him in on Zoe and what I was up to. He said he never gigged again after uni but instead went to work for an advertising firm in Hulme. His girlfriend had recently kicked him out of their one-bed so he was newly single and planning to work abroad for a year. He was leaving on Monday.

Well if this wasn't a sign for him to be my new boyfriend then baby you need to write clearer signs! Larry was being super flirtatious and complimentary. He was really impressed with what I had achieved. He wasn't threatened or intimidated by it; he actually seemed quite turned on by my alpha-ness. He tried to kiss me but I turned him down. I have been here before, I am not going to be someone's sloppy seconds.

Instead we just kept chatting and he kept calling me beautiful and telling me how golden my skin was. Thailand was still showing. He said I looked like a goddess and I took that as another sign (hello, surely only a future boyfriend would call you a goddess). But I kept my sensible hat on, I mean sure, this was all very nice, but I still wasn't going to have sex with him. He is leaving the country. I hadn't had sex in two years and then I had it with Juice. Look how that turned out. No siree, no more sex for me!

But I was tired, tired of fighting, tired of waiting for it to be right, and tired of wanking, by myself, alone. Here was this gorgeous man, who I'd known for years, offering me attention, yes he will never be my boyfriend, yes he is leaving the country, but would it be so bad to enjoy his attention? Am I making the same mistake again like with Marley, Klaus, Dave and Juice?! The signs are here Luisa (the 'no, he is not your boyfriend' ones). He is not available!! I did what I do in all these crossroad situations, and called every one of my best friends. The first and only one to answer was Pas. Thanks Pas.

Pas is very balanced and very good at making informed decisions. (One time when a guy dumped her she just never called him again. I know, right? Not even an email. Weirdo.) I broke down my dilemma (like Nelly to Kelly, lol), and called on the Kelly in my life.

'Pas there's this really sexy guy who I fancy and have known for years. He is randomly staying at the same hotel as me tonight, I am at the bar with him, and he keeps stroking my skin and my body really likes it, I think he is offering me sex but the only problem is he has just been dumped and is leaving the country on Monday so I don't think he is going to be in a position to marry me. But he did just call me a golden goddess, what do I do?'

Pas said, 'Hey Luisa, he absolutely might come back after travelling and propose or he might die in a horrific plane crash. So, either way, probably best if you just fuck him. Just for tonight anyway, just in case.'

'Thanks Pas, you're the best!'

Long story short, we fucked. We fucked all night and all day. Never had I met someone where the sex was so good from the beginning, bam. Or wham bam! Hello! Sorry. I think this was the universe's way of telling me I was doing the right thing. It was some of the best sex of my entire life. It was as if we had fucked before in a past life. We fucked on the floor, on the bed, on the windowsill, in the shower. It was on point. He treated me like a goddess and just kept telling me how beautiful he found me and how amazing it felt to be lying next to me. And that felt nice. Jesus, all this time, this was what I'd wanted and needed. Some human spirit interaction, not just a physical connection but some sensuality.

I'd missed that, I don't think I'd ever had it. I left the following evening knowing full well I wasn't going to see him again. I felt amazing, I'd had the nicest time and had allowed myself to just let go. There was no disappointment to be had; I knew exactly where I stood. I'm just a girl, standing in front of a boy who fucked her brains out and was leaving the country. Perfect.

I ended up selling four more private shows as perks (as in my comedy shows, not my all-night-banging ones). It's safe to say I have the best audiences in the world. Within 30 days I had beaten my target and raised £11,500. Filming was on!

I'd got my team of friends, a director, five cameras, sound, runners, a neon sign that spelt out my name. The funds would cover the filming and that was enough for now. With editing and website the costs were coming closer to £21,500, but I could worry about that later. I set up a production company and started paying for the extras in instalments. My mate Darshan said I could take the website costs off for now and pay him when I had it; now I just needed £6,000 to help with the filming costs. I got paid £3,000 from my Australian tour and that went straight to my DVD fund.

BBC3 offered some money to do a taster tape for an online pilot, so not a pilot but some money towards a tape that if I did have a pilot would be what my pilot looked like. They were after an entertainment documentary-style show, I know it sounds bad, after all my yearning to get some TV, but I just didn't care; I needed help with my download recording. That was the only show I wanted to put on TV, that and Beyoncé.

The recording couldn't have gone better. The audience were exceptional and I had all the footage. The following Monday I got an email from Debi: ITV2 had come back and said they thought they'd made a mistake and would like to offer me a pilot. I went in for a meeting with them. They said, 'It's difficult with you as an artist on your own, we need to put you with a team you will listen to.' Debi set up some meetings and I met some more production houses. I met with a production company called King Bert. I warmed to them instantly, it was all women I met on the team, and between them they had worked on *Miranda, Absolutely Fabulous* and *The Vicar of Dibley*. I liked this production company.

However, the ITV2 pilot would take a few months to organise and right now my priority was my recorded show, I had pre orders I needed to fulfil, I couldn't let my audiences down.

I went up to the Edinburgh Festival again and played a few nights in a 500-seater of 'Am I Right Ladies?!' My shows generated approximately £15,000; I got paid approximately £2,000. I am playing to 500 people, self-funding a DVD and yet still have cling film on my windows.

The money went straight towards my editing costs. I know, I know I keep saying you have to speculate to accumulate, but how about speculating so things are easy for a while and then I can have a bedroom with double frickin' glazing, huh?

Ummm glazing, I love yum yums, I digress.

I was £4,000 short for my editing costs and was feeling the stress and the burden of getting my show up online. I was organising it all myself and I couldn't focus on any-thing else. People had invested their money in me and right now I wasn't earning enough to pay for an editor to edit my show to send out to people. I didn't like where I was at. I had gone my own way, but I didn't see myself as having any other choice. My going my own way was hard.

It shouldn't be like this, so I called Debi; I wanted to talk to her because I wasn't happy and I didn't under-stand why.

Her response was: 'What are you not happy about now? Are you not happy about the ITV pilot they have come back and offered, or the BBC3 pilot, which I am discussing tomorrow, or are you not happy about your book deal or about the fact that I have confirmed dates for you in Australia next year, or are you not happy that you might be going to America again at the end of the year? Which of these are you not happy about Luisa?'

And I said, 'All of them.' I don't know why I said that, it's what came out. I was just tired and a bit burnt out. I hadn't really stopped apart from my holiday in Thailand and I had spent most of that crying.

Every time something amazing would happen, like my Bloomsbury show, I would feel fantastic but then wouldn't be able to deal with any disappointment, TV stuff, filming costs, tour budgets, etc. My highs were really high and I spent all my time trying to chase them. I could only deal with one project at a time, I want to do one thing and make that one thing excellent. I couldn't cope with several plates spinning. The downloads, the pilots, the book (hello you), the shows.

I love comedy and don't want to do anything else, every penny I make I pour back into my next project. But four years of touring and four years of being up and down and up and down and with no savings in the bank to show for it just made me question all my choices up to this point.

I loved Debi, I loved Mick, I loved all the people I worked with, but I felt completely burnt out. I think the industry represented stress for me, so Debi just felt like stress too, even though she was my biggest supporter. I worked until I got sick and then worked again. I was emotionally drained, didn't have much of a personal life, no love life and I was in desperate need of some emotional support. Something had to give. Debi, my promoter, my PR, I just wanted out from all of them. I was at my happiest in control and I felt that I had lost all of it.

'Do you know what Luisa, I cannot work any harder for you, I'm done. If you're not happy now, I don't know what more you want. I am going to call everyone and let them know I am no longer representing you, OK? I'll call them now. I've got to go, I've got clients to look after.' And she put the phone down on me.

I cancelled my gigs that week and disappeared to my mum's. I didn't get out of bed or face the world and just watched *Sons of Anarchy*. There's a blackbird perched outside my window, I hear him calling, I hear him sing. Juice liked singing. Then I self-harmed. Not with drugs, not with alcohol, not with blades; no, I did the modern-world version of self-flagellation and went on Juice's social media. I shouldn't have done that. He seemed so happy. Oh fuck. Stop crying Luisa; everything looks better on Instagram.

28

MY MOTHER'S LOVE

I honestly believe that everything that happens to you happens for a reason. And whether you like it or not, when you go through a shit period and difficult times, maybe rather than berating yourself for it, it's another opportunity to bring yourself closer to happiness.

Basically I had emotionally ruined myself. I was an emotional wreck and couldn't handle all the good things that were in front of me. I had spent four years hustling and now it was time to stop and take a break, a proper one. I quickly developed a chest infection and my knees decided to buckle. I needed time out. What would Beyoncé do?!

My mum is amazing; she took such good care of me. There is no one in the world I love more, she is amazing and kind and creative and smart and hilarious and beautiful! Like the wisest owl! She is like the only person who can always fix me, whatever the problem, she treats me like a princess and makes me believe that I can achieve anything I set my mind to, I just have to be the best version of myself.

My pum-pum was annoyed at me. It hadn't felt right since my night of hard-core sexy times with Larry, but I'd been gigging so much I'd just ignored it. I don't know if it was angry at me because I had left it so long, or because I had managed to get an STD. Great, just my luck, no sex for years and then the one time I catch a dick I catch something.

I wanted to go and get checked out. I asked my mum if I could borrow her car. This is a good thing about being in the Midlands: I don't know anyone, so the chances of bumping into a mate at the local STD clinic are slim.

'Where are you going?'

'Er I just need to pop out to the doctor's.'

'What for?'

'Er my knees?'

'You went yesterday for your knees.'

'OK, I'm going to the walk-in clinic.'

'Walk-in for your knees? That's funny, get it, walk-in?'

'Er yes, that not why I'm going.'

'What? You said you were going to the walk-in.'

'I am.'

'OK, well why are you going if it's not for your knees?'

'Mum!!!! Fine, I'm just going to make sure that I haven't got anything, you know *whispers*, down there.'

'Oh, do you have problems?' *Sips her tea*

'No, I just want to make sure.'

'I can drop you off.'

'No honestly, I'm fine.'

'You can't drive Luisa, you're not insured. I will drop you off.'

Finishes her tea, puts it in the sink, washes the cup, puts it on the side, grabs the tea towel, dries the cup, puts it in the cupboard, wipes the table and then finally gets her car keys

'OK, thank you!'

So as she pulls up outside the STD clinic I give her a 'well this isn't awkward' smile and she says, 'I'm here now so I may as well come in with you. I've never been to one of these before.' She parks up and jumps out.

Oh great, this is embarrassing, a family outing to the STD clinic.

First of all, why are the staff at the STD clinic always so cheery? They are so friendly and nice, and almost too friendly. You come in and cannot look at anyone. The scene needs Western film music. Everyone avoids eye contact: let's just all pretend that none of us are in here. Deal, everyone? Deal! As we walk through the waiting room to the reception area, I judge everyone I walk past and I can see they are all judging me.

The nurse asks which one of us is here for a checkup, and my mum howls.

'It's not that funny.'

'No, sorry, it's just funny that, you know, I don't have sex!'

OK Mum. We sit down and she starts reading a magazine. There are a couple of young men sat to my right.

'You know this is probably not a bad place to meet someone. At least you know they are responsible.'

I can see the other guys heard her, as they go bright red and put their heads down. My mum is so embarrassing and hilarious. We both crack up laughing but have to be quiet as the atmosphere is intense.

My mum elbows me and whispers, 'Hey Luisa, look, STD . . . what does it stand for? I know, Sex To Die for . . . get it?'

We both start quietly crying with laughter, trying to stifle our amusement.

The receptionist calls me over and offers me a tissue for my mum. I say, oh she's not crying, she is just making up jokes. I love that I am sat in the STD clinic with my mum cracking jokes. I love having this relationship with her; no matter where I am, however I am feeling, she just makes everything better. Her love is the purest.

We are still giggling when I get a text message from Larry. *I think you have ruined me, nothing is ever going to be as good.* The message makes me so happy, I show it to my mum.

'Ahh Mum, look, he says I was the best sex he ever had.' I click my fingers and do a little victory dance.

My mum says, 'Yes, very impressive, that's why you are sat here.'

She keeps me in check.

It's my turn to be seen and my mum asks if I want her to come in with me. I'm like, we don't need to be that close. The nurse closes the door and asks me to get ready. I start praying to the STD angels, please just be thrush, please just be thrush.

Legs hoisted up in the stirrups and a woman with a torch looking deep into my vagina. 'You look very tanned.'

'Well you are quite close to my white bits.'

'Have you been on holiday recently?'

Why do they ask these questions? You have my vagina in your face, I don't want to be talking to you about my holidays, this really does not make me relax.

'Er yeah, Thailand a few months ago.'

'Oh Thailand, was it nice?'

'Er yeah, lots of elephants.'

Lots of elephants? Why did I say that? I saw one elephant. I am failing this small talk and finding it really difficult to not get turned on. It's not my fault I like fingering.

She looks up at my face. 'Just relax, it's nearly over. Ooh, what's your badge say? 'What Would Beyoncé Do?!' Oh that's funny, what *would* Beyoncé do?'

I laugh awkwardly. 'Er yeah, I'm a comedian and it's the title of one of my shows.'

'A comedian! Oh wow, I don't think I've had a comedian here before. Hey, I hope you're not going to put this into your act.'

'Er probably not, no.'

'I love Beyoncé.'

'Yep, me too.' My body swallowed the speculum.

Please be thrush, please be thrush, please be thrush.

Afterwards I see the doctor. 'Nothing to worry about Luisa, just thrush.' Wahoo! I have never been so excited to have 'just thrush' in my life. I come out and do another victory dance for my mum, who tells me I still have tissue hanging out my trousers and takes me to the car.

It felt so good to just kick back and be close to my mum. It's important to listen to yourself when you are tired or depressed or hurting. Please reach out and just be with someone, just sit with people that love you, it's good for the soul. It's when we don't listen to these little signposts that we get floored. There is a reason why you might be feeling tired and hurt and emotional and overwhelmed. I had been exhausted; I felt like my soul was tired. Oh well, at least I only had thrush. Win.

I spent most of Christmas either happy to be off and home with my mum or crying my eyes out feeling sorry for myself. With time on my hands, my brain would do this little trick where I would get anxious over my career. It was in the moments of being alone that self-doubt would come along and kick in.

Who do you think you are? Why should anyone pay you for comedy? Why are you trying to be a comedian? You know you're gonna fail, right? You haven't even finished your download yet, people are going to hate you. Why have you left Debi, even though she left you? What are you going to do now? Why can't you just play by the rules? You didn't have to record your stupid show. That's why they don't book you for *Live at the Apollo*, that's why your agent dumped you, because you are not good enough. Sure you have moments, but are moments enough?

Why should anybody listen to what I have to say? Maybe my dad was right, I'm just a dumb bitch ranting.

Why aren't I just plugged into the system and working? Having a normal life? Who do I think I am to stand out? I could go to DFS and buy a sofa, how nice would it be to buy a sofa, to paint my own walls and have a home, a routine. Wake up at 8 every morning and be in bed by 11 at night. Get up and go to work. Have a car and pay my car insurance and car tax on time. Drive to my job, which is 15 minutes down the road. Get into the office, put my bag down on the desk and make myself a cup of tea and have the usual banter with Kelly and Rachel about my weekend. Put my headset on, log in and start taking calls.

Have lunch in the staff room, take out my plastic lunch box and eat a boring salad. Only take half an hour because I feel bad and so I'm back at my desk by 1. Finish at 5.30 but to be honest it would be better if I stayed a little bit longer because I don't want to look like the first person to leave. So at 6.10 eventually turn my computer off and tidy my desk, wash my mug in the sink, grab my coat and say goodbye to everyone, get in the car and head to the gym. I do a class there three times a week, sometimes boxercise, sometimes Zumba. Have a shower at the gym and drive back home where my partner is also back from work and has made dinner. My partner? I met him online, he actually went to the same school as my brother's mate. We get on so well, he loves rugby (I have no interest in rugby). Eat dinner with a glass of wine and go to bed. We cuddle and have sex if we're not too tired.

Wake up the next day and it's pay day, I get paid at the same time of the month, every month, and have organised all my bills to come out the next day so I don't need to worry about it. Council tax, telephone, internet, heating (finally!), electric, Sky subscription, mobile, gym. Monthly payment on the Peugeot because there is no way I can buy one outright, but this way it's good because I have a nice car to drive. It's only a couple of years old, plus the monthly repayment includes insurance. And then oops, I haven't got much left over this month because there's a friend's wedding and we're saving for our summer holiday, which means no going out for a few weeks, no cinema or restaurants, but I can invite the girls round and have a glass of wine or three, ooh cheeky! Book a doctor's appointment for my bad knees, the doctor knows me, the neighbours know my name. Take my pet to the vet for its latest jabs. Oh no, and I've got a parking ticket for being parked outside the vet's at 7.50 when free parking is from 8. That's going to cost me even more money, right, definitely no eating out for the next few weeks. And repeat. For 40 years.

Why don't I just have that life? Beyoncé doesn't have that life. I bet Beyoncé doesn't have to worry about getting car insurance or paying the bills on time or what she is going to cook for dinner. I bet Beyoncé wakes up and it's like the opening credits to *Grease* and birds put her clothes on for her. I bet she doesn't even need to wash or brush her teeth, she just 'woke up like dis'.

I reckon Beyoncé has a gospel choir for an alarm clock who sing 'Oh Happy Day' from her balcony. Then her personal butler says, 'Good morning Beyoncé, lovely to see you, we have everything laid out for you, when you are ready, please get into the car that is waiting for you.' She'll have some great sex with Jay, have a shower in her walk-in Thai-inspired bathroom, pick any outfit, because she is Beyoncé and they all look amazing, kiss Jay goodbye, sing to Blue and get into her chauffeur-driven car ready to take care of business.

Beyonce's people give her forms to sign, you know, to take care of the wi-fi bills; Yoncé is cool, she asks them to shop around and see if Sky is doing a better deal than TalkTalk. I bet they bloody answer the phone to Beyoncé when Beyoncé calls and complains that her wi-fi ALWAYS FUCKING DROPS! I bet she doesn't have to be on hold for an hour. Imagine, I bet when Beyoncé goes on holiday she doesn't even have to turn off her data settings, she just goes abroad and leaves her phone exactly as it is. I bet she doesn't even put it on airplane mode, the rebel.

I bet they don't even make Beyoncé take her shoes off at the airport.

Who am I kidding, she has her own airport, she can walk around barefoot if she wants to.

She isn't using Uber on her iPhone and praying something sturdier than the van from *Only Fools and Horses* shows up. I mean she might use Uber, she is on Airbnb after all.

I bet when Beyoncé is sick, she doesn't have to wait a week for an appointment and when she does go, she doesn't have to wait 45 minutes in the waiting room surrounded by other sick people before risking it and running out of the surgery to put more money in the meter only to come back in and have missed her slot. I bet when the doctor does finally see her he doesn't say, 'Well, I get that you can't breathe but it's probably a chest infection, and yes, your knees keep giving in but you are probably just overweight. If it doesn't get better in three weeks, come back.'

I bet Beyoncé doesn't have to look for change for the bus only for the bus to leave as soon as she approaches the stop.

I bet Beyoncé doesn't have guys who go 'Look, I like you as a friend, I'm just not ready for a girlfriend' and then dump her and get a girlfriend.

I bet Beyoncé doesn't have to sleep in a coat and hat because the room she lives in is so fucking freezing.

I bet Beyoncé doesn't make her own double glazing out of cling film.

I bet Beyoncé gets paid more than £31 for a show.

I bet Beyoncé doesn't have to ask herself if she will die alone or wonder if she is weird because she hasn't had sex in two years.

I bet Beyoncé doesn't get thrush.

I bet Beyoncé can watch *Sons of Anarchy* all the way through without the internet connection dropping. Fucking wi-fi!

See, why can't I just have that life? Why do I choose comedy? Comedy is hard. Actually that is a complete lie. Comedy is easy, the artform is easy; you just have to keep working at it. Comedy guides you, you can be up and down but it always guides you.

What is hard is the bullshit business around the artform. The UK comedy industry can feel pants for women; we all gotta be grateful and know our place and not rock the boat, not post anything public. Otherwise you get met with 'Why are you complaining? You are doing well!' Yes, because I have busted my ass. Mainstreamwise, it's still a closed shop, unless they can box you. Are you a 'feminist comedian'? Well that's political and hot right now so we can use you. We are all fucking feminists, mate. And it's not just women but people from working-class backgrounds too. They will box you, on your race, on your sex, on your class. It's still who you know and who you are with. It's fine, the rest of just have to work harder.

But the shows, the shows I do leave me feeling elated. I get to travel the world; OK, so I cry all the way there and back, but I get to see the world. Doing the shows, I feel like I am part of something. Like I belong, like I have a voice. We all have a voice and I want to use mine. I want to perform and I want to earn a proper living for doing so, not 10 per cent of ticket sales. I want to feel like I am making something for myself, securing a future. I want my soul to sing.

That's all I want. I want to make my soul sing, every day and for everything else to just take care of itself.

My mum wakes me up with a cup of tea and a plate of berries.

'Luisa darling. Do you think Beyoncé has it easy? Of course not, she gets up and she works hard, she doesn't quit. I bet she has so many people making demands on her and judging her. I bet it's very difficult to balance her life and meet people's expectations. I am sure Beyoncé is somewhere thinking, I wish, every once in a while, that I was just like any other normal girl, not in the public eye. I wish I could just have a day off and relax and cry. I bet Beyoncé can't get the night bus home and sing the *Sister Act* selfie melody with Delia. I bet she can't leave the house wearing her pyjamas and get away with not washing her hair for a week. I bet Beyoncé can't sit on her bottom and watch *Anarchic Sons*—'

'*Sons of Anarchy*, Mum.'

'Whatever, for three days without anyone bothering her. I bet Beyoncé can't go down to her local Chinese and just ask for a pot of hoisin sauce and prawn crackers and eat them on a park bench. I bet Beyoncé can't have sex with a stranger in a hotel.'

'He wasn't a stranger Mum, I did know him.'

'Well, either way, I bet she can't have sex with a strange man and then go with her mum to the STD clinic, can she? Can she? No. See, it's not always easier, now eat your berries.'

'I don't like berries.'

'They are good for you, they will clean up your PH balances. I bet Beyoncé eats her berries, that's why Beyoncé never gets thrush. Come on, drink up your tea, let's go for a swim.'

Healing and chilling with my mum and family for the rest of Christmas was amazing. I slowly started feeling happier and lighter and more positive. Until I caught the final episode of *Sons of Anarchy* and then I was sad again. But apart from that, my brothers were good, my sister was good. I liked being around that energy. Seeing my family happy. No one was arguing, no one had any fights, no one had any drama and that was nice. It felt nourishing.

Sarah my director helped me find an editor and he let me pay him in instalments. My show was ready, my website was up and running and I sent out the link to every one of my pre-orders. The response was fantastic. The quality of the show looked fantastic. My fans were downloading my show and sharing the link with their friends.

I kept getting requests for hard-copy DVDS as well as downloads, so I got some made and me and my mum posted them out. I sold enough to pay back Darshan, my editor and Rosie my producer. I broke even; my mum suggested I make some more 'Mind the Gap' knickers, so we did that too. We had a little factory thing going on the living-room floor. DVDs and knickers next to envelopes and address labels. Me and my mum, doing it together. Our own little business. I liked it.

My mum is my Wonder Woman. Give women more power, give women more opportunities, give women more control. Because the one in my life can kinda fix everything.

29

PINK LEMONADE

So it's 2016 and this is where we are at.

I am feeling good. I haven't got an agent in the UK at the moment and am taking care of myself. I was really sad to leave Debi, I love Debi, she is amazing. I don't know if it was the right move or not, but I can't have been much fun to work with. I was stressed and resentful, impatient at best. At least now I can have some time out and re-address what is best for me to do next. A chance for me to sort out what I want. I think I just want one person who can help me take care of everything, someone who has the time to help me manage a career plan. For now, that person is me.

I went away on a retreat, turned off my laptop and phone and did a lot of crying. Cried about leaving Debi, cried about the uncertainty in my career, cried about my father, occasionally I'll think about him and feel really sad and miss him. I think that's probably quite normal, most children want to love their parents and feel loved by them, so it's hard when something interrupts that. But I came away from the retreat feeling totally cleansed, refreshed, new even. Like I had allowed myself to take time out and get nourished.

The past can and will affect you; it will keep biting you in the arse. And maybe rather than avoiding it or pushing it down, ask it what it wants. So that's what I started doing, listening to what I want and to what I need. What do I need to be OK? Whatever it is, however small, listen to it. I spent New Year's Eve with Pas, we had a ball and I got recognised twice! I wonder if that's an omen for the year ahead. I reckon it should be.

I am not waiting on any guy. I know I should probably go on Tinder, but feigning interest is hard. All my male comedian friends get laid all the time, no problem.

I wish it worked the other way around, but if anything, it's like the opposite. I go on Tinder and I gotta laugh along with these amateurs. We all just want sex, mate, but if I've done my bit and pretended to find you interesting, the least you can do is act as if you wanna meet for coffee first.

I swear if I was a man I would get so much sex from loads of different women. I would be so nice to them and understanding and thoughtful. They would feel amazing and be like 'Oh my gosh, thank you so much' afterwards and I would be like 'You are very welcome!' Wow, what a guy.

So for now, no guy on the scene and I like it. I really want to learn what it would be like if I just fell in love with myself first. That is difficult to even write down. This notion of loving yourself. I am so quick to dismiss it as selfish, or stupid or pointless. I need to stop doing that, because my version of love hasn't been working.

Stop looking at other people's lives through an Instagram filter. What other people have is not necessarily what I want; unless those people are Carrie and Big from *Sex and the City*, I am someone who is looking for love, real love, ridiculous, all-consuming, cannot-live-without-the-other-person kind of love. That's what I want. I want the kind of love where I am a whole woman and he is a whole man, where we are individually complete but we choose to lie next to each other because we want to. The kind where he is free to go and cheat and so am I, but you know what? We don't, because both of us prefer what we have with each other. Idealistic or not, I want a soulmate, a playmate, a sex mate. I want someone to fuck on every level and for us to get lost in each other's worlds. But safely, from the comfort of my own sense of self. That's what I want to take time out for now. That's what I want to work on.

Sure, someone will pay me some attention and be nice to me, then ignore me, and it will all go out of the window and catnip here I come. But for now, I want to get good at being present with just me.

So it's coming up to Valentine's Day again and I get a message from my old promoter: Luisa, don't forget we pencilled in the Forum for you at Kentish Town, you might want to cancel it.

It's 800 capacity seated. I asked them to pencil it in the year before and now things have changed. It would cost £6,000 to hire just for one night. But I don't want to cancel it. There's no bad blood with my promoter; they're happy for me to do my own thing, and now here I am staring at this massive venue. Valentine's is my gig. It has become like tradition. I don't want to not do a show on Valentine's Day, but come on, this is ridiculous. £6,000 just to hire?

For the last three years Valentine's Day has been my favourite show. It's one of the only ones that reminds me of my early days in Edinburgh. Rushing across a bridge to get to the stage in time to introduce my mate. Collecting donations at the door. OK, so I'm not running across a bridge or collecting money, but I feel that same level of excitement, of achievement, that same desire to make it really special because my audience is really special. I mean sure, I feel like that about every show. But on Valentine's, the day of the year when single women usually feel crap, I want to give them something to celebrate.

So what do I do? Without the promoter covering the costs, it would mean somehow fronting it all myself. How can I do that with the classic £800 in my bank? Well, before I say no and let myself down with reality, I may as well speak to the venue. It would be rude not to.

So I do. Venue hire £6k. PR £900. Advertising £2k minimum. Then there is insurance, musical licensing, DJ, staff, decorations. I am now looking at a budget of

£10,600. And that is with minimum costs. I make a mental list.

Cons:

1. Huge financial risk.
2. No safety of agent or promoter.
3. Even if it sells I will only just break even. So essentially putting in a lot of work to pay for services.

Pros:

1. An epic night of magnificent proportions that my audience will love and remember.

I call my mum. 'Mum, I don't know what to do, what shall I do?' 'Luisa! What would Beyoncé do?'

I went to the bank of stepdad Johnny with a business proposal. He lent me £10,000 on the understanding that I would pay it back by the end of March. Fuck it, you got to speculate to accumulate, right?

The Valentine's party was on!

I hired Eve, my favourite tech from Soho Theatre, and asked my boy Olly, my Musical Bingo partner in crime, to DJ. He was up for it; we were going to make this epic.

It's one night only, it has to be for everyone, I wanted single women, couples to come and have an epic night out. I had done 'Am I Right' recently with the download record so what better time to bring back, for one night only, my original debut show 'What Would Beyoncé Do?!' and follow it with RnB, '90s garage, '80s power ballads and the odd 'Say Yes' by Michelle Williams? Perfect! Pas said she would help out on the night and my flatmates were up for decorating the venue with me! I knew I would be comfortable with this team around me. I wanted this night to be magnificent.

I looked at YouTube tutorials on Photoshop and made up some quick memes for social media. The party was going to be on 13 February, which was a Saturday. That was perfect, because it meant I could attract couples as well as singles – people could still do their romantic thing on the Sunday and I could have a full house. This was my USP: a Valentine's party that appealed to both single women and couples.

I got my mate Darshan, who'd built my website, to do a mail-out to anyone who had shown interest in the site. One of the guys who worked for Darshan helped design a new poster. I got my live agent Charlotte on board to help with the venue-set-up admin side. She put me in touch with an advertising company and I paid £1,500 for tube adverts at Kentish Town station. I was so happy when I saw my poster coming up the escalator!

I got Katie Phillips, my old PR team, to help out, they started sending mail-outs to press. I tweeted to party companies, props companies, photo companies, cocktail companies, gyms, Virgin Holidays, anyone I could think of. I got in touch with all the London magazines and jour- nalists, who were really helpful. My PR got me a gig at a *Stylist* magazine exhibition event. After I'd done my spot, I did a shout-out about my show and offered the audience first dibs on front-row tickets. At the exhibition there were loads of really cool brands, so I tried to utilise my social media following. I saw this gorgeous pink faux-fur coat from River Island hanging on a press rack. I tried it on and took a picture of me wearing it, then tagged the shop saying *I love your coat River Island, would love your support #WhatWouldBeyonceDo?!!* The picture got over 2k likes, and a reply from River Island: *Hi Luisa, here is a link to buy the coat on the website. Thank you, RI team.*

FFS, this shit would never happen to Beyoncé.

Most of the companies I contacted ignored me, but I did get a response from a company called LookLook, who specialised in photo machines for events. They were amazing and donated a GIF machine, which meant my audience could have their photo taken and the machine would turn it into a GIF, so that every time someone shared their picture it had all my social media handles on it.

A company called Tommy Poprcorn responded to Charlotte and offered free popcorn. Free popcorn! We arrived at the venue and 20 boxes full of the stuff were waiting for us! My audience loved it!

I went a little bit crazy on a party website and ordered 100 helium balloons plus hearts and banners, but me, Pas and my flatmate Kat had fun trying to blow them all up. I wanted it to feel like a school prom. I found a kissing booth. It cost £150. Fuck it, if you can't have a kissing booth on Valentine's Day, when can you? Delivery was another £150. Fuck it, I have a loan, it's all relative and it will all be worth it. Altogether now . . . 'You have to speculate to accumulate.'

Opposite the Forum there is a cocktail bar that used to be a public toilet. It's now a swanky bar (only in London). It's actually really cool and called Ladies and Gents. Every night they have this big cinema-style sign lit up outside with jokes and puns on cocktails. I decided to email the manager and ask if he would consider putting my show details on the sign. In exchange I would plug his bar as the place to go for pre-show and after-show cocktails. He did it, he didn't mind! I had *#WhatWouldBeyonceDo?! At The Forum This Sat* lit up for three days.

Remember how I loved the tuck shop at school? What better place to bring the tuck shop back than at your own party. I ordered £200-worth of penny sweets and spent the night before making up bags for £1. I couldn't get any pink lemonade so pick and mix would have to do. There wasn't going to be any profit on them, but I would cover my costs and I figured it would be a nice touch for the audience. It took me and Kat ages to pack them up, but we had so much fun dancing around, drinking Prosecco. My other flatmate Sophie helped by making signs for the tuck shop. It was all coming together. Some of the sweet bags may have had more flying saucers in them than others; I wanted people to feel spoilt. Other bags may have had more turtles, I'm very sorry about that team, my generous maths on flying saucers may have backfired.

To help me bring in some actual money, I decided to make up some merchandise. I had never done it before because I didn't want to upset Beyoncé by using her name on things and I preferred to concentrate on the shows. However, for this one-off, I designed some T-shirts and jumpers with my show title on and got them made up.

If I was lucky, I could break even. I *was* lucky. Valentine's Day 2016 was by far one of the most epic nights of my entire career. I had 800 people; the venue was packed. Olly was on form, Pas was gorgeous, the event was a huge success. The crowd went crazy for the show, I was so worried I wouldn't be able to deliver it as well as I wanted because of all the stress of organising. But the audience's love and laughter just made the show fly. It was perfect!

We all danced until one in the morning. I broke even from the ticket sales, and I felt proud, proud that this event was mine. Proud that I had pulled it off. Proud that no one else had a handle on it, I'd controlled all of it, and as bad as that sounds, I loved it. I loved having my team of friends helping me. I loved every aspect of it, and it meant that when I pulled the gig off, I could enjoy all the sense of satisfaction and happiness that came with it. This was a beautiful gig and for once, Valentine's wasn't spoiled by a boy. I was there with some of my best friends and 800 beautiful audience members. We danced until the cows came home.

The next day, as I came back to the venue to collect my kissing booth, I was a hot, sweaty mess. The *Kerrang!* tour was happening and their crew was arriving. As I walked past them carrying my stuff and saw the team of about 20 staff all kitted out in *Kerrang!* lanyards setting up the stage. I felt an enormous sense of pride. The day before I'd had my crew in here setting up my stage, only my crew were my friends. Beyoncé probably wouldn't have to carry her own kissing booth the night after a show, but I didn't mind. I liked carrying my own kissing booth. Besides, it's now in my mum's garage waiting for when I can buy my own flat and put it in the bathroom. Or in the kitchen, next to my Smeg.

I liked that I could put on an event and create a working world where I just got to play, like I was showing off in front of my grandma reciting *Sister Act*. I liked that my mum taught me to work for things, that sometimes you have to go to the garden and look for a stick to break up poo. I liked that Salford taught me that no one is going to give it to you. The world owes you nothing. You owe your gift to the world. I might not know yet where I am going in life, I might not have my own home, I might not have a boyfriend, I might still have cling film on my windows, and I might only have earned £300 from a gig that generated nearly £12,000, but when I look back on my life, my most precious memories have been those shows. Valentine's Day was beautiful and that memory is mine for keeps.

I need to work smarter at my career, and I feel like I have such a long way to go, but I hope and think I will always find comedy, because from every situation or emotion, comedy saves me. I will always have that. But balance and rest are just as important as working. Taking time out is good.

This year I have set some intentions. I want to be able to buy my own home one day; I want to have a baby and meet someone nice and hopefully get married. I want my kids to see 'love Mum and Dad' on their birthday cards. I want to look after my mum and buy her a new kitchen. And if I want these things then I need to allow myself to become the woman I am meant to be.

If I had listened to caution, and advice, and fear, I never would have experienced the sense of achievement or the highs that I have. When people tell you that you can't do something, it's usually coming from their own sense of fear. Most people are scared. And that's OK. Life *is* scary, but you are a goddess. A very capable goddess. With or without crying.

There is no greater feeling than listening to your heart and following your instinct and chasing your dreams. Because I swear down, no matter what happens, no matter how hard it is, when you allow yourself to live authentically, to truly listen to and follow your heart's goal, life falls into place. So go get 'em bitches, I cannot wait to see what we become.

ACKNOWLEDGEMENTS

I would like to thank all the men in my life, the plot points of my story; I wish you a lifetime of love and happiness. Thank you for helping me grow.

I want to thank the women in my life who have carried me, shaped me, loved me, listened to me, inspired me, supported me, wiped away my tears, held my hand and continue to make me absolutely howl with laughter.

Big love to Delia, the most talented person I know, thank you for your amazing illustrations. Katerina Vranarama for being such a generous goddess of a woman. Pasqualey, my date for all my Valentine's Days and adventures. Zoe, wifey and comedy sister from Lord knows who.

Della, angel of my life, one of the kindest people I know. Wendy, for all the teens, twenties and ages to come! Smirnoff Ices, jelly-leg dancing and green tea. Ray Ray for being so kind and loving and keeping sand out of my mouth when I was high on Valium and wanted to be a mermaid. Lau Lau for awesome boy analogies and wise words. Am I factually correct in my assumptions?! #GoldenSuitcase. To Ellie T for being an absolute legend. Sajeela for being my comedy mamma. Suzi for the best Old Skool Exhibit days. PS FYI.

Vicci promo 4 life.

Flat party: Kat for actively encouraging my 'go big or stay at home and cry' ideas. Sophie for your endless hair-braiding skills. And Birdy for being such a kind, sweet soul.

Thank you to George, who read and re-read my drafts even though he was bored to tears and helped me go on Tinder. 'Oi-oi, what do we want?' 'Deep and meaningfuls.' 'When do we want them?' 'Now!' Olly for the Meat Loaf and Beenie Man tunes!

Thank you to Mark Bishop for believing in me from the days of the derelict classroom, and Debi Allen who believed in me from the days of a derelict room above a pub.

For Padraig for aways sharing his chips and for Muirrean for being part of the family.

For Francesca who has shown a ridiculous amount of patience and has gently dragged my procrastinating butt all the way through to publication.

Thank you Johnny for always encouraging and support-ing me. To my brothers, who I love and adore (butt-butts). To Joasia, I don't care how old you are, to me you will always be my favourite twelve-year-old of all time.

And thank you to my mumma, the woman who has shown me more love from one parent than I could know in a lifetime from two.

Finally, for you, my beautiful audiences who come and play with me, thank you for making my dreams come true and my heart sing.

Big Love
Luisa xxxx